BRITAIN AND AFRICA UNDER BLAIR

Manchester University Press

This book is dedicated to the students at Nyamhondoro Secondary School

BRITAIN AND AFRICA UNDER BLAIR
In pursuit of the good state

Julia Gallagher

Manchester University Press
Manchester and New York
distributed in the United States exclusively by Palgrave Macmillan

Published by Manchester University Press
Oxford Road, Manchester M13 9NR, UK
and Room 400, 175 Fifth Avenue, New York, NY 10010, USA
www.manchesteruniversitypress.co.uk

Distributed in the United States exclusively by
Palgrave Macmillan, 175 Fifth Avenue,
New York, NY 10010, USA

Distributed in Canada exclusively by
UBC Press, University of British Columbia, 2029 West Mall,
Vancouver, BC, Canada V6T 1Z2

British Library Cataloguing-in-Publication Data is available

Library of Congress Cataloging-in-Publication Data is available

ISBN 978 0 7190 9117 9 paperback

First published by Manchester University Press in hardback 2011

This paperback edition first published 2013

Printed by Lightning Source

Contents

List of abbreviations

APPG	All-Party Parliamentary Group
DfID	Department for International Development
EU	European Union
FCO	Foreign and Commonwealth Office
G8	Group of Eight (industrialised nations)
GNI	Gross National Index
IFI	International financial institution
ILP	Independent Labour Party
IMF	International Monetary Fund
INGO	International non-governmental organisation
IPPR	Institute for Public Policy Research
IR	International Relations
MDG	Millennium Development Goal
NEPAD	New Partnership for African Development
NGO	Non-Governmental Organisation
NLC	Nigerian Labour Congress
OECD	Organisation for Economic Cooperation and Development
UN	United Nations

Preface

When Princess Diana died in August 1997, Sierra Leone's elected Government was holed up in a disused Chinese restaurant in Guinea. The British High Commissioner, Peter Penfold, who had gone into exile with President Kabbah and his ministers, and was advising them to act as much as possible like a government, suggested that the Foreign Minister write a letter of condolence to the Queen. He hoped that this would project a picture of a government in control, even though in reality it had been pushed out of Freetown by a ragged and disorganised rebel movement, leaving Sierra Leone in chaos. At the same moment, Tony Blair was making one of his most famous and statesman-like speeches. Speaking movingly of the 'people's princess', he managed to embody British reaction to and emotion at Diana's death, and at the same time represented a focus of containment and reassurance. This brief and relatively slight moment in Blair's prime ministership is nevertheless one of the best examples of his ability to express a sense of the capacity of his government to embody Britain. It occurred in the days before Britons had learned to distrust him, when his newness and ambition to unite the country still appeared credible.

This book is about the idea of state capacity – in particular, state capacity to embody and represent good. It looks at the ways in which New Labour harnessed a broader British imagination of Africa in order to do this, pursuing it through Blair's attempts to 'do good' in Africa. At the time this story begins, the state of Sierra Leone barely existed. It had collapsed, unable to meet any basic functions; the Government had fled, and was being supported in exile by the British. It represented utter failure, its feeble attempts to demonstrate capacity under the direction of a British official. In contrast, Britain under Blair appeared to have a new moral strength: New Labour had breathed it back into the idea of the British state. There was a reinvigoration of morality in public life; the New Labour Government appeared able to encapsulate a sense of British brilliance and assertiveness; the state itself was at the heart of a far happier British national story. The significance of the idea of the moral strength of the state, the difficulties of maintaining it, and the way in which the stories of Britain and Sierra Leone became entwined, lie at the heart of this book. In particular, it explores the way in which people in Britain – and particularly the political elites that represent them – collectively imagine Africa and project an idealised Britain onto it, in order to conceive a sense of their own 'good state'.

The idea for this book came about through my own observation of New Labour in power when I worked at the Foreign Office in the early 2000s and saw the way in which Africa policy was set apart from the rest of foreign policy. I became fascinated by the idea of Africa as a 'good project' and what this might mean. This built on a lifelong interest around the question of 'doing good' in Africa, which began with questions to my exiled South African mother about white, or non-African, involvement in the anti-apartheid struggle, and then in my own time working in a rural secondary school in Zimbabwe in the early 1990s. It continues today, when I hear from my children that they are being taught in school about starvation and poverty in Africa, and from my students that their ambition is to work for a non-governmental organisation (NGO) and solve Africa's development problems. I, and they, and many other millions of British people, grow up believing that Africa is somehow special and apart, particularly desperate and needy, and that we can and should help. Why and how did a continent come to occupy this particular place in the collective imagination; and why and how is this preoccupation expressed through politics?

I was fortunate to have the support of many people to help me realise this project. Donal Cruise-O'Brien was the first to encourage me to pursue my ideas academically. I am particularly grateful to Stephen Chan, my supervisor at SOAS, for setting an example in adventurous scholarship and encouraging me to persist with ideas and approaches that strayed from the conventional. Other members of the SOAS politics department offered support and many helpful comments, particularly Tom Young, Laleh Khalili, Rochana Bajpai, Matt Nelson, Stephen Hopgood, Marie Gibert, Henrik Aspengren, Hannes Baumann, Sambaiah Gundimeda, Dan Large, Dave Harris, Polly Pallister-Wilkins, Manjeet Ramgotra and Dan Neep. Thanks too to Kimberly Hutchings, Andrew Williams, Radha Upadhyaya, Susan Newman and Crispin Branfoot for suggestions and advice; and to the friends I made in Sierra Leone and Nigeria, particularly Maude, Prince and James. I am very grateful to the British MPs and officials and Nigerian and Sierra Leoneans who agreed to be interviewed. This project has been helped in different ways by my whole family; my parents who first excited in me many of the ideas that propel it; Sophie who helped me understand Melanie Klein; and Christina who became my 'big sister'. Finally, thank you to Shona and Connie who came home from school and made me stop, and Shaun without whom I never would have begun.

Early drafts of Chapters 4, 5 and 6 appeared as articles in *Millennium: Journal of International Politics* and *African Affairs* in 2009.

1

New Labour: doing good in Africa

Introduction

This book is about fantasy and idealisation, about how international relationships provide opportunities to create and pursue them, and why they are essential for political communities. In its transcendence of the domestic, political realm, the field of international relations (IR) provides fantasy and idealisation in a variety of ways: for realists, it depicts a place of anarchy and free-flowing aggression; for liberal-utopians, it is potentially a place of harmony and idealism. In both cases, the international realm is thin enough (empty, even) to enable an escape from the moral complexity and banality of the normal, allowing the projection of extremes.

Of course this is a crude depiction. Many attempts have been made to qualify or reconcile the classic dichotomies of IR theory, to find ways forward in describing a thicker conception of an ethics of the international (see in particular, Cochran, 1999; Linklater, 1998). But still, for theorists and practitioners, some areas of IR remain a potentially rarefied realm, into which ideas can be projected in purer forms than would be allowed in a messier domestic context.

Britain's policy in Africa can be viewed in such terms. By practitioners themselves, it can be seen as distinct from 'politics as usual', an example of an ethical approach to politics, in which self-interest and power have little share. It is described in terms of certain and universal conceptions of what it means to be 'good', enabling a sense of the transcendence of a grubbier conception of politics. And, although much of the analysis of the policy has questioned this depiction, it too, in different ways, has attempted to understand it within a flattened context which focuses exclusively on power and self-interest to the exclusion of an ethical or humanitarian dimension.

Coming from a more pragmatic, social democratic perspective, which accepts as inevitable the complexities, the lack of conclusions and the chaotic quality of politics, I start out with the question of what role such idealisations play in political communities. To what degree is the creation of an ideal space, apart from 'politics as usual', a necessity; in what ways might the international realm provide one; and how can we begin to understand the ways such a space underpins the health of the political community?

I begin from a constructivist position. This roots ideas, actions and motivations within wider society, meaning that any examination of the way political communities approach foreign policy assumes that policies emanate from the ideas and culture of the community, and are not imposed by a distinct stratum of political elites. Instead, under investigation is a complex web of state actors who are reflecting and attempting to shape wider community ideas. It is meaningless, within this paradigm, to examine the motivations of politicians in isolation, as for example Grainger does (Grainger, 2005).[1] Instead my approach is to assume that Tony Blair's interest in Africa, his conception of what it is and what Britain does for it, are entwined with British approaches and conceptions, taking in historical experiences of Britain's role there, and responding to contemporary political pressures and ideas.

The political community mediates and concentrates such ideas upon the state itself; state actors, as the chief protectors and representatives of the state, embody a distillation of the ways in which these processes can be related to the state in much the same way that the formal state itself can be thought of as a distillation of the wider state defined by Hegel as 'the community as a whole with all its institutions' – including the family and civil society as well as the political institutions (Hegel, 1991: xxv). Community at the state level carries a particular significance and is at once vital and problematic. First, in a Hegelian sense, the political state as the highest organising authority confers an essential part of identity and source of wellbeing. This is realised both in the degree to which the state embodies society's ideas and values, and in how well the state projects itself internationally. Second, in its wider meaning, the state is the community we all belong to and, aside from the small numbers of people who emigrate, membership is involuntary. The degree of involvement also varies, but overt support does not necessarily entail more involvement than resistance: both recognise the importance of the state. I agree with David Miller's description of the origins and complexity of national identity. 'One is forced to bear a national identity regardless of choice, simply by virtue of participating in this way of life' (Miller, 1995: 42). The virtue in this is that, like a family, despite periods of frustration and unhappiness, we remain engaged with the state. This iterative, unending and often painful process has been described by Michael Walzer as constituting a 'thick' ethical dimension (Walzer, 1994). Within states, people must develop ways of distributing goods. Walzer says they can do this, more or less well, because they share deep cultural and moral norms by virtue of their having lived together for so long. Walzer I think tends to over-simplify cultural homogeneity and glosses over the multiple and diverse types of community which under- and overlay the state community. We must allow for the fact that members of the state community bring complex identities to their membership (Adler, 2005) – a fact that makes sorting out distribution even messier, but no less thick. Because membership is inescapable, we have to resolve, or reconcile, or find a way to live with our differences to make the state work. However, the extra complexity makes the Hegelian notion of the 'good state', which successfully embodies society's norms and then reflects them out to the wider world a deeply difficult process.

Beyond the state lies the state-system, a collection, in classic IR terms, of self-contained entities which interact independently of any higher authority. From the orthodox communitarian perspective, there is little shared between different state communities. Relations between states are voluntary, or at least fluid, shared norms are at best weak or, in Walzer's terms, 'thin', because they are basic, fundamental and ideal.[2] They can allow us to identify intensely at times with people from other parts of the world who are struggling to achieve goals we share – self-determination or freedom from oppression, for example – but they cannot be the basis for sorting out complicated distributive issues because they are idealised and not rooted in thick community norms.

What interests me is the relationship between the two spheres – the state and the international; the thick and the thin – and the importance of the ideal in the state's ability to inspire wellbeing. If domestic issues are clogged up with thick, complicated and messy negotiations, what happens to ideals, to the sense we all share of reaching for something grander, more profound?

Emile Durkheim's work on the role of religion in the creation and nurturing of community is helpful here. Durkheim argues that individuals together conceive of an ideal society by way of shared religious belief and practice. 'It is a simple idea that consciously expresses our more or less obscure aspirations towards the good, the beautiful, the ideal. Now these aspirations have their roots in us; they come from the very depths of our being' (Durkheim, 2001: 315). In a discussion of modern secular society's search for a replacement for religion, Durkheim dismisses science as a possibility, giving a clear insight into the particular role religion has played. Faith, he argues, includes 'an impulse to act', in which speculation is essential. 'Science is fragmentary, incomplete; it progresses slowly and can never finish: life cannot wait' (*Ibid*: 325). In the religious life of the community, 'the obscure intuitions of sensation and sentiment often take the place of logic' (*Ibid*: 326). In the end, science will not do because it is an expression of collective opinion and not outside social life at all. Durkheim then suggests a number of ways in which people collectively imagine an ideal society, including the need for speculation, the importance of sensation and sentiment, an impulse to act and the search for something beyond our social life.

This search for an ideal community is, Durkheim maintains, 'not a kind of luxury that man might do without but a condition of his existence' (*Ibid*: 318) and, as such, a necessary part of a community's health. If a state community's imagination of itself must have a strong ideal element, isn't this most easily achieved in relation to the wider world? Can we transcend – by escaping or enhancing – our messy, thick domestic social life by reaching up to the thin and pure international realm?

The classic way for a state community to reinforce itself is through war, and war has been the preoccupation of many IR theorists (Waltz, 1959; Bull,

1995; Kagan, 2003). Hegel writes that war is necessary for states to prevent the stagnation that he argues perpetual peace would bring: 'The state is an individual, and negation is an essential component of individuality... Not only do peoples emerge from wars with added strength, but nations troubled by civil dissension gain internal peace as a result of wars with their external enemies' (Hegel, 1991: 362). War as an 'ethical moment' confers and reinforces subjectivity; it is part of the way in which states are aware of each other as different, but also related. It is through mutual recognition that states become subjects.

Mutual recognition and doing good in Africa

New Labour's was an era of the language of idealism in foreign policy, beginning with Robin Cook's 'ethical element', and continuing through Blair's 'humanitarian wars'. It is at best questionable how far British subjectivity under New Labour was enhanced by war. Blair's wars – among them interventions in Kosovo, Sierra Leone, Afghanistan and Iraq – had a mixed record in terms of creating the 'Dunkirk Spirit' effect that Chris Brown suggests is the essence of Hegel's 'cleansing feature of war' (Brown, 1992: 70). Blair's approach to Africa, however, grounded in utopian and cosmopolitan ideas and highly idealised, in a different way offered a grand, heroic identity for Britain. It embodied Durkheim's 'more or less obscure aspirations towards the good, the beautiful and the ideal' and was firmly predicated on the 'impulse to act'. Moreover, in a very concrete way, it offered escape into a realm 'beyond social life'. My argument is that the idea of Africa and Britain's help for Africa has worked as a way to create the sense of an ideal society in Britain, and most particularly to affirm the 'good state'.

To understand Britain's approach to Africa, I want to find a place for it within international relations theories on state-systems. I will look at two IR debates. The first is the traditional utopianism/realism debate which held sway through most of the twentieth century. Although this debate no longer dominates IR discourse, it is useful here because the utopian approach which characterised late nineteenth-century colonial policy – Britain's era of 'do-good' imperialism[3] – has strongly influenced the Labour Party's foreign policy and echoes strongly through current ethical approaches to foreign policy. Moreover, in the tradition of unearthing latent interests, examining current policy on Africa within the utopian/realist paradigm helps towards a richer conception of how British interests are defined and sheds light on the benefits of the policy for Britain.

However, although the realist/utopian discussion helps us think about the way a state looks out at the world, it is less useful in explaining how foreign policy reflects back *within* a state, a key objective of this book. Therefore, I want to look at a second theoretical framework, contemporary IR theory on cosmopolitanism and communitarianism. As Brown suggests, a communitarian approach helps us see how the way we look out at the world underpins wellbeing within the state: foreign policy is no longer seen as purely externally focused but as a positive good that a state can offer its citizens (Brown, 1992). Second, New Labour rhetoric is strongly cosmopolitan: an examination of the cosmopolitan approach should help towards an understanding of the way the Government – and I will argue Britain more widely – sees itself in relation to Africa.

But none of this allows a sufficient development of ideas about what it means for its members that the state is 'good'. They set off the idea of a relationship between individuals and the 'good state', but conventional IR approaches constrain further exploration along this path in two ways. First, they have traditionally sidelined the personal and the emotional; and second, where they have examined ideas of projection, have tended to privilege the destructive and the negative elements, particularly in their focus on war. In my attempt to explore how state engagement in 'good' internationally underwrites the emotional as well as physical wellbeing of the community, I will draw on the psychoanalytic work of Melanie Klein. Klein deals with the development of individual subjectivity through relationships. Most compelling is her analysis of the way in which thin, far-off relationships can be used to support and mend more fraught, thick, close relationships, something she argues is done through the splitting and projection of aggression and idealisation. Against a background of European political thought about the nature of 'good', of where it is imagined to be, and of the essential importance of making a connection to it, Klein's work helps locate the immanent need for good, its source and corruption within relationships, and the ways in which individuals attempt to recreate, recapture and use it to resolve the difficulties of human ambiguity.

The rest of this chapter is divided into three sections. The first outlines the basis of the book, giving an account of how New Labour's interest in Africa grew between 1997 and 2007. The second explores the book's argument in more depth and outlines the theoretical context. Finally, there is a brief discussion of its methodology.

New Labour, ethical foreign policy and Africa

There were three main elements to New Labour's interest in helping Africa and these can be boiled down to ideology, issues of power and contingency. First, the Government inherited old Labour traditions and ideology, mostly developed during the Party's periods in opposition. Rooted in ideas of internationalism and often antithetical to notions of British power, these explicitly focused on how foreign policy could serve to improve the world, rather than narrowly defined British interests (Gordon, 1969; Vickers, 2003; Callaghan, 2007; Phythian, 2007). From the Party's beginnings in the early twentieth century, ideas on a new role for Britain were developed in an attempt to move beyond Britain's imperial past, and the Party has grappled with them ever since. These developed during the long opposition years of the 1980s in the Party's hostile attitude towards the arms trade and its desire to promote human rights. Of particular significance to this discussion is the Party's policy on nuclear unilateralism, painfully abandoned in the late 1980s, and for many a deep hole in what had been a highly ethical stance on defence. Could development and the ethical approach to foreign policy help fill it? The personalities, ideas and ambitions of key New Labour figures also drove foreign policy towards both political and morally based objectives. The ambitious Robin Cook wanted to make foreign policy count at home; Tony Blair and Gordon Brown, searching for a moral cause, found it more easily abroad than at home.

Second, the Government wanted to make sure that Britain was a major world player – an ambition sometimes at odds with the old Labour ambivalence towards power. It did this in the context of the British preoccupation with decline and the search for an international role. How could Britain be made to count in the world once again, without recourse to the realist approach of previous governments? Luckily, the international conditions in the late 1990s, post-Cold War, promoted a development discourse which suited both New Labour's ideological direction and the search for a role. This was rooted in the idealised power of the liberal values of human rights, democracy and better governance in effecting material change in the lives of people in the Third World. By wholeheartedly pursuing these values New Labour could become an influential member of the international community – perhaps even a leader in a new moral crusade. Blair's desire to be closely identified with the US reinforced this tendency too, particularly after 9/11, when his ideas on international community and intervention hardened into a far more aggressive manifestation of the ethical foreign policy.

Third was the role of contingency in the shaping of policy. Events in Sierra Leone and Kosovo, and then 9/11, allowed Blair to articulate and begin to effect his ideas on international community and the doctrine of intervention. He successfully used his moments in the world's spotlight to demonstrate his moral commitment to Africa.

An ethical beginning

Tony Blair's Labour Party was preoccupied by domestic policy while in opposition,[4] but when the Party came to power in May 1997, two early initiatives set the scene for the Government's approach to foreign policy and these were to take on increasing importance. The first was the establishment of the Department for International Development (DfID), now a department in its own right with a cabinet post, filled by the energetic and engaging Clare Short.[5] The second was Foreign Secretary Robin Cook's presentation on 12 May of a foreign policy mission statement with an 'ethical dimension' (Cook, 1997a), immediately labelled 'the ethical foreign policy' by the media.

The new Development Secretary was determined to make development a key government priority. She quickly committed the Government to the UN development aid target of 0.7 per cent of Gross National Index (GNI),[6] and published two white papers – in 1997 and 2000 – iterating the ethical dimension of development.

> It is our duty to care about other people, in particular those less well off than ourselves. We have a moral duty to reach out to the poor and needy. But we also owe it to our children and our grandchildren to address these issues as a matter of urgency. If we do not do so there is a real danger that, by the middle of the next century, the world will simply not be sustainable ... In this area we could give a lead which would make us all very proud of our country and also secure a safe and decent future for us all. (DfID, 1997)

This theme – morality working in tandem with enlightened self-interest – was to become a defining feature of the Government's approach to foreign policy.

Cook, ambitious and highly political, was anxious to maintain his domestic profile as he entered the Foreign and Commonwealth Office (FCO). He was driven by the need both to cement his left-wing credentials within the Party and to keep up with his rival Gordon Brown who had grabbed the limelight by granting independence to the Bank of England as his first action as Chancellor (Wickham-Jones, 2000: 107). The ethical dimension was the last of four foreign policy objectives, designed to 'secure the respect of other nations for Britain's contribution to keeping the peace of the world and promoting democracy around the world'.[7] Two months later Cook explained that the foundations of the ethical dimension were based on the doctrine of universal human rights, and mapped out twelve policies which would demonstrate the Government's approach. These included condemnation of governments which 'grotesquely violate human rights', support for sanctions applied by the international community, a ban on military exports to human rights-abusing regimes, support for a new international criminal court, practical assistance to free media working in repressive regimes, human rights training for foreign armed forces and an annual report on government efforts to promote human rights abroad (Cook, 1997b).

The main flavour of Cook's ethical dimension was the curtailment of British interests where they interfered with the ending of egregious human rights abuses elsewhere. Like Short, Cook was keen to stress moral responsibility: 'The Labour Government does not accept that political values can be left behind when we check in our passports to travel on diplomatic business. Our foreign policy must have an ethical dimension and must support the demands of other peoples for the democratic rights on which we insist for ourselves' (Cook, 1997a). The policy was understood to mean that sometimes Britain would be prepared to act at some cost to itself in the interests of wider principle. Cook's recipe for principled action looks rather cautious now, followed as it was by the more assertive international interventions of the Labour Government: he was anxious to work within international legal frameworks, and at this early stage there did not appear to be wider government commitment to the ethical dimension to justify anything grander than tough words alongside political and economic sanctions.

If pressed, Cook would argue, like Short, that there was a harmony between British interests and the promotion of 'our values'. For example:

> I am constantly being lectured that the work of the Foreign Office should only be about the national interest. Actually, I agree with that. But I also believe that promoting our values, taking pride in our principles is in the national interest. We will be better able to trade with countries that are stable and free. We will be more secure the more democracy replaces dictatorship. (Cook, 1998)

Africa featured for both DfID and the FCO, but in neither was it singled out for special treatment at this stage. For DfID, African countries made up the majority of the world's poorest, and, as former colonial possessions, many already had close development assistance relationships in place. For the FCO, several African states fitted immediately into Cook's ethical element – notably Nigeria under Sani Abacha's military regime, mentioned specifically in the July speech,[8] Sierra Leone, suspended by the Commonwealth the same month after a coup to oust the elected Ahmad Tejan Kabbah's government and Kenya, where elections which returned Daniel Arap Moi to power were widely criticised as flawed. But Africa has never been a high priority for the FCO, which tends to see the continent in a development rather than diplomatic framework. Cook was more immediately, dramatically and problematically occupied by human rights issues in Indonesia, Burma, Pakistan and Iraq.

Despite New Labour's claims to newness, both the ethical dimension and the enhanced importance of international development can be traced back to older Labour approaches to foreign policy. Development had had a higher profile in the Labour governments in the 1960s and 1970s, particularly under two influential development ministers, both from the left of the Party, Barbara Castle, created Minister for Overseas Development in 1964, and Judith Hart, who filled the position twice in the 1970s. At the same time, Cook's ethical dimension – although 'new' in its terminology – was rooted in two long-held Labour Party ideas: the limiting of arms sales to unsavoury regimes and the promotion of human rights internationally.[9] Both were pursued throughout the 1980s, were included in the Party's 1983 general election manifesto and continued to be a preoccupation thereafter. Neil Kinnock in his introduction to the general election manifesto in 1992 said: 'In this increasingly interdependent world there are no distant crises. The Labour Government will therefore, as a matter of moral obligation and in the material interests of our country, foster the development and trade relationships necessary for the advance of economic security, political democracy and respect for human rights' (quoted in Little and Wickham-Jones, 2000: 96).

Cook and Short could more credibly claim newness in comparison with the previous Thatcher and Major governments. By 1997, development aid had been whittled down to just 0.26 per cent of GNI and, in line with the approved Cold War approach, development aid was often used to buy political support rather than in support of developmental or human rights-respecting governments (Cumming, 2001). Aid, moreover, had often been linked to promoting British trade, a practice that had become publicly discredited after the Pergau Dam scandal, and was ended by New Labour.[10] Finally, John Major's government had been scarred by secret arms sales to Iraq during Saddam Hussein's repression of the Iraqi Kurds.[11] The ethical foreign policy and focus on poverty reduction in the Third World were a conscious attempt to show that New Labour offered something different from the sleaze and selfishness of its Conservative predecessors.

However, Labour came to power at a time when international approaches, in particular to the Third World, were already being overhauled. Political conditionalities based on human rights and democracy were routinely attached to both multilateral and bilateral aid, part of a strong post-Cold War push to promote liberal ideology in the Third World. Mark Duffield discusses the growing hegemony of 'liberal peace' as an ideological system shared through a network of international non-governmental organisations (INGOs), governments and international financial institutions (IFIs) which seeks to transform societies by concentrating on principles – economic liberalism, democracy, human rights – rather than previous efforts to support more prosaic development projects: 'Effecting social transformation is itself now a direct and explicit policy aim' (Duffield, 2002: 39), part of the post-Cold War sense of the end of history and the triumph of western values. The idea was that state–society relations needed to be reformed, in order to make development flow, an approach that has had particular traction in Africa (Young, 1995). The ethical dimension fitted well within these emerging international norms, and the New Labour Government eagerly began to participate in a congenial aid regime.

Blair gets interested

Both development and the ethical dimension came to be extremely important to New Labour in the way it dealt with foreign policy. This can be seen clearly through Blair's interest in foreign policy, which, during his first year in office, was limited. He made only one speech on the subject – at the annual Lord Mayor's banquet, an occasion traditionally devoted to foreign policy – in which he described his domestic policy agenda in relation to the promotion of Britain overseas (Blair, 1997). His main areas of concern focused on how to keep Britain firmly within Europe and in close partnership with the USA, a theme he returned to in his two foreign policy speeches of 1998 (Blair, 1998a; 1998b).

However, foreign policy was increasingly shaped for Blair by events early on in his first term. In 1997, a British firm, Sandline, was found to have been breaking UN sanctions by supplying arms to Sierra Leone's exiled government, with the knowledge of Foreign Office officials including the High Commissioner to Sierra Leone, Peter Penfold. There was a scandal – which was embarrassing for Cook who was unaware of what had been going on – but Blair shrugged off suggestions of impropriety, arguing that it was morally right to help reinstate the democratically elected Kabbah regime.[12] The British Government went on to demonstrate a significant commitment to Sierra Leone by later sending troops and then large amounts of aid to prop up Kabbah's besieged government (Kargbo, 2006; Williams, 2001). A second event was the military action in Kosovo in 1999, where NATO-led forces countered Serbian-inspired violence against Kosovan Muslims by aggressive aerial bombardment. Britain contributed forces and Blair energetically and successfully drew in international support, including that of the US.

Sierra Leone and Kosovo became for New Labour supreme examples of an ethical approach to foreign policy. Blair, on British action in Sierra Leone, said:

> I know there are those, of course, who believe that we should do nothing beyond offer some words of sympathy and condemnation. But that would be to turn our back in effect on those poor defenceless people in Sierra Leone, when we could do something to help them. It's one of the reasons why Britain counts in the world. Britain is seen to have values and be prepared to back them up. (Blair, 2000)

Cook said of the Kosovo action: 'The place where human rights, democracy and freedom have been challenged over this past year has been in Kosovo and we've asserted these values' (*New Statesman* interview, 1999). Both were presented as clear successes, the triumph of 'our values'; both conferred international status. They provided Blair success in a way that messier domestic policy, subject to closer media scrutiny, could not.

Foreign policy came alive for Blair and he increasingly took charge. Cook had been politically weakened by a series of arms scandals and diplomatic blunders (most notably, arms sales to Indonesia, the Sandline affair and gaffes over Israel and Palestine), as well as by the public and humiliating break-up of his marriage. Never a popular figure in the parliamentary Labour Party, these left him dependent on Blair's patronage – which is why, as Wickham-Jones suggests, he began to introduce Blair's pet 'third way' theme into foreign policy speeches from 1998 (Wickham-Jones, 2000: 17). He exerted uneasy authority over the Foreign Office brief, failing to win the trust of his officials, and was demoted after the 2001 election. His successor, Jack Straw, uncomfortable with the Foreign Office brief from the first, proved even less able to wrest control of foreign policy from Blair.

The events in Kosovo informed Blair's most significant statement of foreign policy, his 'doctrine of the international community', made in Chicago in 1999 (*Ibid*: 17). In it, Blair discussed how the world's states increasingly face similar problems, caused by globalisation and environmental change, and extended a favourite domestic theme – community – to the international sphere.

> Today we are more than ever before mutually dependent ... national interest is to a significant extent governed by international collaboration ... Just as within domestic politics, the notion of community – the belief that partnership and cooperation are essential to advance self-interest – is coming into its own; so it needs to find its own international echo. (Blair, 1999)

Blair argued that the international community, faced with common problems and motivated by 'enlightened self-interest', must intervene where necessary to promote its shared values because 'the spread of our values makes us safer'. Blair was by this time proposing a far more aggressive 'ethical policy' than that suggested by Cook's more cautious 1997 plan.

The themes of Blair's Chicago speech – mutual interests between states, the importance of the spread of values, the need on occasion for intervention – were dramatically reinforced for him by the attacks by al-Qaeda on Washington and New York in 2001. 9/11 was a seminal moment for Blair, not because it caused him to change his ideas or foreign policy direction but because it demonstrated compellingly to him that his existing ideas were right. The 2001 speech to the Labour Party conference, days after 9/11, was billed as a return to the Chicago speech. In it he spoke of 'our values' as 'the right values for our age', and developed his theme of the moral responsibility of the West to promote and extend them, through war if necessary, but through help for the less fortunate too. For Blair, the war on terror and development in Africa were elements of the same programme. In the conference speech he insisted that the international community, working together, could and should tackle the world's problems, including terrorism, climate change and poverty: 'A partnership for Africa, between the developed and the developing world based around the New African Initiative, is there to be done if we find the will ... The state of Africa is a scar on the conscience of the world. But if the world as a community focused on it, we could heal it. And if we don't, it will become deeper and angrier' (Blair, 2001).

Africa becomes 'a passion'

During his first term, Africa had not been a key issue for Blair. His speeches occasionally referred to the importance of tackling Third World debt and ending trade protection in the West, but these were not principal concerns and Africa did not feature strongly. However, Blair made a commitment to take an interest in the continent during his second term and Africa was certainly on the agenda by the end of 2001, its development and future firmly tied into Blair's wider world community agenda. The roots of Blair's interest in Africa are discussed by, among others, John Kampfner and Anthony Seldon, both of whom emphasise its religious aspect. Seldon, drawing on interviews with Blair's colleagues and senior civil servants, suggests that Blair liked to see Africa in moral terms – a place where Britain could do good things (Seldon, 2004: 529). Alongside the moral imperative, it could not have been lost on Blair that making Africa a priority would give him an attractive international point of differentiation, an idea suggested to him by Bill Clinton (Kampfner, 2004: 73). Blair might also have looked abroad for alternative approaches to Africa.[13]

Blair made constant references to Africa in his foreign policy speeches from this point: 'Africa for me is a passion,' he said in a speech to the World Summit on Sustainable Development in 2002 (Blair, 2002b), arguing on another occasion that 'because it is morally right and because ultimately it must be in our own interest, it is clear that the spotlight of attention of the whole of the international community should be focused on Africa' (Blair, 2004). In practical terms, DfID's budget continued to rise, with a significant proportion going to African countries.[14] Gordon Brown was another government minister with a history of interest in development. According to his biographer Tom Bower, 'helping the Third World had been a special interest for Brown since childhood' (Bower, 2004: 206). He took significant steps to cut bilateral and multilateral debt to the world's poorest countries, the majority of which are African. Efforts culminated, in 2005, with a 'year for Africa', during which Brown announced a 'Marshall Plan for Africa', including more debt forgiveness and a new aid initiative (Brown, 2005), Blair presided over a Commission for Africa, set up to find the answers to Africa's problems, and made Africa and the environment the subjects of the Group of Eight (G8) meeting under the UK presidency.

The Government's approach to Africa comprised four elements. First, there were greater commitments to aid and debt relief for impoverished countries. The Government responded to crises during Malawi's floods (2000), famines in Sudan (2001), and southern Africa (2002), and pumped large amounts of development aid into Ethiopia, Sierra Leone and Mozambique, among others. Second, there was a greater willingness to criticise corruption and mismanagement, both of African governments and British companies that colluded with them. Nigeria was the defining example for Cook in 1997; later others were singled out. For example, in July 2004, the British High Commissioner in Kenya, Edward Clay, became so incensed with Kenyan corruption that he spoke publicly of corrupt ministers 'eating like gluttons' and 'vomiting on the shoes of donors' (BBC, 2004). Third, greater efforts were made to work within international bodies to isolate countries subject to conflict and chaos (military action – according to Blair's Chicago speech – could be an option here, was floated as an idea for Sudan in 2004, but only tried in Sierra Leone). And fourth, Blair's government took steps to work in partnership with 'sound' African leaders to develop an overarching strategy. Blair started this in 2001 with a meeting held in the UK with the presidents of Nigeria, Ghana, Botswana, Senegal and Mozambique to discuss priorities for development in Africa, and a similar approach was used in the Africa Commission and support for the New Africa Partnership for Development (NEPAD). On the whole this played well in Britain, judging by the media coverage for anything Africa-related. One significant irritant was Zimbabwe, which regularly disrupted this smooth representation of Africa, its problems and their solutions. Robert Mugabe refused to fit a category, and British attempts to persuade or pressure him into conformity met with failure and embarrassment. Other African leaders wouldn't condemn or put pressure on him over controversial land reform, his intimidation of opposition activists or his worsening human rights record; the Commonwealth for a long time was split by the issue; Mugabe made the British look foolish through personal attacks on ministers and references to colonialism and broken promises on compensation for land reform (Taylor and Williams, 2002; Chan, 2003b).

Zimbabwe aside, Blair's score-sheet on Africa has been perceived as relatively clean. For Blair, Africa was intrinsic to the doctrine of international community, part of his wider plan to make the world better: it was, according to one political rival, Blair's 'badge of morality, moral honour … [Africa came] to embody the ethical dimension of foreign policy'.[15] For many who were critical of the war on terror, it was the great exception to it. While one million people marched through London in protest against the proposed Iraq war in 2003, similar numbers (many of them the same people) were involved in the Make Poverty History campaign pushing Blair to deliver on his commitment to solve Africa's crisis in 2005. While Blair saw a coherent foreign policy, for his critics it had splintered into two.[16] War, which Hegel suggests should help to bolster the state, became deeply divisive and made his government unpopular. Help for Africa – which might strengthen it in a Durkheimian sense – was popular and unifying.

The arguments

Analysis of New Labour's interest in Africa has tended to develop in one of two ways. In the first, the intention to 'do good' is taken at face value and policies are assessed in terms of how effectively they help African states to develop politically and economically. Critics ask, for example, whether more aid is the answer; or, more sophisticatedly, whether conditionalities can induce African regimes to change their behaviour (Dixon and Williams, 2001; Mistry, 2005; Porteous, 2005; Taylor, 2005, Ware, 2006; Williams, 2005). In picking through New Labour's choice of policies, such questions can illustrate the paucity of its analysis of Africa's problems, suggesting that underneath the earnestness lies a careless interest in the wellbeing of the continent. The second approach looks behind or beyond the avowed intention for latent interests or unexpected outcomes. David Chandler, for example, argues that the ethical foreign policy was a grander, more ideologically attractive policy used by the Government to counteract negative feelings engendered in the Labour Party by its cautious, conservative domestic policy (Chandler, 2003). Here the ethical policy is used deliberately as a domestic tool to shore up the Government, almost as an ethical as opposed to bellicose version of Waltz's 'second image'. David Slater and Morag Bell, in an analysis of the DfID white papers of 1997 and 2000, look at how existing power relations between the UK and countries on the receiving end of its ethical and development policies are reinforced by the ways in which the aid discourse is framed (Slater and Bell, 2002). They argue that British aid policy worked to maintain a dependency relationship between the UK and poorer powers (often former colonies). Paul Cammack, in similar vein, argues that the Commission for Africa was organised around the objective of creating capitalist markets and extending and entrenching capitalist power-relations (Cammack, 2006). Rita Abrahamsen and Paul Williams suggest that the key outcome of the UK's ethical foreign policy has been to give it a higher profile internationally, although the policy's effects on poverty in the developing world have been minimal (Abrahamsen and Williams, 2001). Whatever the motivation, the effect has been to enhance Britain's international reputation.

Whether these objectives are pursued explicitly (as Chandler argues of his), unconsciously or 'mistakishly', here are suggestions that attempts to do good in Africa serve British interests: prestige, internal political stability, continuing dominance of international relationships. Perhaps the ethical foreign policy amounted to little more than an attempt to spin a more comfortable interpretation from the realist view of foreign policy as power? Was the ethical element simply attractive window-dressing for politics as usual in a more squeamish age?

Interests in harmony

The realist argument that reduces all international politics to a pursuit of power makes a parody of a profession pursued for all sorts of reasons. For example, Hans Morgenthau, writing at the height of Cold War realism, says: 'We assume that statesmen think and act in terms of interest defined as power, and the evidence of history bears that assumption out... A realist theory of international politics, then, will guard against two popular fallacies: the concern with motives and the concern with ideological preferences' (Morgenthau, 1993: 5). But, as Andrew Williams argues, few would remove morality entirely from politics. 'Policy-makers... are motivated by instincts other than national interest. To assume otherwise is to assume that policy makers are not moral beings, a curious position to take, or that national interest does not have a moral component' (Williams, 2006: 12).

More subtle realist arguments point out debilitating flaws in utopian thinking and uncover some of the less tangible interests pursued through foreign policy. E. H. Carr's characterisation of nineteenth-century utopianism as rooted in the assumption of a harmony of interests resonates strikingly with New Labour's approach. As it came to office in 1997, New Labour displayed several characteristics of utopian thinking.[17] There was the assumption that difference and argument were to be overcome, rather than accepted as an inevitable and endless part of politics. David Marquand argues that this assumption underpinned New Labour's absorption of a wide range of different interests – not just traditional labour, but big business and financial interests – and the belief that it could develop a set of policies to suit all. Older forms of Labourism – trade unionism, libertarian leftism, even social democracy – spoke in terms of struggle and of conflicting interests between labour and capital (Marquand, 1999). New Labour, by contrast, suggested it could transcend political argument by the power of argument and reason. Explicitly, there was a break with old left ideas that fairer wealth distribution could only be pursued at the *expense* of capital, replaced by the idea that it was possible to create a climate where promoting wealth creation would deliver social justice: a perfect harmony of interests.

The notion of harmonious interests proved difficult to sustain in domestic policy but worked in the thinner international atmosphere. Here Blair appeared better able to exert the power of reason and persuasion to solve disagreements. He tended to reduce unavoidable conflict to a dichotomy of 'good guys' and 'bad guys'.[18] The bad guys (Saddam Hussein, the Taliban, Robert Mugabe) – beyond rationality – were to be written off, got rid of. 'Some regimes,' as Robin Cook explained, 'such as Iraq, may simply be beyond rational persuasion' (Cook, 1997b). The good guys, evidently, were either already persuaded or capable of responding to reason. There was no room in the world for different perspectives on the way forward.

The New Labour Government found a ready-made consensus in international political and development discourse into which it could fit: its self-evidential universal norms were already being pursued by like-minded donor countries and international bodies such as the United Nations (UN), the IFIs and the European Union (EU). They were expressed in terms of human rights, democracy and free trade, and their pursuit for the benefit of all. In development circles, there was a high level of agreement: that the key solutions to underdevelopment were more aid, fair trade and less debt; good governance, universal human rights and democracy; and development to remove the causes of conflict. This consensus extended increasingly between the international development agencies and the IFIs. Although the development agencies tended to be critical of World Bank and International Monetary Fund (IMF) economic policies in the developing world, particularly of the ways in which economic liberalisation had undermined welfare provision and hurt the poor, by the late 1990s this approach was changing. The conditions for agreement were already favourable in the sense that the IFIs had long favoured the use of the private/NGO sector rather than governments as service providers, a policy that had seen a substantial increased in the NGO sector in the Third World (Chabbott, 1999). But by the late 1990s, the IFIs had largely abandoned the extreme market liberalisation policies they had promoted in the 1980s and were more interested in the types of political reform – democratisation, human rights and the development of civil society – favoured by the development agencies. The large-scale Make Poverty History campaign in 2005 was an example of the consensus on international development: INGOs, religious groups and political organisations such as trade unions joined forces in an attempt to ensure that the Government delivered on its great year of initiative on Africa. The approach of the international development lobby was attractive both for its internal consensus about the nature of the problems to be tackled and the ways in which to do it, and because, as Duffield suggests, it tended to be technocratic and ostensibly apolitical, echoing a nineteenth-century rationalism and belief in scientific progress (Duffield, 2002). Both these characteristics appealed to the utopian side of New Labour.

Carr criticises utopians for the damage they cause by clinging to the idea of an 'invisible hand' dispensing rational international order. The notion that, by reason and a natural harmony of interests, different parties can be brought to agree, leads to a situation in which international affairs are determined by the strong on behalf of the weak. 'The clash of interests is real and inevitable; and the whole nature of the problem is distorted by an attempt to disguise it' (Carr, 2001: 57). What results is the promotion of the values and interests of the powerful nations and the preservation of the status quo (Duffield's description of 'liberal peace'). 'The bankruptcy of utopianism resides, not in its failure to live up to its principles, but in the exposure of its inability to provide any absolute and disinterested standard for the conduct of international affairs' (*Ibid*: 80). Carr suggests that when world leaders gloss over immanent conflicts of interests, replacing them, magically, with an assumption that 'our interests' are 'your interests', they ultimately serve self-interest far more closely than the interests of intended beneficiaries. Under this interpretation, utopians fail to escape the inevitability of realism, though they may delude themselves and others in the attempt.

What interests are being served? Following Carr, and power-based arguments, these could be the extension of Western or liberal hegemony, the status quo in which Britain is a significant world power, the reinforcement of values that make us safe. However, a substantial 'interest', I believe, comes from the fact of being utopian in itself. Frank Manuel, in discussing the important psychological role utopianism plays, identifies it as a 'kind of dream writ large, where a dream derives its content from a need denied or a wish suppressed… the utopia may well be a sensitive indicator of where the sharpest anguish of an age lies' (Manuel, 1973: 70). For the Labour Party explicitly, a return to utopianism was important to its recovery of self. Adam Utam, in a discussion of socialism, suggests that utopian ideas based on rationalism have been key to the left's portrayal of its ideals. Writing in the 1960s, he suggests that 'the decline of utopian thinking… has seriously damaged the capacity of socialism to stir up emotions of fear or hope' (Utam, 1967: 117). After eighteen years of opposition, during which much cherished ideology was jettisoned, the Party may well have needed a utopian standard around which to collect itself. Wickham-Jones, in a discussion of the role of unilateralism in the Labour Party during the 1980s, and the effect on the Party when it was abandoned, suggests that in the ethical foreign policy the Party found a kind of redemption: in it they had a means to restore their own sense of value as a force for good in the world, and, particularly pleasing, a popular initiative with which they could bring the rest of Britain with them (Wickham-Jones, 2000).

Does utopianism serve Britain too? Utopias are far away places – in space or in time – ideal and perfect; inevitably unreal. Thomas More's ironical *Utopia* fashions a world of self-conscious fantasy. Utopias are mirages of perfection: an ideal society of the imagination. Because they are far away, they exist in a purer realm; they are populated by thinner norms; their foundations are universal. They create in our minds a conception of the ideal of our own society. Blair's enormous appeal in opposition lay in his ability to present himself as a potential leader of a 'young country', to project the concept of a reborn Britain, to capture the longing for an end to hard-headed realism, sleaze and cynicism. A little bit of this idealism continued in his interest in Africa – his 'one moral cause' – which gave Britain its better, cleaner, ethical sense of itself.

Beyond billiard balls

The older utopian/realism theoretical framework couches international relations in terms of how states look out at each other, without attempting to understand how this relates to domestic policy. Although I have already suggested how utopianism does reflect back on British society by helping it conceive of itself as ideal, current IR debates which centre around the dichotomy of cosmopolitanism and communitarianism can add depth to an analysis of the ways in which foreign policy helps secure domestic wellbeing. I will look at the communitarian approach later. I begin here with a discussion of cosmopolitan ideas and how these have influenced New Labour.

A cosmopolitan approach to human relations is based on ideas of shared humanity transcending ethnic, cultural, religious or other differences. Group – even family – allegiances are not more important than others, and therefore the state demands no particular loyalty; neither should it give preference to its own members. Chris Brown traces cosmopolitan thought from the Greek Stoic definition of citizenship based on the *cosmos* rather than the *polis*, through Kant with his advocacy of universal moral law and perpetual peace between nations, utilitarian ideas about the promotion of happiness as widely as possible, irrespective of identity, to Marxist arguments for an international workers' solidarity (Brown, 1992).

The Labour Party's ideas on foreign policy have been heavily influenced by cosmopolitanism, which flows from several ideological roots of the Party. These have held sway particularly in periods in opposition when Labour politicians and activists have enjoyed a more romantic vision of international relationships. The Party's foreign policy thrust in government – typified by two of its most significant Foreign and Defence Secretaries, Ernest Bevin and Denis Healey – has been unashamedly realist (see Bullock's 1983 biography of Bevin, and Healey's 1991 collection of essays on international relations). One cosmopolitan influence on the Labour Party came from Marxist ideas of international solidarity. The concept of extending solidarity throughout the international movement has had particular resonance with the trade union movement. This angle on cosmopolitanism shares some characteristics with the Christian socialist view of the world – a second significant influence within the Labour Party – which promotes universal moral principles and concepts of shared humanity. The Marxist and Christian forms of cosmopolitanism – like those of the philosophers of the Enlightenment – look for a higher universalism under a common set of values, be they the interests of the proletariat, divine morality or pure reason.

Third, cosmopolitanism has influenced the libertarian wing of the Party, keen to disrupt loyalty to organisations, ideas of nationalism or patriotism, and generally concerned with overcoming sources of authority, particularly – in the twentieth century – the state. As Julia Kristeva suggests, the extreme libertarian view 'emerges from the core of a global movement that makes a clean sweep of laws, differences, and prohibitions ... by defying the *polis* and its jurisdiction [it] implicitly challenges the founding prohibitions of established society' (Kristeva, 1991: 60).

These forms of cosmopolitanism have tended to inform those from the idealist left of the Party. However, the mainstream also absorbed a cosmopolitan outlook, one that grew in part out of attempts to reform utopianism as the Labour Party developed its critical stance on both domestic and foreign policy in the early twentieth century and could be described as particularly interested in international institutionalism. The work of Leonard Woolf is an example of this. Writing for the Labour Party and the Fabian Society in the first part of the twentieth century, Woolf attempted to reform or reclaim nineteenth-century utopianism from the imperialists whom he saw as exploiting Africa in the pursuit of British economic interests (Woolf, 1998). Although in many ways a utopian – Woolf argued that humans could reshape the world and overcome power politics – his break with classic utopianism (as defined by Carr) came with the rejection of the idea of harmony of interests. Woolf believed that it was possible for people to work together for common interests, but not easily to do so within the constraints of nation-states. According to Peter Wilson: 'Throughout the nineteenth century, Woolf contended, international interests had been gathering strength at the expense of traditionally conceived national interests. By this he meant that the interests of individuals and groups within the state increasingly corresponded to the interests of similar individuals and groups in other states' (Wilson, 2003: 33). Concluding that Africa needed help, but that Britain wasn't giving it disinterestedly, Woolf advocated that the job should be taken on by new forms of world authority which, free from the distorting dogma of national interests and ideology, could act with international welfare in mind.

Thus cosmopolitanism within the Labour Party ranges from the search for an authority higher than the state – the search for universal principles and possibly universal forms of government – to an anarchic end to all authority which, although emanating from the edges of the Party, exerted a powerful suggestiveness of the unease felt by many in the Party with the aggressive power of the state.

Cook's foreign policy was dominated from the beginning by the cosmopolitan desire to promote universal principles, particularly through international institutions and law. His first key speech on human rights spelt this out.

> My starting point is that in the modern world all nations belong to the same international community ... If every country is a member of an international community, then it is reasonable to require every government to abide by the rules of membership. They are set out in the Universal Declaration of Human Rights ... These are rights which we claim for ourselves and which we therefore have a duty to demand for those who do not yet enjoy them ... The right to enjoy our freedoms comes with the obligation to support the human rights of others. (Cook, 1997b)

New Labour's close relationship with the development agencies reinforced its universalistic approach to international relationships. Since the 1980s, INGOs had become increasingly focused on a cosmopolitan 'rights-based approach' to development, using the UN Declaration of Human Rights as an organising rationale for their work. If a government does not or cannot fulfil those rights – to healthcare, or education, for example – it falls on donors to do so.[19] The two assumptions of this approach – shared apparently by Cook – are that, first, the definition of goods is universal and uncontested and, second, that it matters less who provides the goods than that they are provided.

The Government also found the idea of globalisation supportive of its cosmopolitan approach. Peter Hain, a junior Foreign Office minister, described his ideas of a global community (in ways strongly echoing Blair's doctrine of international community) as based less on common humanity than on common problems – specifically environmental degradation, AIDS and poverty. Explaining his views in a book called *The End of Foreign Policy?* he explicitly dismisses a realist approach, calling for political leaders to 'align the way their nations see their own interests with the new global imperative. Before asking "How can we use our diplomatic tools to secure maximum national benefit?" they should ask "How can our nation best contribute to the attainment of the global goals we all share?"' (Hain, 2001: 7). Further on he refers to 'the beginnings of a global culture' and discusses the opportunities afforded by 'the interconnected world' (*Ibid*: 19). These themes are echoed in DfID's 2000 white paper, which was devoted exclusively to globalisation. Blair's introduction said:

> Globalisation created unprecedented new opportunities and risks. If the poorest countries can be drawn into the global economy and get increasing access to modern knowledge and technology, it could lead to a rapid reduction in global poverty – as well as bringing new trade and investment

> opportunities for all. But if this is not done, the poorest countries will become more marginalised, and suffering and division will grow. And we will all be affected by the consequences. (DfID, 2000)

They extend the ideas of mutual interests and responsibility for action: everyone is now involved in everyone else's problems. Hain's cosmopolitanism overrides the notion of discrete nation-states bouncing off each other like billiard balls and the foreign and the domestic become inseparable; hence 'the end of foreign policy'.

New Labour's borrowing from development NGOs further reinforced this sense of the transcendence of politics. Hugo Slim, drawing on Weber in his discussion of the work of NGOs involved in disaster relief, has described the 'prophet' role many adopted in the 1980s and compares it to the 'priestly' approach traditionally used by governments (Slim, 1998). 'Prophets' are attractive, heroic figures who see past worldly political perspectives straight to the problem, while 'priests' are deeply embroiled in politics. The priestly approach became discredited when both recipient and donor governments were seen to be using aid for their own purposes – recipient governments to line their pockets; donors to buy diplomatic or economic advantage. This is why development agencies have liked to portray themselves as apolitical, basing their work on moral authority which they see as more straightforward. The prophet approach – so successfully used by Bob Geldof in his fundraising efforts for Ethiopia in the 1980s – clearly has greater appeal than the more bureaucratic and politically suspect 'priestly' approach.

Because they see politics as (at best) an irrelevance, prophets are inherently cosmopolitan in their outlook. They favour a direct approach, bypassing governments when they can. They see need in universal terms, irrespective of time and place, typified in their interest in universal human rights. It is easy to see why New Labour might be drawn to this approach.[20] It is at once heroic and technocratic. Its heroic quality comes from its putting the self at the centre of the action, both as one who knows what has to be done and as the one to do it. It is technocratic in its transcendence of politics and its closeness to Enlightenment approaches, which assume that there is a right way to do things, which is beyond discussion.

Cosmopolitanism is thus a useful way to escape a messy domestic scene. Escape enables transcendence to a rarefied arena of more certain, 'thinner' ideals where problems and solutions appear more straightforward. The escape is part of the overthrowing of authority; the projection of ourselves into this purer context allows new possibilities of self-idealisation, and perhaps the establishment of a new, controllable and universal authority.

Africa as a refused place

The projected self is idealised in two ways. First, as discussed above, because of the 'mess' of the domestic scene it leaves behind as it situates itself within a purer sphere. But there is a second source of idealisation to do with the displacement of internal messiness. Kristeva identifies a tendency to export the strangeness or nastiness intolerable in oneself as part of cosmopolitan approaches throughout European history. Freud explained it as the 'narcissistic self…[which] projects out of itself what it experiences as dangerous or unpleasant in itself, making of it an alien double, uncanny and demoniacal' (Kristeva, 1991: 183). This attempt to evacuate and control the uncomfortable or 'uncanny' in ourselves leads to a form of cosmopolitanism that defines otherness on one's own terms and seeks to subject it to supposedly universal principles. 'There is no uncanny strangeness for the person enjoying an acknowledged power and a resplendent image. Uncanniness, for that person, is changed into management and authorised expenditure: strangeness is for the "subjects", the sovereign ignores it, knowing how to have it administered' (*Ibid*: 190).

Africa, as a strange subject, has long existed in European imagination. The Victorians were fascinated by explorers of Africa, and this was reflected in popular literature of the time which, according to Elleke Boehmer, described the dark continent in lurid terms, pitted against heroic British explorers (Boehmer, 2005) – very much along orientalist lines (Said, 2003). Building on Said's work, V. Y. Mudimbe argues that Africa provides the ultimate benchmark of 'otherness' for Europeans, a 'refused place', a place to deposit its own unacceptable facets.

> The discourse is autocentered. It explicitly promotes an unequivocal cultural vocation it wants to convey, counterbalances the identity of its spatial and historical experience to that or those occupying the margins of its concrete as well as its symbolic space. The 'savage' is the one living in the bush, in the forest, indeed away from the *polis*, the *urbs*; and, by extension, 'savage' can designate any marginal being, foreigner, the unknown, whoever is different and who as such becomes the unthinkable…the Other cannot be but the other side, the negative proposition of oneself that should be mastered in its very contradiction and absolutely converted to the ideals of one's truth. (Mudimbe, 1994: 15)

In Mudimbe's description of Africa as a 'refused place', Kristeva's 'alien double' finds its natural home. But, as Achille Mbembe suggests, Africa's otherness is particularly characterised by its apparent emptiness, something that allows for positive as well as negative projections.

> More than any other region, Africa thus stands out as the receptacle of the West's obsession with, and circular discourse about, the facts of 'absence', 'lack' and 'non-being' of identity and difference, of negativeness – in short, of nothingness…In fact, here is a principle of language and classificatory systems in which *to differ* from something or someone is not simply *not to be like* (in the sense of being non-identical or being-other); it is also *not to be at all* (non-being). More, it is *being nothing* (nothingness)…The continent becomes the very figure of what is null, abolished, and, in essence, in opposition to what is the very expression of that nothing whose special feature is to be nothing at all. (Italics in original, Mbembe, 2001: 4)

Mbembe's description works on two levels. First, the emptiness of Africa – its lack of politics proper, its failed states, its chaotic economic systems – provide the blank sheet necessary to project 'our values' onto.[21] Second, as a yardstick by which to measure Britain's place in the world as something – as we look for a post-imperial role – Africa's nothingness is exemplary.

A resplendent image

I have suggested that the British international persona was conceived by New Labour in utopian and cosmopolitan terms. These were derived from an assumption that common humanity leads to common interests, which can be met through universal norms, policies and systems. This approach demanded a simplified view of otherness. It could not be founded on more complex relationships, which would necessarily involve something messier and thicker – a recognition of conflicting interests and ideas and a necessity to resolve distributive issues within this recognition. It resulted in an idealisation of the self – the 'resplendent image'.

The argument of this book is that in a political context, the projection of the ideal works to reinforce the idea of the 'good state': constant identification with a simplified and controlled 'other' enhances conceptions of a Durkheimian ideal community. The Labour Government might have viewed the world and its relationships within it in idealised cosmopolitan terms. However, this directly contradicts a communitarian framework that sees 'the good' as created within communities, embedded within thick relationships that also constantly muddy its purity and create ambiguity. The remainder of the book will make the argument that the 'resplendent image', the idealised state, the utopia, the 'ideal community', is created in an attempt to deal with this ambiguity.

Methods and map of the book

In Britain, Africa is often seen as an undifferentiated entity based, as I have argued above, largely on British imagination. In government policy terms, the continent is often treated as a whole – subject of a 'Marshall Plan for Africa', a 'Commission for Africa' – and less is said or known publicly about country-specific policies. Therefore, much of this book looks at Africa, through British eyes, as a homogenous whole.

At certain points it will, however, be useful to have a tighter geographical focus, and I have chosen Nigeria and Sierra Leone for this purpose. Since the approach adopted by New Labour has strong echoes of late colonialism in Africa, I wanted to look at the part of Africa that can best illustrate benign British engagement in both eras. West Africa is the most extreme subject of a consciously do-good approach to Africa adopted in Britain, rooted in the abolitionist movement. Freetown, as the home set up for slaves freed by the British, was at the heart of British attempts to end the slave trade; later expansion into the interior above Freetown, Lagos and other coastal towns were part of the European division of Africa and justified by the British in terms of Governor Frederick Lugard's 'dual mandate' (Lugard, 1926). Colonialism in West Africa, intimately tied up with the abolition of slavery and without clear, immediate economic advantages (Robinson, Gallagher and Denny, 1961), was seen by the British as part of their attempt to do good in the world.

In the New Labour era Nigeria and Sierra Leone were identified with different aspects of the ethical approach to foreign policy. Nigeria, which in 1997 was ruled by a particularly brutal military dictator, typified Cook's description of the democratic and human rights abuses he wished to overcome. When Abacha's regime fell a year later, and multi-party elections followed, the new President Olusegun Obasanjo came to embody what Britain saw as a right-thinking, progressive African leader.[22] As discussed, Sierra Leone has become part of the New Labour folklore of an ethical intervention. The conflict had been portrayed in Britain as a straightforward battle between a decently elected government and a criminally led rebel movement. Britain's role in sending military help and then financial and technical support was accepted at home as unambiguously clean and right.

Most of the empirical content of the book is based on fifty interviews and informal discussions conducted in 2007 with British MPs, former ministers and government officials, and with Sierra Leonean and Nigerian political activists, journalists and academics. Interviews were semi-structured and aimed at encouraging subjects to talk about how they viewed Africa and British work there – both their own and that of the Government as a whole. People were very happy to talk to me – even those I contacted 'cold' – and the very positive approach they shared, and the fact they appeared to assume I would share it too, underlined the unambiguously positive role Africa and British work there represented.

The rest of the book plays out in six main chapters. Chapter 2 provides a brief and broad introduction to the European history of ideas of the 'good' as separate from the 'political'. In particular, it examines the expressions and meanings of different forms of utopian thought. Chapter 3 examines the way these forms of utopia have been explored in the history of British engagement in Africa. It discusses the abolitionist movement in the eighteenth century and the colonial expansion into West Africa under Joseph Chamberlain at the end of the nineteenth century. The chapter concludes with a discussion of how the ideas and approaches from these two moments fed into the Labour Party as it emerged at the beginning of the twentieth century. Chapter 4 returns to the theoretical discussion, introducing Klein. It suggests the ways in which her work might be understood as an analogy for state–state relationships and discusses the ways in which British engagement in Africa under Blair might be understood within a Kleinian context. Chapters 5 and 6 draw on the empirical work of the research, Chapter 5 detailing the ways in which British MPs imagine Africa and their role there; and Chapter 6 examining how far officials reinforce this perspective and find it possible to sustain it, particularly when they are posted to African countries. Chapter 7 looks at the wider historical and political context in which New Labour pursued its interest in Africa, discussing why political elites saw the state as damaged, the anxieties caused by such a perception, and the ways in which work in Africa might have helped support ideas of repair. The book concludes with a brief summary of the main argument and discussion of some of the themes and questions arising from it.

Notes

1 Grainger makes an interesting attempt to demonstrate how Blair fits Weber's 'ideal' politician, presenting him as an individual anomaly, but fails to address why a politician of this type might have such wide appeal (Grainger, 2005).

2 For classic IR realists, there are no shared norms at all, a position which Frost has challenged in his description of an implicit international normative framework: 'The person or state who acted as a consistent amoralist would not be recognisable as a man or a state properly so called. This does not imply that all individuals and all states are at all times moral. It also does not imply that any specific moral stance is the right one. What is being argued is that individuals and states must have some moral position, for having such a position is particularly constitutive of what being a person or being a state is' (Frost, 1986: 49).

3 The phrase is used by Frederick Cooper, who sums up the similarity in approaches to Africa used in the nineteenth and late twentieth centuries: 'One might argue that this was the ancestor of the movements we are talking about today – using a universalistic language, making an appeal about the humanity of people who are "different", acknowledging the moral implication of people in one place in the fate befalling people in another' (Cooper, 2001: 29).

4 Books on New Labour's ideas published before the election limited discussion of foreign policy to Europe (see, for example, Mandelson and Liddle, 1996; Blair, 1998c; Sopel, 1995).

5 According to John Kampfner, Blair nearly failed to deliver on the manifesto commitment to create DfID, coming under pressure from Robin Cook who didn't want to see the 'good news' bit of the Foreign Office taken out of his hands (Kampfner, 2004: 64).

6 She could not, however, say when the target would be met. Government spending was tightly controlled in the first term, fulfilling a manifesto commitment designed to demonstrate Labour's financial steadiness (Draper, 1997: 85). However, aid levels did rise over time, to reach 0.46 per cent of GNI by 2005 (DfID website: www.dfid.gov.uk).

7 The other three objectives – which Cook described as based on 'clear national interests' – were security, prosperity and quality of life (Cook, 1997a).

8 'The evidence from Nigerian NGOs before last week's meeting of the Commonwealth Ministerial Action Group confirmed in harrowing detail that the military regime in control of Nigeria falls short of those principles [of the Harare Declaration on Human Rights]. Unless there is a radical transformation in the performance of the government of Nigeria, Britain will be arguing at the Commonwealth Heads of Government Meeting that Nigeria continues to be suspended from membership' (Cook, 1997b).

9 David Owen, Foreign Secretary in the late 1970s, told me that 'the idea that ethical foreign policy was started under New Labour is complete bullshit' (interview with David Owen, London, 26 June 2007).

10 This was actually a departure from old Labour too. Judith Hart had introduced the link between aid and trade, an initiative she saw as a perfect harmony of interests between Third World development and protection of British manufacturing jobs (Bose and Burnell, 1991: 98–9).

11 Cook himself seized one of his most glorious hours in opposition by attacking the Government over the Scott Inquiry into the scandal. 'Many people regard Robin Cook's finest moment in the Commons as his devastating analysis of the Scott report on the arms-to-Iraq scandal. Just two hours after being handed a copy of the 2,000-page document, the then shadow foreign secretary pulled apart the Conservative government's handling of the affair with what was regarded as a bravura performance' (BBC Website, 2005).

12 Cook (who was absolved of any knowledge of the arms supply) was more anguished about the impropriety of breaking UN sanctions, expressing a greater concern with international law. This difference with Blair was demonstrated dramatically in 2003 when Cook resigned from the Government over Blair's decision to take military action in Iraq despite the failure to win UN approval.

13 The French way of developing very close, supportive and personal relationships with Francophone African leaders, for example, was very different from the post-war British preference for multilateral engagement. Others – notably Canada and Australia – may have provided a more direct example for Blair. For an account of various approaches in the post-Cold War era, see: Taylor and Williams, 2004.

14 The 2004 spending review pledged a £6.5 billion budget for DfID, £1.25b of which was earmarked for bilateral aid for African countries (Department for International Development Website: www.dfid.gov.uk). More was channelled through the European Union.

15 Interview with Baroness Shirley Williams, London, 25 April 2007.

16 Timothy Garton Ash, for example, argued that if it were not for Iraq, Blair's foreign policy would be seen as largely successful (Garton Ash, 2006).

17 These are not confined to the UK. See Boyle's discussion of Bush's utopianism (Boyle, 2004).

18 Blair explained this outlook in an interview he gave to US journalists at Downing Street on the eve of his first visit to the newly elected President Bush in 2001, in which he described his approach to foreign policy in terms of alliances between rational states which together would sort out rogue states (discussion with an FCO official, February 2001).

19 Development agencies often see themselves as the most effective service providers in African countries. For example, in Ethiopia the country director of a large UK-based NGO argued that British development aid should come straight through his organisation rather than go to the Ethiopian Government, which 'didn't have the capacity to use it effectively' (discussion with the author, Addis Ababa, September 2004).

20 They aren't the only ones. The Conservative Party understands the attractions of the prophet approach and followed Blair in co-opting Geldof to their development programme at the end of 2005 (*Guardian Online*, 2005).

21 Alice Conklin refines the discussion of the way Europeans viewed Africans as

alien and 'other', arguing that what made the colonial project reconcilable with grander liberal ideologies was the perception of the perfectability of Africans. In other words, although different, Africans contained the seeds of sameness. This contains a particularly fascinating impression of Africans as templates waiting for the breath of Europeans to animate them (Conklin, 1998).

22 In a joint press conference with the newly elected President Obasanjo, Cook said: 'It is the beginning of democratic government in Nigeria and the opportunity for renewal of Nigeria and a renewal of the friendship and partnership with Britain. And as I have assured General Obasanjo today, we will be working in Britain as a partner and a friend of Nigeria, working together to make sure that we develop the economy, that we develop Nigeria's status in Africa and in the international community' (Cook, 1999).

2

Ideas of the good and the political

A foundation question for this book is: what made New Labour want to do good in Africa in contrast to a more conventional, interest-based foreign policy? We have seen how Robin Cook announced the 'ethical element' to foreign policy within days of New Labour's election. What made him do it; what made it such a widely applauded approach; and why has its appeal persisted in the form of the Government's approach towards Africa? In later chapters, I will look at the ideas and history of the Labour Party which fed into this approach; and I will discuss Britain's view of its role in Africa more generally, looking for a wider historical lineage for New Labour's Africa agenda. In this chapter, I want to discuss the wider more theoretical question of why a state might attempt to 'do good' abroad. I am going to do this by thinking about how 'the good' and 'the political' in foreign policy might be viewed as both different from, and related to, each other.

I do this because I think that the approach and language used in relation to this attempt to do good suggests that there is a clear separation between what is 'good' and what is 'political'. The former is perceived as pure and universal, compared with the latter, which is steeped in the conflict, ambiguity, self-interest and imperfectability of human relationships. There is a sense with the policy in Africa that self-interest is being escaped and political conflict left behind: that the policy occupies a realm of certainty and universalism where struggles can be transcended because they are subject to universal good. It is this powerful idea that appeals to policy-makers, and that makes the policy in Africa popular in Britain. Approaches to foreign policy that suggest more complex – perhaps more political – relationships appear to be less attractive. I will discuss in detail how British policy-makers see Africa in such terms in Chapters 5 and 6. I begin here by trying to lay some conceptual foundations by discussing how European thinking about this separation between the good and the political has evolved, how it informs conceptions of personal and community relations to the good, and in what ways having a secure connection to a pure idea of good might provide social and psychological underpinning for the community. I draw broadly on European thought, but at times think about how this has been interpreted through British history and ideas. What I say is meant to be applied to Western thinking about international politics; some will be useful mainly in a British context; how far it might apply more broadly is a question left open.

The good and the political in IR

Various IR schools assign different roles to the political and the good. The realist approach that holds that foreign policy can only be about power relations and self-interest therefore finds no place for altruism in international relations (Waltz, 1959; Morgenthau, 1993; Kissinger, 1994). In this view, the good and the political are viewed as completely separate. The political is about the pursuit of power and involves regular clashes between different parties and interests. It was this philosophy that Cook had identified with the previous Conservative regime and was attempting to overturn. As we have already seen, he wanted to replace it with a policy based on 'enlightened self-interest' – a situation where self-interest and altruism worked in harmony – through the pursuit of policies to promote a wider sense of 'the good', this being broadly defined as political liberties in the shape of democracy and human rights. Later on, both he and Tony Blair justified various foreign policy interventions – notably in Kosovo and Sierra Leone – more straightforwardly in terms of their being 'the right thing to do' rather than because they were in British interests. And, as we have seen in Chapter 1, this approach was most clearly extended into the Africa policy where the self-interest side is least apparent, and the approach can be most explicitly presented as based on more purely disinterested motivations.

So, we begin with two ways in which to view 'the good' and 'the political' in foreign policy: first, the realist view of 'the political' in IR as being completely dominated by the pursuit of power with no room for the good; and second, the Cook notion that 'the political' can be reconciled with a strong element of the ethical or 'the good'. It is worth noting that although self-interest remains in this account of foreign policy, it now has nothing to contest since all interests – self-interest and the pursuit of the good – are in harmony. This is a fine example of Carr's description of a utopian foreign policy in which a higher good apparently aligns all interests in the same direction (Carr, 2001). In the utopian view, conventional politics is essentially neutralised as harmonious interests cannot be in conflict with each other. Older theoretical debates in IR between realism and idealism were rooted in this notion that 'the political' and 'the good' were separate. Either the political dominated international relations – as maintained by the realists – or it could be transcended, replaced, by the pursuit of the good – as the idealists suggested. The essential dichotomy here was whether human organisations could ever evolve beyond squabbles over interests and attain some higher state where the good would reign. Carr, who influentially framed this dichotomy, suggested that self-interest could never be escaped and that attempts to do so ended in the entrenchment of particular interests or ideologies rather than a disinterested 'good'. Carr called the idealists utopians, because, he said, they imagined a perfect state of human government within which different interests could be harmonised away by a universal ethical framework.

There is, implicitly, a third view which holds that 'the good' might dominate some parts of foreign policy, either over-riding self-interest or being pursued for its own sake when no material self-interest is evident. British action in Sierra Leone comes close to this: considerable resources, manpower and political credibility were pumped into a small, politically insignificant country in West Africa, although British officials and politicians who were interviewed for this study were reluctant to express policy ambitions in this form (see Chapters 5 and 6).

More recent IR discussions juxtapose cosmopolitan and communitarian approaches, and it is the latter that provides a radical shift to this perception. The cosmopolitan approach, as Chris Brown suggests, grows out of the idealist tradition, drawing on Kantian ideas that all humans have the same rational powers and are subject to the same moral law (Brown, 1992: 39). This approach is evident in New Labour's rhetoric. The argument runs that in a globalising world the essential differences between people – distance, lack of communication, different economic experiences – have been diminished to the point that interests are united around a basic set of human needs or interests. Politics, if defined as a collection of particular interests, which clash with the interests of other groups, becomes redundant. The cosmopolitan approach essentially combines pure altruism with enlightened self-interest and maintains the separation between the good and the political.

The communitarian approach makes the most radical change to this perception of the relationship between the good and the political because it suggests that they are inescapably fused together. Brown argues that the communitarian approach grows partially out of the realist tradition and he traces it back to anti-Enlightenment thinkers like Rousseau, Herder and Hegel, who all maintained that human failings could not be overcome (*Ibid*: 75). Carr's description of realism makes clear its relationship to communitarianism: 'In this [realist] view, the absolute standard of the utopian is conditioned and dictated by the social order and is therefore political. Morality can only be relative, not universal. Ethics must be interpreted in terms of politics; and the search for an ethical norm outside politics is doomed to frustration' (Carr, 2001: 19). Hard-line communitarians do not believe there are universal human bases for ethics, but view these as specific to communities. If different communities develop different ethical paradigms, there can be no universal ethical standard and thus political differences must remain between them. Sometimes this is presented as the ethical occupying the domain of the community, while the political is left for relations between different communities and it is here that it approaches realism most nearly. But this view is rooted in a very static and uniform version of community, one that sees norms within communities as essentially settled, rather than the subject of ongoing contest.[1] More dynamic accounts of a communitarian basis for ethics allow for continuing internal disputes over norms – an endless project under construction – rendering them more part of a political discourse in which different competing norms are in contest. In this version, the good and the political are not separable; conceptions of the good are a creation of human relationships, and so not universal, even within a small community. And, by extension, they exist within different levels of community, suggesting possibilities of thickening within 'international communities' (Linklater, 1998).

This work begins from the assumption that a straightforward separation of the good and the political presents a thin and unconvincing account of human moral and political activity. And yet, clearly, idealist accounts are highly attractive. Indeed, they have come in the era under discussion to define the way policy-makers talk about the world. The New Labour outlook on the world – in common with contemporary outlooks[2] – fits much more closely to idealist and cosmopolitan views of moral universalism and the unchallenged place of the good in IR.

This needs investigation. I propose that the projection of a pure idealised good into the international realm has more to tell us about the self-idealisation of the community than about the nature or quality of its relations with the outside world. But before I discuss this, I am going to look at how the separation of the good and the political has been conceived in European thought, and how different approaches have fed into forms of utopianism.

Historical conceptions of 'the good'

The idea that the good and the political are separate is deeply embedded in European thought. Early European conceptions of 'the good' placed it beyond the Earth and human realisation. The ancient Greek idea of a golden age put the time of perfect government in the past, a state of grace lost to humankind. Hesiod, for example, in *Works and Days*, compares the Golden Age when people lived 'without sorrow of heart' with the corrupted contemporary Iron Age (Hesiod, 1978). The Greeks had not denied the existence of earthly virtues: the ancient heroic traditions very much tied power and prestige to glory and a particular form of virtue. But these were rarely viewed as the highest forms of 'good'. Plato puts them well below the reason and disinterest in worldly power that are the foundations for order and calm, the sources of a far more profound good (Plato, 1941). For the Greeks, it was the idea of harmony with the celestial – that ideal, abstract and distant order, literally beyond the Earth – that embodied the highest form of good.

The Judeo-Christian tradition of Eden before the Fall reinforces this idea, looking forward as well as back. Eden is juxtaposed with Earth; perfect good with human frailty. Original sin – the powerful idea of human fallibility – underwrites the impossibility of perfect human organisation on

Earth. In the *Book of Isaiah*, the idea of a 'good government' becomes one of extreme idealisation, separated from human life by a chasm crossed only in death. Nature itself must change before Heaven can come to Earth.

> The wolf also shall dwell with the lamb, and the leopard shall lie down with the kid; and the calf and the young lion and the fatling together; and a little child shall lead them. And the cow and the bear shall feed; their young ones shall lie down together: and the lion shall eat straw like the ox. And the sucking child shall play on the hole of the asp, and the weaned child shall put his hand on the cockatrice' den. They shall not hurt nor destroy in all my holy mountain: for the earth shall be full of the knowledge of the LORD, as the waters cover the sea. (Isaiah, chapter 11, verses 6–9)

In Heaven, animals lose their nature; aggression and antagonism are banished; God's good pervades everything. This paradise lost through original sin can never be realised in human life again. Here, the insuperable distinction between the good and the human is laid bare.[3]

From this starting point grew interpretations that informed European philosophy and political organisation. The life and teachings of Jesus are interpreted in ways that at times reinforce and at times challenge this separation of the good and the human. Jesus himself as the personification of good in human form represents the idea of the good entering human life. For some Christians, Jesus's work has a political message and admits the idea that human organisation and government can be brought closer to the good. For example, this strand of thinking is compellingly expressed in Catholic liberation theology which builds on the idea of the Trinity as expressive of difference contained within the person of God – the Father, Son and Holy Spirit – and for the good to be an expression of the relationships between the three persons of God. As diversity is found even within the person of God, more complex explanations of the good are plausible (Boff, 1988). For others, it advocates a purely individual connection to the other-worldly good: personal salvation and preparation for the next world are about endless attempts to shake off the stain of original sin; a mediating organisation is too political and flawed to achieve salvation.

In Europe, Christianity had became closely connected through the Church to political authority. During the Middle Ages, the Church was both political entity and holder of the monopoly on human connections to the unearthly good. However, as R. H. Tawney describes, the nature of this connection changed as the strain caused by this straddled position – the inevitable and extreme corruption of the good within a flawed political organisation – led to the Reformation and the ascendancy of an individualised connection to God (Tawney, 1990). This happened with particular ideological intensity in Britain with the rising influence of Puritan Protestantism. Having rejected the idea of a mediating authority that was human and corruptible, the most individualist forms of Protestantism established an unmediated relationship with the good that allowed a greater preservation of purity because the good was no longer mixed up with the political. Interestingly, as Tawney describes it, the Church of England, too, managed to restore some sense of its own purity by explicitly withdrawing from political life, both in its own right and then through its unwillingness to intervene in the political and social affairs of the state (*Ibid*: 140–96).

The political realm became increasingly identified with earthly, human corruption, to be so distinguished from a disinterested good that, in Machiavelli's famous depiction, the two had nothing to say to each other (Machiavelli, 1992). The political arts ignored morality and effective political leadership became synonymous with expediency and the single-minded pursuit of power. Politics was not an arena of calm and harmony, but one of different interests in constant competition. Whether it was a matter of Hobbesian political systems attempting to overcome the state of nature, or Machiavelli's power struggles, politics has to deal with and to an extent even represent disorder. The most reduced definition sees politics as about struggles over power; but even more nuanced versions of politics still see struggles between competing ideas and ideologies which remain unresolved (Freeden, 2003). Bernard Crick describes this neatly within one strand of political ideology – socialism – which he sees as containing within itself competing political ideas which contradict each other and are in constant tension (Crick, 1987). As Hugh Brogan puts it, the nature of politics is 'as natural a dimension of human life as eating, drinking, sex or commerce; a universal process by which human beings adjust to reality – especially the reality of other people – and adjust reality to themselves. It is messy, never wholly successful, and necessarily incomplete. It is the opposite of Utopia' (Brogan, 2006: 277).

A longing for harmony

Yet the need felt by flawed humans to create a connection to the calmer realm of the good remains a feature of social life, as illustrated by the plethora of utopian writing throughout European history. Lewis Mumford's history of utopian thought demonstrates the ways in which utopias have changed, in reaction to contemporary political and practical problems, and the ways in which they reflect aspirations for a social life of perfect order and harmony, an escape from the messy difficulties of life (Mumford, 1922).

Mumford's account illustrates too the shifting ideas about where and how this good is to be found, a theme that is taken up by Charles Taylor in his description of how 'the good', once viewed as completely outside human life, became gradually internalised (Taylor, 1989). Taylor traces the process from Augustine, through Descartes, down to Locke and other Enlightenment thinkers. Augustine maintained the source of good – truth – as outside human life, arguing that individuals can get closer to it if they choose to reject the perverse side of human nature. The *external source* of morality can be reached by finding and promoting the part inside that resonates with it and rejecting the part which is antithetical to it. This approach encapsulated the Christian philosophy which describes the human as a site of eternal struggle between an affinity towards the pure goodness of God and human failure. Descartes revolutionised moral philosophy by *internalising the source* of good, developing a 'new conception of inwardness, an inwardness of self-sufficiency, of autonomous powers of ordering by reason' (*Ibid*: 158). This internalisation of the good found a fuller manifestation in Locke, who advocated complete disengagement from the transcendent, into a route towards the good through human instinct and reason. In the process good was reduced, for Locke, to an instrumental form, whereby subjective pleasure and pain become synonymous with good and bad. The idealised and other-worldly conception of 'the good' becomes defined as more corporeal 'goods'.

Locke and other Enlightenment thinkers created a revolution in thinking when they described a moral framework which could be completely grasped and owned by humanity. From this, a more rational order of public life would be possible. The Enlightenment held out the intoxicating possibility that the good and the political could be conflated; or rather that the good – the rational – could subordinate political, or natural, conflict.[4] With rationality as the internal paradigm for good, humans were now potentially the owners and creators of their own 'good'.

The liberalism spawned by the Enlightenment was particularly influential in Britain, where political thought and action have followed their various forms for at least 200 years: all three of Britain's main political parties can claim liberal philosophy as a pre-eminent guiding principle. Isaiah Berlin's two liberties provide a useful framework (Berlin, 1969). Positive liberty allows for a grand conception of the realisation of a common good created by human organisation and genius. It is a creative, potent form of good, whereby human potential can be realised through organisation around a rational and improving philosophy. It is interested in forms of enlightened and powerful government and authority, and takes on the idea that good is internal and can be organised by humans. Negative liberty is defined in terms of personal approaches to a good life within a looser framework of mutual tolerance. It more passively enables connections to a higher form of good (which might or might not be based on religion). Only by the removal of human interference can this be achieved, and a flowering of 'natural good' realised. This strand fuses with pre-Enlightenment ideas that the source of good is beyond human life, but can be connected with – even to the extent that human weakness can be overcome by it. Both forms of liberty hold an essential common idea, that with the use of a moral framework – internal or external – the negative forces of human frailty and aggression can be eradicated. Original sin was not an inevitability of the human condition.

We are left with three strands of thought, all of which remain powerful ideas in political theory and practice. The first is that of the complete separation of the good and the political, which lives on in versions of realism which root political behaviour and logic in the pursuit of power and draw on the idea of human frailty and the limiting factor blocking the pursuit of anything morally grander. This approach characterised international relations during the Cold War. It remains powerful in the academy in post-structuralist forms, including the theories of Michel Foucault, who suggests that human subjectivity is created through flows of power and control (Foucault, 1988). The second and third, both descendents of the Enlightenment, view the good as realisable, either through human organisation or through the abdication of human organisation. The first of these, at its height in various modernity theories during the middle of the twentieth century, gave way with the rise of neo-liberalism to the second, which appeared to reach its own pinnacle at the end of the Cold War, trumpeted as the 'end of history' (Fukuyama, 1992). It has dominated the ways in which Western politics has seen and represented itself ever since. It finds intellectual expression in cosmopolitan ideas about the potential for rational international norms and institutions to transcend politics and do good. In this approach, the 'political' or ideological gives way to the pursuit of the good. Berlin describes this approach: 'Where ends are agreed, the only questions left are those of means, and these are not political but technical, that is to say, capable of being settled by experts or machines like arguments between engineers or doctors' (Berlin, 1969: 118). It is this approach that is closest to utopianism or cosmopolitan thought which views political ends as coming together in harmony.

I have attempted, very briefly, to sketch out these European traditions of the view of good, all of which are rooted in the idea that the good and the political are distinct from each other. As Carr describes it, 'Here, then, is the complexity, the fascination and the tragedy of all political life. Politics are made up of two elements – utopia and reality – belonging to two different planes which can never meet' (Carr, 2001: 87). Whether good, and its replacement of politics, is realisable on Earth (as idealists hope), or only to be found in Heaven because human politics cannot be escaped (as realists insist), the distinction between the two is maintained. However, despite our best efforts, the 'good life' remains elusive. Squabbles over distribution, ideological argument, fears about the sordid nature of life, have not been eradicated by the Enlightenment; in international relations, power struggles between nations, and between ideological movements, have not succumbed to the 'end of history'. Humanity remains in a state of aspiration towards the good, rather than master of it; still composing an imagined good life in contrast to the flawed lived life. In the next section I will examine this idealist tendency in more depth, by looking at the nature of utopian thinking.

Ideas of utopia

Utopianism remains a powerful idea throughout political and moral thinking because of the difficulty in realising proximity to the good in real life. Since realists assert that they are comfortable with human frailty, they either reject the possibility of a 'good' life altogether or project it onto a post- or super-human realm. At any rate, such a connection to purity is not realistic for life as lived on earth by humans. However, for most idealists, letting go of the idea that we can get closer to the good is rather more painful. One of the ways of getting past this painfulness is to imagine and describe forms of social organisation that achieve this proximity, and this is essentially the root of utopian thinking. Schemes of a better life project us in imagination into another place, or another time, where we have somehow managed to overcome the pain of conflictual social reality. Ralph Dahrendorf says:

> With few exceptions, the purpose behind utopias has been the criticism, even the indictment of existing societies. The story of utopias is the story of an intensely moral and polemical branch of human thinking…They [utopian authors] have certainly succeeded in conveying to their times a strong concern with the practical and ethical short-comings of existing institutions and beliefs. (Dahrendorf, 1968: 118–19)

In their descriptions of a perfect life, within a perfect social organisation, utopias express a 'longing for rightness' (Buber, 1969: 7) that resonates because they manage to express a collective sense of the 'anguish of an age' (Manuel, 1973: 70) and help to 'make the world tolerable to us' (Mumford, 1922: 11). Whatever difficulties societies are encountering, utopia allows some opportunity for transcendence, or escape.

Utopian thinking is differentiated from individual fantasy – it is, rather, a collective fantasy – because it 'seizes upon currents already present in society and gives expression to them' (Mannheim, 1985: 207). In other words, it sums up a *collective* sense of dissatisfaction, providing an overarching framework for a society, providing it with goals and a sense of purpose (Ricoeur, 1986: 283).

Utopias allow communities to feel they can transcend ordinary, messy life by imagining the 'good life'. A crucial element to this is the ability they have to express an idealised vision of what life could be like, and this requires distance – in time or space – from real, current life. As Paul Ricoeur argues, 'no connecting point exists between the "here" of social reality and the "elsewhere" of the utopia'. This disjunction 'allows the utopia to avoid any obligation to come to grips with the real difficulties of a given society' (*Ibid*: 17). Or, the disconnect is essential to the capacity of a utopia to create an idealised scheme of living. They exist, says Ricoeur, in an 'empty place' and constitute a 'leap outside' reality (*Ibid*: 15). In a sense, they constantly revive this idea of a distant, external good, one either lost or yet to be created that, as we have seen, dominated older European ideas about the source of good.

Utopias get beyond the present, inescapable tension within social life whose 'real difficulties' are characterised by inherent dissonance and social conflict. Utopias are created in an empty and idealised place, where perfection has been attained and nothing changes: there is no disagreement, no progress. The guiding force behind all utopias, a key to their attractiveness, is that they present forms of social system which bind all interests harmoniously together, wiping out dissonance and opposition. All potential opponents 'can be convinced or converted to the New Gospel: their enlightened self-interest urges them in this direction' (Utam, 1967: 128).

Two utopias

Mumford, in his survey of utopian thinking, argues that utopias tend towards one of two approaches: either an attempt to escape reality, akin to an attempt to return to Eden; or an attempt to control reality. 'The first leaves the external world the way it is; the second seeks to change it so that one may have intercourse with it on one's own terms. In one we build impossible castles in the air; in the other we consult a surveyor and an architect and a mason and proceed to build a house which meets our essential needs' (Mumford, 1922: 15).

Ricoeur calls these types of utopia the 'romantic' and the 'radically rationalist' (Ricoeur, 1986: 287). However, both describe idealised realms. The escapist or romantic describes a utopia beyond human life, and reaches past human messiness towards it. In the return to Eden, for example, we see a relinquishment of humanity to a higher good: either a religious good or a rational scheme as suggested by Enlightenment thinkers. Charles Fourier, for example, advocated a utopia that allows us to plug into a higher rationality which will create an order that overcomes human frailty. Having relinquished the wickedness of our ways, we become subject to a universal order (Fourier, 1971).

The controlling or radically rationalist utopian idealises human capacity for effecting rationality, for overcoming conflict. This type of utopia is about internalising the capacity to create good through rational human agency. It is typical of an alternative form of Enlightenment thinking, such as that established by Henri de Saint-Simon and his followers, who were concerned with the reformative power of science and education. Such forms of utopianism concentrate on the ways in which human endeavour can be harnessed to organise away human frailty. They are often much more interested in the potential of power and social organisation and many are optimistic about the possibilities for collective self-improvement in human nature.

This dichotomy is clearly resonant with Berlin's description of the two liberties discussed above. An idealised negative liberty suggests that an abdication of human organisation to a higher form of good could enable a full flowering of human potential and good; while an idealised positive liberty describes, for example, the capacity of a state to create a system of good and enlightenment.

What do utopian imaginings achieve? Why have they maintained such a hold throughout the history of European thought? Much of the writing on utopianism is concerned with the ways in which utopian dreams help to transform society. Only if social revolution can be imagined can change be made possible (Mannheim, 1985). Utopias then, are part of the engine of human progress, even if, in their realisation they are damaged and compromised by the realities of human frailty. However, there is another role for utopias, which is concerned with the ways in which communities imagine themselves as perfect and connected to good, and how such imaginations can provide relief for reality, creating a sense of communal repair. Collective fantasies of a good life, the creation of a sacred core at the heart of compromised reality, can provide essential psychological underpinning for a community. This second role ties into Durkheim's suggestion that the existence of a pure, sacred space at the heart of a social organisation is an essential way to maintain a connection to a source of good, and underwrite a community's faith in itself (Durkheim, 2001). The sacred must remain separate from the ordinary, profane activities of human life. Like utopia, it must be removed from the real to avoid contamination.

Africa as utopia

This is the aspect of utopianism that this book is concerned with. We have looked at the nature of utopian thinking and explored two broad types which show the ways in which a perfect social life can be imagined. The argument I want to make is as follows. Most of us appear to need to feel a connection to a higher form of good than is accessible in normal human life. We do this by individually and collectively conceiving better – or perfect – ways of life. When political communities do this – whether they are political parties, pressure groups or states – the compromises of reality inevitably undermine them. But if they are projected, imagined, created far away in space, they can to a far greater extent retain their ideal character. I am concerned here with the community centred on the state, on the ways in which the state creates a sacred core at its centre, a utopian project, a connection to the good. I will argue that Africa has provided an opportunity for the British state to do this. Africa works because it appears particularly far away – in space, obviously, and in time in the ways it is described as a pre-modern place which bears little relation to real, lived life.

Here, in the final part of this chapter, I want to lay out how I am going to explore the utopianisation of Africa by Britain. These ideas divide into two broad types which I will call the 'transcendent' and 'transformative' approaches. They draw on the dichotomies already discussed, in utopian thought as the distinction between the romantic and the radical rationalist; or as described in Berlin's negative and positive liberties. The transcendent approach stems from the traditional *laissez faire* British liberal tradition of Adam Smith and Richard Cobden and seeks to identify with a source of good beyond politics. Suspicious of the state, ill at ease with the messiness of governing, it can be tied up with an overtly religious creed, or with some other form of transcendent good – a politically neutral international organisation or statement of principle or law – an embodiment of Enlightenment ideas about pure reason. The transcendent approach is the mother of cosmopolitanism, in that it carries assumptions about basic humanity and beliefs in the organisation (or non-organisation) of super-national institutions which can eradicate aggression and war. It is predicated on the rejection of human politics and therefore is a form of 'escapist' utopia. The example I will discuss in Chapter 3 is found in the abolitionist movement which overtly attempted to put principle above policy in its cause to end the slave trade. It was expressed in the promotion of free trade and internationalism in the late Victorian period, and its proponents generally opposed imperial expansion. Suspicious of politics and the role of the state as the transcendent approach is, it is unsurprisingly the preferred ideology of opposition, and it heavily influenced the early Independent Labour Party and the trade union movement.

The transformative approach, by contrast, is far more interested in what the state can achieve. It is pushing against forces seeking to restrict or emasculate the state, and wants to recreate it as a potent force, both at home and abroad. In other words, it has a tendency to idealise the capacity of the state. This approach was espoused by the 'social-imperialists' at the end of the nineteenth century and favoured British colonial expansion in Africa. It was informed by two beliefs: first, that widespread colonial possessions would secure British welfare; and second, that colonial rule by the British would bring moral and social improvement to uncivilised parts of the world. One manifestation can be found in the gentlemen colonial officers who, antagonistic towards capitalism which undermined their status at home, attempted to recreate idealised feudal societies in Africa. But other proponents framed it in more progressive ways and, anxious to attempt new ideas of social reform, hoped to find in the empire the means to resource it, and also, when implementation was tricky at home, an arena in which to practise it. This approach, which again will be discussed in Chapter 3, was promoted by Joseph Chamberlain in his radical social agenda, and carried on by the Fabian Society.

There are three points to make about these approaches. First, both manage to protect themselves by projection onto Africa. If ideology can be projected, it gets caught up in the thinner atmosphere of an idealised and flattened utopia. Here, British state capacity becomes absolute. It appears benign and welcome; able to evade sticky problems and dissent. Likewise, the fantasy of a transcendent liberal order – of shared humanity, of the escape from politics – is far easier to maintain. Second, both are engaged in reabsorbing goodness. The transcendent approach essentially makes Africa the tool in the rescue of British goodness; the transformative approach sees Africa as an explicit means of rescuing Britain from economic and social malaise, extending into an implicit means of rescuing the British state from the attacks of the proponents of *laissez faire*. Because of this, both are involved in the activity of repairing the community.[5] Third, although these ideologies were in direct confrontation over colonial expansion at the end of the nineteenth century, when it came to Africa, dividing lines were less clear. The transcendent case was weaker in Africa than in other parts of the empire: cosmopolitanism, the idea that people share interests and values, was all very well up to a point but it wasn't clear to many that Africans fell within that point. At the same time, the transformative approach borrowed heavily from the transcendent when it came to Africa, aligning the British cause in Africa with the grander project of abolition, and, as Jack Gratus points out, many of the descendents (literal and ideological) of the abolition movement were keen to extend the ideas of liberation and enlightenment in Africa through British influence, and many entered or supported the colonial service (Gratus, 1973: 67).

These two approaches, which characterise Britain's approach to Africa at the end of the nineteenth century, were absorbed by the Labour Party, emerging at the same time, influencing both its ideas about the state and politics and its attitude towards colonial and foreign policy and explicitly Africa. As I have already indicated, New Labour's characterisation of Africa and Britain's role there was not original. It is rather in part a resurrection of historic ways in which Britain has seen the continent and its relation to it.

Notes

1 Amitai Etzioni provides a more static and uniform account of communitarianism (Etzioni, 1995). This approach has been quite reasonably criticised for presenting a too uniform, too static view of society (Kymlicka, 2002).

2 See, for example, Stephen Chan's description of the US tendency to view foreign policy challenges in terms of good and evil (Chan, 2005b).

3 More tangible and political forms of utopia did, of course, become the ambition of succeeding generations of Jews.

4 This more Kantian formulation is described by Kimberly Hutchings, who suggests that Kant himself held a more ambivalent idea of the relationship between the good and the political: 'On the one hand, in so far as politics relies on the mechanisms of natural determination it is completely opposed to morality. On the other hand... the purpose of politics (ie, the establishment of state and law) remains governed by the demands not of pragmatism but of a purely rational principle of right which is inextricably bound up with the demands of moral law... ultimately politics is in the service of morality' (Hutchings, 1999: 8).

5 Early attempts to define what this community is are uncomfortable with the idea of the state as the embodiment of the community. Even Chamberlain carried his Liberal suspicions of the state, arguing in favour of municipally driven welfare. But his ideas did give way to an increasingly state-focused logic, carried to its fullest extent by the inheritors of his ideas, including the Fabian Society (see Chapter 3).

3

How the British found utopia in Africa

This chapter explores the ways in which Africa has offered opportunities for idealisation in the history of British engagement with the continent. This is not an attempt at a history of Britain in Africa; nor am I trying to suggest that the British have always seen themselves as behaving with altruism and selflessness – there are too many examples of naked aggression and calculations of self-interest in the history of Britain's dealings with Africa to justify such a claim. However, there are key episodes and streams of ideas relating Africa to Britain which were seen as 'good' by those involved in them.[1] And many of them feed into modern British conceptions of what the continent is, and specifically into Labour Party ideas about a British role in Africa.

I will explore the roots and development of ideas about the ways Britain connected to a sense of 'the good' in its dealings with Africa, and about the ways in which these appeared to effect a sense of the repair of the state, as described by several key moments of British policy towards Africa. First, I discuss the ways in which British involvement in West Africa has been described, as a backdrop to ideas about Britain's role of 'doing good' in Africa. In the second and third sections, I discuss two key movements and streams of thinking about Britain in Africa. I look first at the abolition movement in the early nineteenth century, and argue that its concentration on a repudiation of politics in favour of a higher moral authority or framework represents an example of the transcendent approach. Second, I examine the late nineteenth-century colonial expansion into West Africa under Joseph Chamberlain, and I argue that his attempts to invigorate state capacity led to the idealisation of the colonial state, as a way to repair material damage not just in Britain, but in Africa too. This is an example of the transformative approach. Finally, I look at how these two periods in history, and the ideas that guided them, fed via different streams into the Labour Party, causing internal tension over the issue of colonial possession, and ultimately becoming fused into one glorious idealisation of Africa and British history and policy there. It was this fused idealisation that informed the Party's approach to Africa under Blair.

The account given in this chapter relies heavily on the writing and speeches of a number of key players: in particular, I discuss the ideas of William Wilberforce, Joseph Chamberlain, Frederick Lugard, Leonard

Woolf and Fenner Brockway. This is not meant to suggest that history is shaped primarily by individuals, or even that these men were uniquely representative of the ideas they expressed and the movements they led and belonged to. Rather than give an account of history, I am discussing the history of the ideas contained in the various movements and initiatives which these men represented particularly clearly. Ideas cannot be found in the account of events, but in the way those involved understood and explained them. Therefore I think it reasonable to draw on their depiction of the ideas that motivated them, and that they used to justify and popularise what they were doing.

Britain and Africa: the 'ethical' history

British imperialism in Africa was relatively short-lived: the tiny colony of Sierra Leone was established under self-rule by British abolitionists in 1787, becoming a crown colony in 1807, and the Cape of Good Hope was only occupied by the British in 1795. Apart from the odd toe-hold on the continent, the British preferred to operate through spheres of influence, granting charters to British trading companies, some of which pursued ambitious administrative projects. After the Berlin Conference in 1884–85, the question of whether to formalise control over the 'British bits' – in southern, eastern and West Africa – became a more pressing question, although state control by Britain only became properly established at the very end of the nineteenth century and less than sixty years later decolonisation had begun. As Charles Allen points out, it was once relatively easy to find people in Africa who could remember both the advent and demise of British colonial government (Allen, 1979). However, this is not to underestimate the effects of colonial rule, both during its operation and afterwards, a theme dwelt on with particular force by African novelists and intellectuals (see, for example: Achebe, 1958; Achebe, 1986; Ekeh, 1975; Mamdani, 1996).

The parts of Africa I focus on are Sierra Leone and Nigeria in West Africa, during the period in which Britain attempted to consolidate and extend its hold there at the end of the nineteenth and beginning of the twentieth centuries. There are good reasons that make this period and these countries suitable cases in which to look for evidence of the origins and development of the British idealised approach.

First, and in contrast to other parts of colonised Africa, West Africa held few immediate economic or strategic attractions. Minerals were as yet undiscovered and potential markets for British goods were at best a long-term prospect. Without white settler communities, commercial farming was also going to be more of a challenge. The position of West Africa, far from the strategically and economically more important imperial concerns in India and increasingly the Middle East, made it strategically peripheral. Ardent imperialists could attempt to justify colonial expansion in West Africa only on the basis of *potential* economic interests, and, more immediately, and popularly, to make do with the interest of keeping the French at bay.[2] However, West Africa was perhaps more effectively tied in the British imagination to the sacrifice of self-interest in pursuit of a higher good. In 1807, the Act of the Abolition of the Slave Trade had defined a British role in West Africa as one of altruism and principle over self-interest and politics. British ships had patrolled the West African coastline and captured slave ships, returning their cargoes to the newly-created and poignantly named Freetown, a colony set up by abolition campaigners in 1787. Writing about the history of Sierra Leone, J. J. Crooks wrote in 1903: 'The initial cause of the British forming this colony, which was, and is, practically useless as an outlet for Great Britain's surplus population, such as other colonies have been, may be summed up in one word, SLAVERY' (emphasis in original, Crooks, 1972: 20).

Second, this key moment in British history – the long debate and public mobilisation which eventually led to the demise of the slave trade – had succeeded in uniting British opinion around a grand and noble cause; it had created in fact a consensus, which continued to shape its role and the sense of what its business was in the world. The abolition of the slave trade was viewed as a moment in history that defined the elevation of principle over self-interest (Howse, 1952). It had differentiated Britain from its more venal European neighbours, and created an imagined role for Britain as one defined by William Wilberforce: 'Wherever the sun shines, let us go round the world with him, diffusing our beneficence.'[3] This view of Africa and Britain's key role in undermining the slave trade and then slavery itself was to inform subsequent policy approaches to the continent, no more so than in West Africa, the site of Britain's moment of altruism.

Third, and tied into the relative lack of direct interests, in contrast to colonies in southern and eastern Africa, Britain's four West African colonial possessions were not considered suitable for white settlers – the climate killed too many of them. This meant that a handful of British colonial officers ran colonies predominantly made up of indigenous and resettled black populations.[4] This enabled a far thinner relationship between the governing and the governed. In settled colonies like South Africa and Kenya, white communities made often unreasonable demands about labour conditions, and there were tensions over unequal political and economic distribution which caused 'permanent headaches' to British politicians and officials (Gann and Duigan, 1978: 8). These contentious issues could only thicken political and social organisation as the authorities were pulled in to resolve differences and to take sides and ultimately led to much more violent independence struggles. It was much more difficult in these conditions to present policy as disinterested and non-partisan. In West Africa, the colonial government did not have to deal with the same kinds of conflicting community interests and was therefore better able to see and present itself as principally concerned with the welfare of the native populations. With the local population broadly on a par, it was easier to portray policy as being in the interests of all.[5]

Fourth, again linked to the points above, the relative lack of self-interest meant that British government in West Africa was always going to be more poorly resourced and widely stretched than in other parts of the empire. Attempts to make these colonies pay their own way were deeply problematic, and without the promise of economic reward the Treasury was reluctant and always having to be persuaded to provide funding. This meant that the colonial state itself had to be thinner, and to rely on local collaborators and structures of authority (see Owusu, 1970; Berman, 1990). Although deals with local strongmen were necessary, and could create friction and even conflict, it was also true that indirect rule must remove large areas of direct control from the hands of the state, thus increasingly thinning the ways in which it conceived of itself and its relationship to those it purported to rule. In ways that rather echo modern descriptions of the rulers and ruled, African elites might well be viewed as corrupt and difficult; but African populations, at greater remove from the colonial authorities, were relatively flat and idealised.

Fifth and finally, the expansion of the colonies in West Africa occurred during a period in which liberal views about the role and capacity of the state in shaping and improving social, economic and moral life was gaining traction in Britain. Colonial rule in these new possessions could be and was expressed in terms of this approach, in ways that projected an uncomplicated sense of the capacity of the British state. At this period it was more allowable to exercise these new ideas of the state in a far-off British colony than in Britain itself. One of their chief proponents, Joseph Chamberlain, a radical liberal in favour of social reform in a Conservative government, asked for the job of Colonial Secretary for this very reason. 'The Colonial Office ... would provide him with an unrivalled chance to promote the material wellbeing of Britain through a business-like re-ordering of imperial trade and the proper use of imperial resources' (Judd, 1977: 185). And presenting the approach as uncomplicated might have been more feasible in far-off Africa, where scrutiny was less minute. When things did go wrong, or when problems became visible back in Britain – as they did, for example, in 1898 when the colonial authorities in Sierra Leone met violent resistance to their attempts to impose a hut tax – the reaction in Britain was horrified and focused on how and why the relationship between the governor and the local population had gone so bad.[6]

Transcending politics: the oppositionist abolitionists

The British slave trade operated throughout the eighteenth century, and for most of this period, there was little public concern that the practice was inconsistent with domestic principles of liberty. During the height of the trade, British ships transported up to one million Africans to America and the West Indies (Gratus, 1973: 39).[7] However, towards the end of the century, opposition to the trade began to grow, precipitated, claims Linda Colley, by the loss of the American colonies. 'Many of them [the abolitionists] now sought to explain what appeared an almost inexplicable defeat at the hands of colonists by reference to their own failings in the sight of God. They had been corrupt and presumptuous ... and they had been duly punished' (Colley, 2005: 353). The slave trade, and the riches Britain had won by it, began to appear morally unsupportable.

The campaign, then, was propelled by a sense of national unease; it responded to feelings of guilt and damage done by Britain to the wider world and to its own national virtue; and it was directly concerned with attempts at reparation. As I shall argue, this was done through an attempt to repudiate politics and interest by reaching for a source of higher good. As Ernest Marshall Howse describes the movement, it was 'an illuminating reminder that spiritual factors in civilisation may outweigh material factors' (Howse, 1952: vi).

The oppositionist abolitionists

The debate over the abolition of the slave trade lasted more than twenty years and saw many attempts to introduce legislation to ban the trade. It began as bitterly contentious, and it ended attracting overwhelming support, uniting the political parties – both William Pitt and Charles Fox spoke and voted in favour of abolition – and claimed such intellectual luminaries as John Wesley, Adam Smith, Beilby Porteous and Jeremy Bentham as supporters. The campaign succeeded in mobilising popular support, and much of its success was due to mass lobbying and petitioning of Parliament (Colley, 2005: 354–5). Finally, its success in 1807 conferred a nation-wide feeling of involvement in a noble cause which could be described by the historian W. E. H. Lecky as 'among the three or four perfectly virtuous pages comprised in the history of nations' (quoted in Coupland, 1964: 250–1).

The abolitionists explicitly presented the issue as a contradiction between interest and principle, between the political and the good. The interests of the West Indian plantation owners, of the British ports that serviced the trade, of the traders and transporters themselves, and of the wider British economy, were pitted against the immorality of a trade that led to the transportation of thousands of Africans each year on British ships in the most appalling of conditions: 'Let any one imagine to himself six or 700 of these wretches chained two and two, surrounded with every object that is nauseous and disgusting, diseased, and struggling under every kind of wretchedness! How can we bear to think of such a scene as this?' (Wilberforce, Slave Trade Debate, 1789: 45–6).

There was no harmony of interests here; just a full-blooded attempt to overcome the political with the good. In an early attempt to end the trade, Wilberforce said:

> Policy, sir, is not my principle, and I am not ashamed to say it. There is a principle above everything that is political; and when I reflect on the command which says, 'Thou shall not do murder,' believing the authority to

> be divine, how can I dare to set up any reasonings of my own against it? (*Ibid*: 62–3)

In the face of which the unashamedly corporeal and archetypal realist Alderman Newnham represented a straightforward dismissal of the abolitionists' arguments in favour of principle over interests. Its supporters, he argued, 'did it from motives that would gain [them] merit in another world, for with him he was sure it would gain none here. He objected to the motion as destructive of the commerce and revenue of the country' (Alderman Newnham, Slave Trade Debate, 1795: 1,332).

The interests under attack were substantial. Sir William Young, in the debate in 1796, argued not just against abolition on the grounds of pressing economic interests, but against the criminalisation of 'gentlemen of rank in society, of polished manners and of extensive connexions [*sic*]':

> He felt for the West India merchants and planters, who would be consigned to inevitable ruin ... and he felt for his own property in the West Indies, of which this measure would necessarily deprive him ... Every gentleman of character and fortune would be liable to lose his reputation, to suffer in his estate, and be separated from his wife, his children, his country and his dearest connexions [*sic*]. Nor would the interests of the West Indies be injured only, but the interests of this country, which he was ashamed to call the mother country, since, by this bill, it had already forfeited that appellation, would be injured with them. The bill might, with propriety, be called a bill of general foreclosure. (Sir W. Young, Slave Trade Debate, 1796: 866–8)

The repudiation of politics and the prioritisation of the good in public life felt like an attempt to overthrow the natural order, a sense reinforced by the wider contemporary backdrop of a religious revival. The movement's key protagonists did feel that the cause demanded religious principles be brought into the political sphere (Coupland, 1964). For Wilberforce, abolition was a cause 'which appealed to his new-found conscience, untainted by party interest, involving the moral and physical welfare of countless human beings, a challenge to a Christian and a patriot to redeem his country from sin, a real crusade' (*Ibid*: 74). For Buxton, the political life in pursuit of the cause of abolition was 'the sphere in which I could do most for my Master's service' (quoted in *Ibid*: 119).

The moral force behind the argument was drawn from the idea that mere human 'reasoning' was powerless in the face of divine commandment. The higher good could not be reached through human means, but by an abdication of human frailty and self-interest in favour of a higher, essentially non-human order. Wilberforce rooted his approach in the concept of inescapable original sin: humans could only achieve salvation by resort to a higher good. In his book, *A Practical View*, he writes:

> The Holy Scriptures speak of us as fallen creatures; in almost every page we shall find something that is calculated to abate the loftiness and silence

> the pretensions of man. The imagination of man's heart is evil from his youth [...] They are all gone aside; they are altogether become filthy; there is none that doeth good, no not one ... a thorough change, a renovation of our nature, [is] necessary to our becoming true Christians ... holy men refer their good dispositions and affections to the immediate agency of the Supreme Being. (Wilberforce, 1958: 28–9)

Wilberforce's frequent applications to divine law were an explicit illustration both of the goodness of this higher authority and its position of opposition to the man-made world. 'I could not believe', he said, 'that the same Being who forbids rapine and bloodshed, had made rapine and bloodshed necessary to the wellbeing of any part of the universe' (Wilberforce, Slave Trade Debate, 1789: 48–9).

A strong theme of the abolitionists was that of the destructiveness of British interference in Africa. This approach underwrites the connection between the abolitionists' cause and a negative liberalism: interference and over-involvement do harm. The trade was a degrading one, which corrupted and despoiled both the exploited and the exploiters. For example, Wilberforce asks whether: 'civilisation [in Africa] must be checked; that her barbarous manners must be made more barbarous; and that the happiness of her millions of inhabitants must be prejudiced with her intercourse with Britain?' (Wilberforce, Slave Trade Debate, 1789: 43) The cause itself was one of removal and reversal – a negative rather than a positive demand. In common with the later anti-colonial and anti-apartheid movements, this cause maintained purity by taking an oppositionist position.

Weariness and disgust with real life generated guilt that frailty and interest had so dramatically overcome divine right and law. Guilt gave the impetus for action through reparation. Transcendence of politics was a restorative action.

> I mean not to accuse anyone, but to take the shame upon myself, in common, indeed, with the whole parliament of Great Britain, for having suffered this horrid trade to be carried on under their authority. We are all guilty – we ought all to plead guilty, and not to exculpate ourselves by throwing the blame on others ... What a mortification must we feel at having so long neglected to think of our guilt, or to attempt any reparation! (*Ibid*: 42)

However instinctively oppositionist, however individualist its philosophical origins, and however much it shared an affinity with the state-sceptic free-trade and liberal movements, the movement did represent a concern with the health of the British as a nation and in the health of the state. Jack Gratus, in his very critical account of the movement, argues that the abolitionists were far more interested in their own personal salvation than in the welfare of Africans. 'So insistent were these critics of the imminence of God's punishment that it is not clear what was more important to them – the sufferings of the slaves, or the souls of the white Christians engaged in the system' (Gratus, 1973: 45). But they were interested in more than securing their own place in Heaven. For them, the realignment of good with public life was of great significance. Colley links their cause to the growing realisation of British identity, a crucial part of which was an identification of Britain with 'the good'. 'Successful abolitionism became one of the vital underpinnings of British supremacy in the Victorian era, offering – as it seemed to do – irrefutable proof that British power was founded on religion, on freedom and on moral calibre, not just on a superior stock of armaments and capital' (Colley, 2005: 359).

We see in the debates the theme of the damage done to the 'national conscience' (Buxton, 1968: 531), expressed in the idea of the degradation of the British nation, and of the British state that had allowed the trade. One abolitionist could argue that, 'we shall, by voting the abolition of the trade, have wiped out a foul blot from our national character' (Hobhouse, Slave Trade Debate, 1797: 572), while another suggested that, 'if this country did not wipe away the foul stain of iniquity by which it had been polluted, it was liable to a responsibility unequalled by any which the human mind could picture to itself' (Whitbread, Slave Trade Debate, 1795: 1,331), and Wilberforce referred to the trade as 'destructive to the human race…disgraceful to the character of the British nation' (Wilberforce, Slave Trade Debate, 1796: 737). 'If ever there was a national sin,' he said, 'the slave trade surely was of that description' (Wilberforce, Slave Trade Debate, 1795: 1,328).

The Act of Abolition, when it finally came in 1807, was rooted in the idea that politics could be transcended; however it also fed into direct state activity through the patrol of the West African coastline and the recapture of slaves, and in the moment when the British state took responsibility for Sierra Leone.The moral triumph of abolition, a success story in which everyone wanted to claim a share, shaped British approaches towards Africa in several directions. One turned into a more proactive approach to British policy in Africa, to the development of humanitarianism and the colonial project. This will be discussed in the next section. Another, maintaining more of the escapist flavour, became manifest in the anti-colonial movement, which I will come to in the final part of the chapter.

Transforming politics: the potent state

The legacy of the abolition of the slave trade, and its ideas of connecting the state to a source of good, were gradually absorbed into a more proactive form of liberalism. This was shaped perhaps by shifting perceptions as to the source and manifestation of British malaise. Whereas the abolitionists made a stand against an apparently aggressive and selfish state, the new liberalism took up a position against the inadequacies of an over-passive state. The more radical liberalism that developed towards the end of the nineteenth century increasingly sought to redefine the concept of freedom to encompass notions of social reform by means of collective political activity, gradually solidifying into state activity. Traditional liberalism – personified by William Gladstone[8] – was pushed into a corner by two decades of economic depression and a wider electoral franchise demanding more of government, and now had a vigorous rival which contemplated more social, positive conceptions of freedom and a far wider remit for the state in effecting it. The ideas of the radical liberals were shared within other parts of the left, among them elements of the fledgling Labour Party and the trade union movement, and reached their peak of influence with John Maynard Keynes and William Beveridge after the Second World War.

The radical liberals were optimistic about the ability of collective political action to direct and promote social wellbeing. Driven by concern for domestic welfare, this group promoted ideas that would shape colonial policy, both in terms of what it could do for British welfare, but then too in terms of what it could do for the welfare of the colonised. Part of this development, argues Bernard Semmel, was a reaction to the growth and perceived threat of socialism which was increasingly making demands on the state to better represent and provide for the working classes. As an alternative to the socialist espousal of internationalism, the radical liberals developed a form of 'social imperialism', 'designed to draw all classes together in defence of the nation and empire and aimed to prove to the least well-to-do classes that its interests were inseparable from those of the nation' (Semmel, 1960: 24). Semmel's point is that the social aspect of imperialism was crafted in reaction to potential political instability at home; but this is not the whole story, particularly when it came to Chamberlain himself, who saw empire both in terms of the concrete ways it could enhance British welfare and through a 'desire to associate imperialism with some tangible and popular programme [motivated by] his sense of the urgent need to rouse the people from apathy or domestic quarrels to some larger purpose' (Fraser, 1966: xv).

Chamberlain, with his experiments in 'municipal socialism' in Birmingham, was a standard-bearer for the radical liberals. His politics were guided by his belief that government should be an active provider of welfare and a protector of British industry. His break with the Liberal Party over Irish home rule (which he opposed), his aggressive imperialism, and his subsequent commitment to tariff reform were all informed by this political imperative (Judd, 1977). Chamberlain articulated a contemporary reaction to the perceived damage done by *laissez faire* policies. Britain in the 1880s and 1890s appeared to be in relative decline: export growth had been consistently slowing for some years in comparison with European competitors, and industrial upheaval continued to bring 'poverty, misery and depravity' to Britain's industrial cities (Gann and Duigan, 1978: 3). Chamberlain's ideas about empire and reform were thus rooted in anxiety and dissatisfaction with the domestic situation.[9] His imperialism would feel its way towards two utopias: the first created the idea of a new industrial phase which would bring material benefits to Britain's manufacturers and workers through cooperation with 'fellow subjects'. Chamberlain, in a speech made in 1998, said: 'There is another duty which, I think, is incumbent upon the British Government, and that is to draw closer to our colonies (cheers), to the sister nations of our race across the seas (cheers), and to seek in our own family the strength and support which we shall never find from foreign nations (cheers).'[10]

This is repair at its most visceral, in which Chamberlain's argument for the empire depicts it as an area of protected trade that could directly support British industry and jobs and pay for domestic welfare. It is at its most graphic when Britain could display a map of the world that was dominated by large blocks of imperial red.[11] The second utopia, which emerged more gradually, became a powerful idea of an idealised British state developing the welfare of Africans. It was developed by colonial officers like Frederick Lugard. The idea that Britain worked for the benefit of the colonised was not new; but that the state could be the engine of these benefits was. Partly it developed because it was a popular idea;[12] and partly it developed because the very idea of the ideal state, which is difficult to sustain in the domestic arena, worked so much better when it was projected onto Africa.

What I am now describing is a new ideal; whereas the abolitionists rejected politics in favour of the good, the new approach envisaged the state itself as the source of good. This was a re-absorption, or internalisation of the capacity to create the good by the state: the state itself is the engine of good.

Josephus Africanus[13]

Chamberlain was appointed Colonial Secretary in 1895, and immediately initiated a more assertive colonial policy. In particular, the new African colonies would be actively developed by the state. In his widely reported and applauded first speech to the House of Commons, the new Colonial Secretary said:

> I regard many of our colonies as being in the condition of undeveloped estates, and estates which can never be developed without Imperial assistance. (Cheers.) ... Cases have already come to my knowledge of colonies which have been British colonies, perhaps, for more than 100 years, in which up to the present time British rule has done absolutely nothing: and if we left them today we should leave them in the same condition as that in which we found them. How can we expect, therefore, either with advantage to them or to ourselves that trade with such places can be developed? I shall be prepared to consider very carefully myself, and then, if I am satisfied, to confidently submit to the House, any case which may occur in which, by the judicious investment of British money, those estates which belong to the British crown may be developed for the benefit of the population and for the benefit of the greater population which is outside. (Cheers.) (Chamberlain, House of Commons, 1895, 640–52)

Chamberlain admitted that his material approach amounted to a 'squalid argument' and was also ready to use more romantic arguments – about the need to save and reform backward, suffering Africans – in favour of empire (Semmel, 1960: 95). The success and popularity of the British role in the abolition of the slave trade created solid foundations for the projection of a moral role for Britain in taking over parts of Africa in order to eradicate slave ownership and other barbaric practices, such as fetishism and twin-murder, which excited British imaginations.

These were not new ideas and they resonated comfortably in Britain.[14] There was continuity with older British conceptions about imperialism, which, Cain and Hopkins point out, had been driven by gentlemen-capitalists and financiers, who felt that, in comparison with profit-seeking industrialists, they pursued a 'service ethic', and an understanding that it was the job of the privileged to serve the poor. 'The empire was a superb arena for gentlemanly endeavour, the ultimate testing ground for the idea of a responsible progress, for the battle against evil, for the performance of duty, and for the achievement of honour' (Cain and Hopkins, 1993: 34). This was, they argue, about the projection of a British superiority, realised in British ability to improve and bring enlightenment to the world. Africa was the continent most in need of enlightenment. 'Africa, the Dark Continent, had a special appeal; for there, in the aftermath of the Atlantic slave trade, it seemed that economic backwardness, moral degeneration had reached the lowest possible levels, and it was there, consequently, that the ultimate test of the supremacy of western culture and skills was to be found' (*Ibid*: 353–4).

The heroic leaders of the chartered companies – men like Cecil Rhodes and George Taubman Goldie – had managed to personify this ethic and were glorified in the press.[15] Now this heroic garb was to be borrowed by the state itself. For example, the *Pall Mall Gazette* says of Chamberlain: 'Whereas too many of his predecessors have been fertile only in evasions of responsibility, he has boldly adventured upon a policy of construction. If we are right in our interpretation of his speech last night, his views are practically identical to those of Mr Cecil Rhodes' (*Pall Mall Gazette*, 1895: 1). And on another day: 'If British policy has not been continuous, Anglo-Saxon character has, and the success of our colonial career has been due not to our administrators, but to our colonists' (*Ibid*, 1898: 4).

At the same time, the state's potential role was even grander and more creative, rising above individual self-glory. This reflected far wider shifts in perceptions about the role of the state which Chamberlain represented. A leader column in *The Times* on the occasion of Chamberlain's first speech captured this:

> Just as it was the custom to think that the less we had to do with the colonies the better for all concerned, so people were accustomed to suppose that trade and commerce were always capable of looking after themselves, and were much better without assistance from the state ... The erection and worship of fetishes is a weakness of human nature which civilization hardly

> seems to modify and certainly has not yet eradicated. The fetishes of the Manchester School are no longer universally believed in under penalty of denunciation for impenetrable stupidity, but they still sway a considerable number of persons whose ideas lost their elasticity some fifteen or twenty years ago ... Our rivals perceived very early that a nation industrially backward may profit enormously by bringing in the organised power of the state to second the efforts of individual adventurers ... Mr Chamberlain's speech is only one of many significant acknowledgements that a new conception of the duty of the state to its subjects holds sway among contemporary politicians. (*Times*, 1897: 7)

For Chamberlain, a rejection of the 'fetish of the Manchester School' meant that the British state took direct, formal control of the territories from the chartered companies. His belief in the relative ability of the state vis-à-vis the private sector to best represent British interests laid the groundwork for a new relationship between the state and the expanding electorate, one in which an active state could become an engine for social reform and success. The state could be not only as heroic and brave as Goldie and Rhodes but more capable and good.[16] This point is demonstrated in the parliamentary debates during 1895 over Chamberlain's bill to buy out the Royal Niger Company. The bill's supporters saw it as representing the triumph of collective over private interests. 'What was the real and true objection, not only to this chartered company, but to every chartered company? That they were mixing up totally dissimilar things – things not only dissimilar, but which ought on every principle of ethics and good sense to be eternally dissociated – the right to govern men and the desire to make money. (Hear, hear!)' (H. O. Arnold Foster, Queen's Speech Debate, 1885: 289–94).

What marked this sense of the separation between the good and the political as different from that of the transcendent abolitionists was the notion of human capacity – found in the state – to effect good. The new agenda for governing West Africa involved a substantial set of objectives, which the Company was now considered unequal to, including keeping the predatory French at bay; effecting the eradication of slave ownership; and making West Africa economically viable. Chamberlain describes the nature of a state-sponsored colony, which involves a far deeper role and set of obligations on the part of the Government than could be demanded of a chartered company.

> When we have made a treaty with a native state, we accord it our protection. At the same time we are bound as a civilised power to accompany that with certain conditions. We expect, for instance, that the practice of slave raiding, and the observance of these fetish superstitions, which have caused so much bloodshed in Africa, and which – slave-trading especially – has desolated the country, and has destroyed for centuries the possibilities of trade – we expect that these practices will be given up. In return, we have to guarantee the security and the order and peace of these districts if they are threatened from outside. (Chamberlain, Supply Debate, 1898, Hansard: 1,617–28)

In particular, the state's capacity was the key to its goodness.

> In the Niger Company's territories the legal status of slavery has been abolished. No doubt that was a most excellent arrangement, but at the same time I must point out that it is to a large extent a paper arrangement, because in a very large portion of this gigantic country of Sokoto and Bornu no white man has ever been, and nothing like the control has been established which would enable us to interfere in any way with such a matter, for instance, as domestic slavery [...] What we shall do, of course, is to influence the customs of the country as far as that is possible, and, as our effective control extends, so also will extend our laws and arrangements with regard to slavery. In the meantime, what we are doing is something the effect of which can hardly be over-estimated. We are destroying everywhere in our protectorates and in our spheres of influence, as well as in our territories, slave raiding, and it is slave raiding which has been the great curse of Africa. (Chamberlain, Royal Niger Company Bill 1899: 1,292–5)

Chamberlain got his bill and the money to fund the West African possessions. The support he had for his ideas of a more potent state then fed into grander ideas about the colonial project, and it was in this spirit that conquest of the West African colonies began. The press promoted popular support for the policies of expansion and imperialism as inherent to a newly shaped national cohesion and pride, as this *Daily Mail* comment on the occasion of the Queen's Jubilee demonstrates.

> Up they came, more and more, new types, new realms at every couple of yards, an anthropological museum – a living gazetteer of the British Empire. With them came their English officers, whom they obey and follow like children. And you began to understand, as never before, what the Empire amounts to. Not only that we possess all these remote outlandish places ... but also that all these people are working, not simply under us, but with us – that we send out a boy here and a boy there, and the boy takes hold of the savages of the part he comes to, and teaches them to march and shoot as he tells them, to obey him and believe in him and die for him and the Queen. A plain, stupid, uninspired people, they call us, and yet we are doing this with every kind of savage man there is. And each one of us – you and I, and that man in his shirt-sleeves at the corner – is a working part of this world-shaping force. How small you must feel in face of the stupendous whole, and yet how great to be a unit in it! (quoted, Judd, 1977: 211)

Lugard: hero administrator

> Lugard's records of the occupation [of Northern Nigeria] seem to pulse with the urgency and enthusiasm of those crowded months of his life ... The moral theme runs strongly through the reports – Lugard and his envoys seem to dash about the country like knights-errant, punishing wicked people and liberating the oppressed, overthrowing cruel kings and elevating good ones. This was what Lugard willed to do and what he believed himself to be doing. (Perham, 1956: 52–3)

No colonial governor so well represented the idea of the noble state as Frederick Lugard. He is arguably one of the most influential and significant British colonial officers of this period, the first British governor of Northern Nigeria in 1900, formalising the British ownership of the region and becoming governor of the whole of Nigeria in 1912. He was a great publicist for the nobler ideas of empire, through his own writing and assisted by his wife, Flora Shaw, who was a colonial correspondent for *The Times*. In particular, Lugard's book *The Dual Mandate in British Tropical Africa*, published in 1929 after his retirement, carries a very full explanation of the imperial project, from its grander ambitions to the details of its practice in Nigeria.

The 'material' is very evident in the book. There are chapters devoted to the economic benefits for Britain of colonial possessions, detailing the costs and revenues from the colony. The final chapter is a passionate defence of the imperial project to its detractors in the Labour Party. Lugard wrote, for example, about the ways in which colonial products and wealth have bettered the lives of the British poor. He asked his reader to:

> contrast the condition of squalor and misery in which the bulk of the people of these islands lived in 1816, with the conditions prevailing in 1891, [and] he will realise how insistent had become the demand alike for the food-supplies and for the raw materials which were the product of the tropics ... Who can deny the right of the hungry people of Europe to utilise the wasted bounties of nature? (Lugard, 1926: 61)

This is good, but it is a material good; a return to Chamberlain's 'squalid argument', and Lugard had grander ambitions. He understood and shared in the popular fascination and pride in the project of the empire:

> It has been well said that a nation, like an individual, must have some task higher than the pursuit of material gain, if it is to escape the benumbing influence of parochialism and to fulfil its higher destiny. If high standards are maintained, the control of the subject races must have an effect on national character which is not measurable in terms of material profit and loss. And what is true for the nation is equally true for the individual officers employed. If lower standards are adopted – the arrogant display of power, or the selfish pursuit of profit – the result is equally fatal to the nation and the individual. Misuse of opportunity carries with it a relentless nemesis, deteriorating the moral fibre of the individual, and permeating the nation. (*Ibid*: 59)

Lugard argued that the colonial authorities – the proxy for the British state – had enormous potential for creating good by bringing benefits to Africans, as well as people in Britain. His immodest ambition was the ultimate capable and ideal state. 'It was the task of civilisation to put an end to slavery, to establish courts of law, to inculcate in the natives a sense of individual responsibility, of liberty, and of justice, and to teach their rulers how to apply these principles; above all, to produce happiness and progress' (*Ibid*: 5).

Lugard faced crippling limits on how far such ambitions could be realised, caused largely by the reluctant Treasury and the difficulties in wringing economic benefits from the West African colonies in particular. He famously rationalised the limited reach of the colonial state through his description (and idealisation) of indirect rule, for which he came to be criticised by the next generation of colonial officers and reformers.[17] Therefore, the initial ideal of a capable and all-providing state – or even of a state which could extract the hoped-for material benefits for Britain – was almost impossible to realise.[18]

Lugard's perception of the state as the prime authority extended to the absorption of the role traditionally held by the missions. He regarded their approach to education and the spread of Christianity as essentially unsettling and potentially destructive, and as early as April 1900, he wrote to Chamberlain about the need for the state to take on the education of Africans, arguing that it was 'neither good policy, nor fair upon charitable institutions, that governments should rely upon the pupils of missionary societies and make little or no effort in tropical Africa, to turn out a sufficiency of clerks, artisans and other trained natives to meet at least a part of its own demands – men with a sound secular education'.[19] Limited resources demanded compromise and accommodation with the missions, but Lugard's relationship with the missionaries was always strained: he viewed them as competitors with the state and distrusted the effects of their education on Africans, which he regarded as at once emasculating and endowing unrealistic expectations.[20]

However difficult the reality, Africa provided wonderful opportunities within which to describe an ideal state, particularly to audiences back home. First, the continent presented a large-scale challenge: 'intertribal warfare, slave-raiding, and the ravages of unchecked epidemics ... venereal disease, with its attendant infant mortality' (Lugard, 1926: 66). There was much for a 'good state' to do. And second, Africans were apparently suitably incapable themselves, and appreciative of others' attempts, to help them:

> In character and temperament the typical African of this race-type is a happy, thriftless, excitable person, lacking in self-control, discipline, and foresight, naturally courageous, and naturally courteous and polite, full of personal vanity, with little sense of veracity ... His thoughts are concentrated on the events and feelings of the moment, and he suffers little from apprehension for the future, or grief for the past ... He is by no means lacking in industry, and will work hard with less incentive than most races. He has the courage of a fighting animal – an instinct rather than a moral virtue ... In brief, the virtues and the defects of this race-type are those of attractive children, whose confidence when once it has been won is given ungrudgingly as to an older and wiser superior, without question and without envy. (*Ibid*: 69–70)

Surely this is a description of the perfect subjects? Here was the opportunity for an ideal state to operate with an ideal population. 'Child-like', Africans appeared to respect and even love the authority and good intentions of a benign state which could 'produce happiness and progress'. This ideal state was personified by the British district officer, described by Lugard in Biblical terms: 'To him alike the missionary, the trader, and the miner look for assistance and advice. The leper and the slave find in him a protector' (*Ibid*: 134).

The resulting picture is one of the bravado of initial intention, tempered and twisted by local experience, and finally polished and rationalised to fit back into the initial frame. Between them, Chamberlain, Lugard and the promoters of late Victorian colonialism painted a picture of a state that should, and could, do all. In a thinner, far away Africa, this seemed quite plausible.

Labour takes on Africa

The Labour Party inherited both British traditions of the idea of Britain's engagement with Africa. Ideas about transcending the political and rejecting interests fed into the British anti-colonial movement, while more transformative ideas associated with the idealisation of the colonial state influenced the more mainstream Fabian Society. These two key protagonist types of the Labour Party have been described as the 'anarchists' and the 'bureaucrats' (Beilharz, 1992: 125). John Callaghan argues that various traditions of the British left were able to accommodate each other up until the 1930s when the dissenting, pacifist voices began to gain strength. Widespread popular pro-imperialist sentiment 'blunted, where it failed to eliminate, the critical edge of liberalism and non-conformism in relation to Britain's colonial role' (Callaghan, 2007: 21–2). In addition, the purely anti-imperial sentiments that seemed well justified in more 'civilised' parts of the empire had always tended to be modified in the case of Africa, in which self-government appeared less viable.

The anti-colonial movement found its primary home in the Independent Labour Party (ILP), founded in 1893, a pacifist, egalitarian, non-conformist movement with a strong belief in international solidarity (Vickers, 2003: 35). It also attracted left-wing members of the Labour Party who, according to Richard Crossman, believed that 'power politics are wicked and must be subjugated to the rule of law' (quoted in Callaghan, 2007: 5). During the 1940s and 1950s the anti-colonial movement was headed by the ILP MP Fenner Brockway, whose approach had a close affinity with that of the abolition movement. According to Tony Benn, who joined the cause and worked closely with him, Brockway, like Wilberforce, saw politics as a vehicle for establishing a connection to a moral cause. 'Somebody said to him, find the life force in your period in history and attach yourself to it, and Fenner worked for Indian and African independence…Fenner was an extraordinary man. He never got into high office, of course, because when you get into high office, you are subject to such pressures that you can't do what you want to do.'[21] Charismatic, guided by religious principles (although not a religious believer himself), Brockway wrote: 'The Christian ethic – service inspired by love – is the highest one can know…our present economic system stands condemned because it does not reflect this ethic' (quoted in Howe, 1993: 170).

Idealisation, in a number of forms, was a strong feature of the movement. First, many of the African nationalist leaders – Kenneth Kaunda, Kwame Nkrumah, Jomo Kenyatta and Julius Nyerere – were particularly fascinating to the left in Britain because they represented a revival of the ideas of international socialism that the two world wars and emerging Cold War had appeared to extinguish. Joining their cause was a chance to rekindle that lost ideal. Benn, who was a young MP at the time, said of the African nationalist leaders: 'We worked as closely as we could with them…I think it was a very natural relationship…we saw it as a common struggle. And they saw in us friends.'[22] Second, within the wider objectives of national self-determination and freedom, the personal flaws and ideological differences of these leaders could be gently subsumed, creating notions of a genuinely consensual movement. Brockway himself argued of African nationalist leaders: 'Their one desire is to serve the cause of human freedom and peace' (quoted in Howe, who calls Brockway an example of 'an inverted racist who is blind to all human flaws in people of colour' 1993: 172). Third, there was a poignancy in the oppression of Africans, and heroic causes like that of Seretse Khama played a crucial role in galvanising the movement.[23]

There are further echoes of abolitionist thinking. Guilt was a significant feature, as was the feeling that British interference was inevitably degenerating: Brockway believed, says Howe, that 'the colonial relationship inevitably distorted and hampered the development of subject territories' (*Ibid*: 172). There were also corresponding traces of a belief that a return to a moral outlook would overturn the corruption of a human-made, political institution. Brockway argued: 'Empires have fallen before, but this is the first time that the conscience of man has repudiated the actual existence of empires. We are thus witnessing more than the end of an age; the whole course of human relations over many thousands of years of history has changed' (quoted in *Ibid*: 172–3).

While the anti-colonialists represented a repudiation of politics, and found their home in the left of British politics, the Fabian Colonial Bureau, established in 1940, remained preoccupied by a state-centred approach and fed directly and with increasing influence into the Party's leadership. The Fabian Society, according to George Bernard Shaw, was in favour of a 'lofty and public-spirited imperialism' (quoted in Semmel, 1960: 68). Shaw wrote, in the first Fabian treatise on the subject, *Fabianism and the Empire*: 'A Great Power, consciously or unconsciously, must govern in the interests of civilisation as a whole; and it is not to those interests that such mighty forces as goldfields, and the formidable armaments that can be built upon them, should be wielded irresponsibly by small communities of frontiersmen.' Instead, Shaw advocated the 'effective social organisation of the whole Empire' (*Ibid*: 71).

The Fabian Society was London-based and middle-class, espoused science rather than religion as a guiding principle of social organisation, and promoted the idea that an educated elite could bring about an enlightened and harmonious society (Vickers, 2003: 37).[24] For the Fabians, the state was the central driver of such progress: 'virility in government' was required, argued its founder Sydney Webb (quoted in Semmel, 1960: 73). It was influential within the Labour Party leadership and the post-war government, with a key member, Arthur Creech-Jones, becoming Colonial Secretary.

Socially radical in domestic policy, the 1945 government stressed continuity in foreign affairs, under a realist foreign secretary.[25] It managed to carry both approaches into the colonial project, attempting at once to maintain and actively develop the remains of the empire, particularly in Africa where, it was believed, substantial development was required before independence would be feasible (Hinden and Brailsford, 1945). This was partly a revival of the 'squalid argument' – post-war Britain needed all the economic advantages it could muster. But it was also a quite natural extension of the ideas that the state could and should plan and organise development, and an espousal of the ethical approach proposed by the Fabians, and in particular a key contributor to the policy of its Colonial Bureau, Leonard Woolf.

Woolf combined the transcendent and transformative approaches in his idealisation of international organisation, and shaped a philosophy which is reflected by the modern Labour Party in its understanding of Africa and British policy there. Woolf expressed the Fabian belief in the centrality of the state, the way in which it could be an expression of the national will, and its power: 'Man's past was caused by what man desired and believed: the future will be caused by what we desire and believe ... policy is a kind of immaterial tissue of communal desires and beliefs, woven out of what we desire and believe the state to be, and what we desire and believe the state can attain for us in relation with other states' (Woolf, 1998: 9).

Woolf didn't believe in a rosy African past: European rule was desirable in the interests of Africans who lived in squalid, primitive conditions and who had been, in 1880, 'completely helpless in the hands of a trader or an adventurer armed with a modern rifle' (Woolf, 1971: 77). But he was critical of European greed and selfishness in its dealings with Africa – the 'atrocities, exploitations and hypocrisy' (*Ibid*: 79) practised during the scramble for Africa – which he argued had been exclusively about the economic advantages to be gained by Europe. What was required was a change in the way the Europeans behaved: 'If the European state is to become an instrument for good rather than evil in Africa, the economic beliefs and desires of Europeans must suffer a change [...] These proposals will, of course, appear utopian, a demand for a change in human nature' (Woolf, 1998: 361–3).

Having arrived by logic at the need for a utopian change of human nature, Woolf laid bare the belief he had in human organisation. Human organisation, in the form of exploitative economic and imperial systems, had contributed to many 'dark pages in the world's record' (*Ibid*: 355), but, an alternative was achievable: 'There are, it is quite true, no utopias in the world, but that is because the world does not desire utopias' (*Ibid*: 366). However, Woolf carried a distrust of the idea that states can be transformed to this degree and, like many Labour politicians since, was more comfortable with international forms of government which, he believed, could transcend power politics. He felt, though, that various historical currents were on the side of such reform, including globalisation. It was, he wrote,

> no longer a world of isolated units moving majestically along their own orbits; it is a world of states, nations and peoples, all closely-inter-related parts of a vast international society with its own economic and political organisation. No part of this whole has either the right, or in fact the power to pursue its own interests without reference to the interests and will of the other parts. (Woolf, 1971: 116)

Within such a historical context, it might be possible to create an international body which could overcome 'the forcible subjection of one people ... by others' (*Ibid*: 120). Woolf had described the escapist ideal of the supra-political containing principle or order – in the League of Nations, a 'trustee on behalf of civilisation' (*Ibid*: 128) of which he was a passionate advocate – but in his version of the story, this had been created by human agency. It was no less utopian for that: 'I can imagine it supplying experts, administrators, advisors and advisory commissions; they would be free from the kind of suspicion which naturally attached to similar "advisors" provided by the great imperialist powers' (*Ibid*: 123). Woolf brings both transcendent and transformative approaches to British policy in Africa, with his emphasis on European guilt and need to make reparation and in his description of the League of Nations as a super-national, rational, universalising body which could transcend politics.

Differences over Labour's colonial policy are lost to modern popular memory. But the contradiction between the idea of Britain as a capable, statuesque figure on the world stage, and Britain abdicating to a higher good, which is represented by the idea of universal norms and laws, remains. Vickers sums up the ways in which these two contradictory ideologies within the Labour Party have coexisted.

> Labour's commitment to working in the international good, to work in the 'international' interest rather than purely what it perceives to be its national interest has often been based on the idea of Britain's leadership in the world. This reflects the context within which the Labour Party developed, as well as its tendency to have a missionary zeal to reform and shape the world in its likeness, which has sometimes been at odds with its commitment to working through international institutions. (Vickers, 2003: 197)

This chapter has described some of the ways in which British political actors have attempted to transcend or transform difficult politics. The two approaches outlined have sought to do this in different ways – one by rejecting human frailty and politics in search of a higher source of good; the other in creating an idealised version of human capacity and organisation to overcome it. I want to make some final points about the ways in which these two different approaches also share common features.

First, both appear to be a reaction to messy politics at home: to the perception of the degradation of morals or feelings of collective guilt; or to the horrors of industrial and social squalor. Attempts, therefore, to identify with a source of 'the good' appear to constitute throughout an attempt to repair what is wrong at home with current, collective social life. Second, both attempt to do this through the creation of a utopia, an idealised reconnection or recreation of the perfect social life. For both, Africa has been able to represent utopia, as the site of relative emptiness upon which such idealisations can be projected. Third, they have fed, via different streams, into the ways in which the Labour Party has perceived its role in the world. As discussed, their different emphases have conflicted in the past, and caused problems within the Party, but with the ending of colonial control in Africa, they have become far easier to reconcile – the edges have been blurred – so that in current ideas about Britain and Africa, they appear to coexist quite happily. This is a theme to which I will return in Chapter 5. In the next chapter, however, I want to explore the theoretical foundations of such an approach to foreign policy, in particular by looking at this idea of reparation in relation to the damaged state. I will do this through a discussion of communitarian thinking in IR and the psychoanalytic theory of Melanie Klein.

Notes

1 Classic accounts of British engagement and colonialism in Africa that detail more forcefully the selfish motivations are provided by H. A. Hobson and Walter Rodney (Hobson, 1938; Rodney, 1973). Moreover, when British actors were driven by altruism this did not necessarily make for a more enlightened approach. 'They came to Africa puffed up with the virtue of emancipating black slaves – but with the conception of Africans only as slaves, porters, or eunuchs in harems' (Lewis and Foy, 1971: 4).

2 The popularity of West African expansion as constituting a knock to French ambitions there was undeniably potent; the idea of letting the French encroach on British possessions was unthinkable: 'Anything more humiliating, more positively abject, it would be difficult for the worst enemy of England to conceive,' opined *The Star* in a leader column published in support of Chamberlain's plans for expansion (*The Star*, 24 August 1895: 1).

3 William Wilberforce, *Debate on Mr Wilberforce's Resolutions Respecting the Slave Trade, 12 May*. Vol. 28, *Parliamentary History*. London: Hansard, 1789.

4 Sierra Leone, of course, held its own settler population in Freetown, comprising resettled slaves. This group, while seeing itself as distinct from the indigenous population, and although far closer to the British in terms of language, culture and affective ties, was black, and African, and was in important ways lumped in with indigenous groups. For example, Governor Cardew describes the residents of Freetown as 'ignorant and indiscriminating… a people who, from the time

their ancestors were first brought here have always been accustomed to receive at the hands of the Government and never to pay back ... a people without history ... unable to appreciate and enjoy [our free institutions and liberty of the press]'. Governor Cardew, Letter to the Colonial Secretary, 28 May 1898, Government Dispatches.

5 This rather simplified analysis doesn't account for important differences between urban and rural populations which were administered differently by direct and indirect rule, a system which Mamdani has argued is scarcely different to the apartheid system which distinguished between black and white communities in South Africa (Mamdani, 1996). However, I think the point stands if we are considering the ways in which the policy was viewed by the colonial rulers, rather than the different ways in which it affected the ruled.

6 The contemporary Parliamentary debates on the uprising give a strong flavour of the disturbance they caused in British political circles and the anger against what was seen to be Governor Cardew's insensitive handling of the hut tax. It appeared inconceivable that Sierra Leoneans, for whom Britain had done so much, would react in such a violent way unless grossly mistreated. 'It is a story which must make every man who takes a just pride in the name of England, and the traditions of his race, sick at heart to ponder over' (Hedderwick, Appropriation Bill, 1899).

7 Reginald Coupland puts the figure at two million (Coupland, 1964: 21).

8 Inheriting the liberalism of Mill and Cobden, Gladstone argued in 1838 that there was 'no exception to the unvarying and melancholy story of colonization. Whenever settlers from a people in advanced stage of civilization came into contact with the aborigines of a barbarous country, the result was always prejudicial to both countries, and most dishonourable to the former' (quoted in Butler, 1968: 3).

9 Bernard Porter also makes the fascinating point that as an outsider, Chamberlain's sense of alienation might explain his conception of an imperialism – rooted in tariff reform and imperial preference – that required the total transformation of Britain: 'Free trade had been embedded in the British national psyche for nearly a century' (Porter, 2007: 232).

10 Chamberlain in a speech to the Liverpool Chamber of Commerce (*Times*, 1898).

11 'The magnitude of our Imperial interests strikes even the least imaginative person who studies a map of the world on which British possessions are coloured red. One might blindfold put one's finger on the atlas, and the odds are heavy that it would light on some British territory ... And as it is with the sense of sight so it is with the sense of hearing. Any stranger seated in the gallery of the House of Commons yesterday afternoon, listening to a debate which ranged over every quarter of the globe, could hardly fail to be convinced that a new interpretation was given to the apophthegm *nihil humanum a me alienum puto.*' ('I consider nothing that is human alien to me.') (*Pall Mall Gazette*, 1895: 1).

12 Semmel argues that the 134-seat majority gained by the Unionist Party in the general election in 1900 demonstrated the high levels of popular support for imperialism (Semmel, 1960: 54). Judd too explores the origins of the popularity of imperialism: 'Herded into factories and workshops, subjected to industrial regulation, and denied full political freedom, it was hardly surprising that many Victorian working men should rejoice at the far-flung exploits of red-coated

infantry, or at the steel shield that the Royal Navy flung across the oceans. Perhaps in this sense, imperialist sentiment was merely an inflated patriotism. It is also tempting to see symptoms of national insecurity intermingled with jingoistic exultation. In the 1890s, Great Britain, for all her territorial pomp and splendour, was without allies and openly disliked by many in Europe and the US. "Splendid isolation" was in fact uncomfortable and costly; a rationalisation of a predicament, not a calculated policy. The rapturous public reactions to the triumph at Omdurman or the relief of Mafeking can thus be seen as the responses of an uncertain people' (Judd, 1977: 188).

13 The *Pall Mall Gazette* used the title in its coverage of Chamberlain's 'excellent beginning' as Secretary of State (*Pall Mall Gazette*, 1895: 1).

14 Nevertheless, Bernard Porter strikes a cautionary note as to how widely or deeply such enthusiasm really ran, arguing that the imperial project met with very different reactions in different parts of society, many of which barely noticed it (Porter, 2007).

15 Thomas Pakenham ascribes Rhodes's charisma to his 'pride in what he called his "big ideas", his sense of being born for greatness, of serving great ideals'; while he describes Goldie as 'a throwback from the Regency, pleasure-loving, Byronic, buccaneering, a man who took pride in his own egotism, and snapped his fingers at the conventions of Society ... [a] romantic imperialist' (Pakenham, 2001: 376; 460).

16 Chamberlain was assisted in his arguments by the bungled Jameson Raid, which in 1895 had confirmed the worst proclivities of a rapacious and irresponsible private approach to empire and brought disrepute on Britain (Butler, 1968).

17 A group of British colonial officers serving in Africa were sharp critics of British policy, which they regarded as too passive in development terms. They became increasingly influential in the 1940s and were closely involved in attempts to resource large-scale development programmes in Africa after the Second World War (Macmillan and Marks, 1989).

18 Although the British administrators were constantly constrained by the lack of resources and difficult local conditions from carrying out their grander projects, on occasion this could work in favour of a larger role for the colonial state. Anne Phillips's discussion of the ways in which the British tried and failed to implement capitalism in West African colonies, for example, suggests not only the limits of the idea of the all-powerful state, but also that the need to adapt did sometimes give rise to a more active role for the colonial state than at first envisaged. Although, she argues, the British planned to create capitalist economies in the colonies, the disturbing effects of large-scale, privately-owned companies on local political relationships, and the potential dangers involved in creating a proletariat class, were in the end thought too damaging to stability. In Phillips's account the idealisation of the resulting state-directed peasant economy was part of the *post hoc* rationalisation of colonialism on the cheap. Thus, rather than contingency undermining the role and extent of the colonial authorities, in this case it actually entrenched them (Phillips, 1989).

19 Lugard to Chamberlain, 23 April, Colonial Office Dispatches, 1900.

20 For example in a heated correspondence with Bishop Tugwell who wanted to set up missions in Northern Nigeria, Lugard criticised him as provocative, sensation-seeking, and liable to undermine the stability and good relations with the native populations. In the matter of eradicating slavery, the apotheosis of

the good to be done via British rule and one of Lugard's great passions, it 'is a matter to be dealt with by the Administration rather than by missions'. Tugwell replied with a grovelling suggestion that one of the key roles of the missions would be to support the colonial state: 'We are all fervently loyal of our country, and its interests, and to your Excellency as Governor of this vast country, and we earnestly desire that your Excellency should feel that far from being a hindrance to the Government we might be a help, our only longing is for the good of these people. By kindness, by medical work the people have been won to us, and innumerable opportunities have occurred with all sorts of people to explain to them the nature and work of British Administration: wrong impressions have been removed, fear, hesitation and even opposition have, we know in a great many cases, and in many towns given way to friendliness, and a desire for the advent of the British Government.' The missions working in the service of the capable good state was an acceptable proposition, and Lugard relented on this occasion. Correspondence between Lugard and Tugwell: Lugard to Tugwell, 1 November 1900; Tugwell to Lugard, 14 February 1901, Colonial Office Dispatches, 1900–01.

21 Interview with Tony Benn, London, 9 May, 2007.

22 *Ibid.*

23 The Seretse Khama case had a significant symbolic importance for the anti-colonial movement, representing the struggle for racial equality, a resistance to pressure from South Africa and support for a progressive, enlightened African leader who faced oppression from the colonial authorities which were motivated by national interests. His exile from British Bechuanaland in 1951 was a pivotal moment for the anti-colonial movement. Michael Dutfield describes the story as one typical of British realism. The 'lies, hypocrisy, cruelty and deceit' of the British Government, he argues, led to the sacrifice of Khama in the pursuit of South African uranium (Dutfield, 1990: xii).

24 It is interesting to note that, although the Fabian Society represented the thinking of a narrow intellectual elite, the ideas it promoted on the empire were far better at attracting popular support than those of the anti-colonialists.

25 Ernest Bevin did not believe that 'governments in practice would (or should) make a unilateral sacrifice of national interests to uphold some international principle', and was 'unmoved by the accusation that, in safeguarding his own country's interests, he was turning his back on Labour's traditional internationalism' (Bullock, 1983: 110). Within the Labour Party there has traditionally been a gap between the pragmatic, often realist, leadership of the party particularly in power – Bevin was just the first of a number of prominent foreign and defence secretaries who took a more realist approach, including Denis Healey and David Owen – and the left and the wider membership which tended to favour the policies brought to the party by the dissenting ILP. A key cause of the left and the membership has been that of international peace and solidarity, and this remains. 'There [i]s no evidence ... that the party membership had been cured of its desire for an ethical foreign policy. Indeed, the idea was taken up by New Labour – which in all other respects was supposed to have broken with the party's past' (Callaghan, 2007: 283–4).

4

The good, the bad and the ambiguous

I discussed two ways of expressing and realising the idea of good in Chapter 3 – the transcendental and transformative – both of which have found expression in the imagination of Africa and Britain's relationships and role there. Historically, these have been expressed directly in relation to religion. Wilberforce and Buxton explicitly tried to recapture a religious idea of the good and relate it to the British state: the 'happy state of a truly Christian nation' (Wilberforce, 1958: 119). Chamberlain and Lugard, neither of them religious men, made explicit references to the idea that a replacement for dwindling religious feeling needed to be found in public life: for Chamberlain, 'the cult of duty, self-sacrifice and service to the community, nation or empire, became increasingly the antidote for waning religious belief and growing materialism' (Fraser, 1966: xv). They described a quasi-religious idea of a state project or mission which would elevate and ennoble the British state.

This chapter develops a theoretical underpinning of the reconnection of the state to a source of good. It develops the ideas behind utopian thinking about the sense of a damaged political system, and the ways in which imagining an ideal might help repair it. It does this, first, by looking at communitarian ideas that locate good within the community and its relationships. These ideas need to grapple with the problem of locating both the good and the political within the same human realm. The first section discusses communitarian approaches and the various ways they attempt to address the problem of the corruption of the good. These tend to reserve the idea of pure good, locating it either within or beyond the community, but it becomes explicitly an idea or an ideal, something that exists to help resolve tension with the ambiguities of the real world. Durkheim, for example, explains the need for a source of pure good – and locates it in the sacred beliefs and practices shared by members of the community. Hegel, in his exploration of a new form of ideal republic, discusses the idea of the 'good state'. For both, the ideal is contained within the community. Hegel, moreover, explores the theme of inter-subjectivity and the ways in which a relation to an 'other' underwrites the idea of the 'good state'. Both are suggestive of the idea of good playing a sort of psychological shoring up of the community: that this expression of and identification with the good give rise to both subjectivity and thereby enable the community to provide a healthy underpinning for individual human development. This is the idea that I explore in more depth in the following three sections of the chapter, in which I discuss the issues raised by the communitarians in relation to the work of psychoanalyst Melanie Klein. First, I describe Klein's work as it relates to the role of relationships and the good in the development of subjectivity. Next, I discuss the degree to which Klein's work can be thought about in relation to the state, and how far it helps an understanding of state subjectivity. Finally, I attempt to link her ideas to those of the communitarians, in particular in thinking about the nature of relationships within and between communities, and the degree to which they depend on each other. As a whole, the discussion aims to more fully realise the roots of the psychological underpinning of the role of good, its relation to the state and its place in the wider community.

The intimacy of the good and the political

Enlightenment conceptions of the good see them approached from the position of and contained within the person of the individual. Through reason, the individual connects with a universal realm of the good. An alternative, communitarian, approach creates a definition of good as a product and producer of relationships between members of a community. This radically different perspective eschews the possibility of both individual and human-wide realisation of the good, so it is at once more and less universalist, occupying instead the middle range of locally shared norms. This difference has implications for the question of the assumed separation between the good and the political, outlined in Chapter 2. If good is necessarily intimately tied up with human relationships and communities, can it be defined as separate from human weakness? If it can't be, in what state is it left? It is necessary to examine how a sense of good is developed within communities before we can answer these questions.

Constructivism underwrites communitarian conceptions of the development of morality within communities. Emanuel Adler describes processes of the development of meaning, values and norms within a community as deriving from collective learning. It is a circular process whereby social 'facts' are established through agreement over collective meanings. 'Consciousness is awakened, reasons emerge, and people act intentionally on behalf of those reasons' (Adler, 2005: 12). Reason is then defined in relation to a negotiated set of norms and ideas. It cannot exist as an abstract ideal or be mastered by an individual working in isolation from the rest of society. For communitarians, the notion that individuals can reason their way towards a moral framework on their own is nonsense. A sense of the good is thus constructed within communities and is particular to the community. Michael Walzer describes morality as standing 'in an intimate descriptive/critical relation with its own society. For what it expresses in its idiomatic, particularist and circumstantial style is the socially constructed idealism of *these* people' (Walzer, 1994: 39).

How this sense of the good is contained, or expressed, has been interpreted in different ways. For Durkheim, the sense of an ideal society is expressed through religious thought and practice. Religion makes a sacred space within the community which embodies its sense of its own proximity to the good. It is shaped by the community's conception of values, and reinforced through religious ritual and practice which concretely build the community's solidaristic ties, as well as members' feeling of connection to the sacred. Durkheim recognises the significance of a connection to a pure good: the capacity to idealise 'is not a kind of luxury that man might do without but a condition of his existence' (Durkheim, 2001: 318). This connection to the good is what makes human frailty bearable. The believer is 'raised above human miseries because he is raised above his condition as man; he believes he is saved from evil' (*Ibid*: 311).

For Durkheim, there is still a strong sense that the good is split off from human frailty – his separation between the sacred and the profane. Even though both are human, contained within the community, they are seen as distinct. Indeed, Durkheim's explicit connecting of the good to religion ties it firmly to the conceptions of the separation of good and sinful, or church and state, as discussed in Chapter 2. This enables the sacred to remain occupant of an uncontested space – unlike the political space where interests and differences and contests remain. Perhaps for Durkheim, the important point is that there is *perceived to be* a separation between the good and the human, which suggests that this splitting of the good plays an important psychological role in nourishing the health of the community. I will return to this point in the next section.

But other communitarians describe a good that is more clearly compromised by the fact that it is embedded and created within human communities. In this communitarian approach the good cannot be separated from the human and idealised: its validity is derived from its historical and cultural thickness. The processes through which moral frameworks evolve within communities are contentious and difficult, characterised, as Walzer describes, by 'qualification, compromise, complexity and disagreement' (Walzer, 1994: 6). It is this immanent clash of different interests within a community that interests Walzer. Thick forms of associational life are deeply rooted in historically negotiated and complex norms, particular to the community. Broad normative paradigms underwrite these processes, but plenty of room is left for contention and negotiation. Over time, these processes lead to shifting normative paradigms, but they remain deeply embedded, specific to and owned by the community in which they sit. Disagreements about social meanings can only occur within a shared view of the world, and ideas of morality are an expression of social meaning, a 'thick understanding of life and death, a human culture' (*Ibid*: 29). In other words, morality is as contested as any other form of human life: norms are deeply embedded in what we might term 'political processes' – messy, human, constantly contested.[1]

For Hegel, a founding father of modern communitarian perspectives in IR (Frost, 1986), it is the state itself that embodies this sense of the ideal community, 'the actuality of the ethical idea' (Hegel, 1991: 275) which, by containing and expressing the community's will, enables individuals within it to best achieve freedom, or self-actualisation. Unlike Durkheim, who regards good as linked to a distinct sacred realm, Hegel ties the good directly to the human and flawed political arena of the state. For Hegel, the state is capable of solidifying collected norms and aspirations in laws which attempt to supersede 'the contingencies of feeling, opinion and the forms of revenge, compassion and selfishness' (*Ibid*: 243) – or, in other words, all of human frailty.

Hegel could have then idealised the state as an organisation capable of overcoming these frailties. But he distinguishes between the *idea* of the good state and its reality. He suggests that, since this sense of the ideal is rooted within relationships and the community, it is inextricable from the weaknesses and corruptions of human life. 'The state is not a work of art; it exists in the world, and hence in the sphere of arbitrariness, contingency and error, and bad behaviour may disfigure it in many respects. But the ugliest man, the criminal, the invalid, or the cripple is still a living human being; the affirmative aspect – life – survives in spite of such deficiencies' (*Ibid*: 279).

Despite its immanent corruption, the community is still able to retain and be nourished by this *idea* of the good state, even when constantly reminded of the imperfections of the *real* state. The community can hold the notions of good and evil, of the ideal and the real, within itself, without needing to split them apart. Hegel's approach strikes me as a more plausible account of a richer and more complex political and moral landscape. But it demands that the community contains an understanding of its own internal differences, that it can tolerate the coexistence of the notion of the good alongside the reality of human failings and that it allows that the good can belong to, and does not transcend, the realm of politics.

For some communitarians this is enough; for others there remains a need for a connection to a non-material form of good that cannot be encompassed within human experience. Simone Weil, for example, wrestles with this problem. She distinguishes between human goods which are the subject of contest in the political realm – liberty, obedience, responsibility, equality, hierarchism, honour, punishment, freedom of opinion, security, risk, private property, collective property, truth – and an impersonal good reached only through private and lonely contemplation by an individual with a sacred, other-worldly realm. The political goods are good in the sense of being essential for moral health, but remain in a state of constant contradiction with each other. The impersonal good rises above difference (Weil: 2005). Taylor, too, maintains the importance for some of a connection to a good beyond human life here and now:

> The aspiration to fullness can be met by building something into one's life, some pattern of higher action, or some meaning; or it can be met by connecting one's life up with some greater reality or story ... [for example] some committed leftists see themselves as part of the socialist Revolution, or the march of human History, and this is what gives meaning, or fuller Being, to their lives. (Taylor, 1989: 43–4)

What interests me here is how far and in what ways the idea of a connection to good can be achieved through the international realm. Political ideas and actions have carried through this longing for the good, as I have suggested in Chapter 3, through the imagination and experience of international relationships. Although some communitarians have not seen the need for a transcendental element to the good, others have looked for it in the international realm. Walzer, for example, describes thin relationships within the international realm as able to express some more fundamental, universal idea of the good, and argues that these are derived from thicker communal relationships (Walzer, 1994). In contrast to Walzer's 'inside-out' approach, Mervyn Frost suggests that international norms are a source of reinforcement for the richer norms of the community – an 'outside-in' approach (Frost, 1986). Frost uses a Hegelian understanding of the centrality of the idea of the good state, and the way its subjectivity is fashioned via external sovereignty. Hegel's insistence of mutual recognition between states as an essential component of the state as an individual provides a basis of understanding of how 'the state's relations to other states are constitutive of its individuality' (Jaeger, 2002: 500).

This is the jumping-off point for the main theoretical contribution I want to make to this discussion. In this chapter I want to explore, first, the idea that good is essential to the community's sense of itself; second, the problems of reconciling the need for good with the ambiguous reality; and third, the idea of mutual regard as constitutive of subjectivity. I want to do this by borrowing an IR tradition of seeing the state as an individual which relates to other individual states, but to bring to this idea Klein's work which also deals with the creation of subjectivity and the ways this is developed through relationships with those close to us and those far away.

Inside/outside; thick/thin

Klein, a follower of Freud, developed new and controversial ways of thinking about emotional and moral development. Working in London from the 1920s until her death in 1960, Klein based her theory on her clinical psychoanalytic work with children. Many of her ideas, which deal with the intense emotions of early life, are difficult and alienating, and her work has been controversial. Yet the Kleinian approach has become one of the key schools of psychoanalysis and continues to provide challenging insights into the workings of the human mind.

Klein's work centres on the way people relate to objects – real objects in the world around them, and the internal objects, or *imagos*, they build unconsciously to reflect and help them make sense of the world.[2] External objects are experienced by the subject through projection; and they are mentally internalised to form the 'internal objects' that enable the growing child to begin to make sense of itself and its relations to the world. 'Good' internal objects are important because they foster a sense of security and wellbeing. 'Bad' internal objects are subject to feelings of aggression and are experienced as frightening and persecuting. In healthy development, internal objects are gradually brought together and come, through a dialectical process, to reflect the reality of the external world – in all its moral complexity – allowing subjects to develop mature relationships.

Klein, drawing on Freud, says that humans are born with powerful senses of love and hatred, arising from the inherent life instinct (or libido) and death instinct. They resonate with the baby's first experiences of life – of security and gratification, and of frustration and pain – and so the very new baby sees the world as expressions of its own internal extremes. The world as experienced by the baby is a series of encounters with 'good' and 'bad' objects at first, and limited to the immediate family, initially to the mother. The baby experiences 'two' mothers, one good, providing gratification and love; one bad, withholding and persecuting. The good – or ideal – mother can be loved, while the bad mother is hated and becomes the object of destructive fantasies. 'The very young infant's emotions are particularly powerful and are dominated by extremes. There are vigorous dividing processes between the two aspects (good and bad) of his first and most important object, the mother, and between his emotions (love and hatred) towards her' (Klein, 1998c: 304).

Klein is interested in the ways in which children reconcile these fractured extremes with the ambiguities, the grey areas of reality. As the baby begins to put its experiences together, it gradually makes a whole object of this good mother – the object of intense love – and this evil mother – the object of destructive, hateful emotions. That these are one and the same is a terrifying, overwhelming realisation. Inadvertently, the baby has been nurturing destructive feelings towards its most loved object – the object, moreover, so intimately bound up with its own identity and survival. 'Feelings of guilt arise in connection with the child's own destructive impulses, which he now fears to be a danger to his loved object [his mother]' (*Ibid*: 293). These destructive impulses are very powerful. First, because of the way in which the baby feels itself omnipotent: it cannot distinguish between its feelings and intentions, and reality. Therefore, when the baby fantasises about killing, destroying its bad mother, it fears it has actually killed and destroyed her. They are powerful too, because of the way external objects constitute the baby's subjectivity. Klein suggested that the small child introjects the objects around it – first the good and bad mother, then the whole, more ambiguous mother, father, siblings and other family members. 'These [internalised] figures grow in importance and acquire independence in the child's mind as time goes on' (*Ibid*: 295). They become the child's means of connecting, through the medium of the ego, to experiences in the world, and the child's ability to cope with them in a positive way.[3] Therefore, the child's fantasised attack on the mother gains poignancy because it is also an attack on its own internal objects, and thus on its own very survival and identity.

At the realisation that good and bad objects are in fact part of the same whole, all good things, 'are felt to be lost, and lost as a result of his own greedy and destructive phantasies' (Klein, 1998b: 345). This appears to be a primordial – and, Klein would suggest, universally experienced – sense of the painfulness of the loss of the ideal, a loss caused, moreover, by the child's own greed and aggression. Klein described this state of realisation as the 'depressive position'.[4]

Attempts are made to defend against the painful depressive position. These involve continuing with the splitting of good and bad, but now pushing them outside the family, into the wider world. Here, aggression and hatred can be safely projected onto people and objects which are remote and unconnected with the important family relationships. These distant objects are less threatening, and can be safely hated from a distance. They also absorb the deflected aggressive feelings the child would otherwise feel within intimate and important relationships. 'The division between the loving and hating attitude fosters the feeling that one can keep love unspoilt…In the last analysis the image of the loved parents is preserved in the unconscious mind as the most precious possession, for it guards against the pain of utter desolation' (Klein, 1998a: 330).

At the same time, the child can project an idealised form of goodness – again, onto people, objects and causes beyond the family. These 'ideal' objects in the outside world can be identified with as a means of denying aggression and re-establishing a connection to a source of good, something the child feels has been lost or destroyed within the intimate family relationships. Such objects could be teachers, good causes, admired celebrities: 'Inner security is derived from the feelings of love, admiration and trust towards them, because, among other reasons, in the unconscious mind these feelings seem to confirm the existence of good parents and of a love relation to them, thus disproving the great hatred, anxiety and guilt' (*Ibid*: 329–30). This process of displacing love onto things – onto 'anything that is felt to give out goodness and beauty, and that calls forth pleasure and satisfaction' (*Ibid*: 333) – helps recreate and restore the lost ideal.

Klein suggests that the recreation of the ideal is part of an essential attempt to repair the damaged internal objects, and a way for the child to resolve the painful depressive position. For example, admiration for a heroic figure re-establishes the possibility of goodness and nobility in the world; getting involved in a good cause, helping someone else, enables the child to take an active repairing role. By 'repairing' external objects in idealised conditions, the child is able to feel that the damaged internal relationships and objects are repaired too. As such, reparation constitutes a vital part of the child's ethical and emotional development, helping to strengthen good internal objects. This helps the child become reconciled to reality and enable more mature forms of love in adult life.

The primary result of successful reparative attempts in the wider world is a sense of the restoration of good internal objects and relationships. Indirectly, attempts to repair external objects are socially useful and constructive. People engaging in 'good' work – aesthetic, perhaps, or socially worthy – help enrich society. The displacement of love is 'of the greatest importance for the development of the personality and of human relationships; indeed, one may say, for the development of culture and civilisation as a whole' (*Ibid*: 326).

Although these processes are essential for children as they develop ways of understanding the world, there should be less need for them as they grow and develop more morally complex internal objects. However, Klein argues that mechanisms that guard against depression are used by adults too. The tension between the need to feel connection to an ideal good, and the frequent reminders of the ambiguous reality inherent in closer relationships, can be difficult to bear, and all people react to overcome it, sometimes with acknowledgement of guilt and attempts at genuine reparation; at other times in defensive, denying ways. Problems arise if a person gets stuck in these processes, failing to acknowledge the depressive position because guilt feels too overwhelming and is refused instead of acknowledged and resolved. Then, more pathological forms of reparation come to dominate the person's relationships with the world. Klein called this 'manic reparation'. Segal describes the term:

> An essential feature of manic reparation is that it has to be done without acknowledgement of guilt, and therefore under special conditions. For instance, manic reparation is never done in relation to the primary objects or internal objects, but always in relation to more remote objects; secondly the object in relation to which reparation is being done must never be experienced as having been damaged by oneself; third, the object must be felt as inferior, dependent and, at depth, contemptible. There can be no true love or esteem for the object or objects that are being repaired, as this would threaten the return of true depressive feelings. Manic reparation can never be completed, because, if it were complete, the object fully restored would again become lovable and esteemed, and free from the manic person's omnipotent control and contempt... The objects that are being repaired are unconsciously, and sometimes consciously, treated with hatred and contempt and are invariably felt as ungrateful and, at least unconsciously, dreaded as potential persecutors. (Segal, 2006: 95–6)

Manic reparation cannot restore an inner sense of good because, guilt denied, a real sense of reparation is impossible. It might bring wider social benefits (some of the most zealous social reformers may well have been driven by an endless and futile attempt to repair a damaged psyche). But as external objects tend to be patronised and controlled in (unacknowledged) aggressive ways in an attempt to recreate infantile feelings of omnipotence, manic reparation can be unhelpful or even destructive to those it is directed towards. In such cases, external objects are treated as props to restore the subject's sense of superiority. I will return to this theme in my discussion of Britain and Africa in Chapters 5 and 6.

Klein and the state

Before exploring how far Klein's ideas help us resolve this question of the relationship between thick and thin realms, I want to argue for Klein's theory as a model for examining the way states relate to each other. This might be attempted from two directions, using her ideas as either constitutive or analogous of the way states behave.

There is a case to be made for a constitutive basis for Klein's theory. This is derived from the way in which the individuals who control and shape the state – principally politicians and officials – carry personal feelings of ambiguity and the need to repair important intimate relationships into their work within the state. As Klein suggests, an engagement in 'good' activity is an important way in which individuals try to repair the damage done to core relationships. She talks about the ways in which this leads some people to engage in caring professions such as teaching or medicine.[5] The same case might be made for those working in politics, many of whom are at least partially motivated by the idea that their lives are dedicated to good causes of public service or social reform. Individuals who constitute the state narrowly defined, therefore, might see it as a vehicle for making such connections, and the state which is involved in 'good' work in the wider world would create affirming resonances for its core protagonists.

For this argument to convince, the reader will have to allow that individuals shape and direct the work of the state, an approach which dominant realist ideas in IR have tended to treat with suspicion. As Stephen Chan argues, Waltz's sharply divided three images generated a discipline that 'sidestepped an entire century of the interiority inaugurated by Freud' (Chan, 2003a: 198). Further, Barrie Paskins suggests that Waltz's model has tended to limit IR by causing us to underestimate the ways in which all three images inform how international relations are formed, both separately and in the ways in which they interact and reinforce each other (Paskins, 1978: 165–6). States and state systems are driven by individuals and the relationships between them – they cannot behave in ways outside human life.

It is here that there could be a danger of slipping into a form of psychoessentialism; of attempting, for example, to somehow assess the psychological state of politicians or officials, either in particular cases, or as a group. To avoid this, I suggest that there may simply be a sense of personal satisfaction and wellbeing to be derived from the connection to 'good' work, and that the state, by engaging in such good work, might help provide a psychological underpinning that is useful for the individuals most closely involved with it. This point is reinforced in my discussion of state actors' feelings about British work in Africa (see Chapters 5 and 6).

Using Klein's ideas by way of analogy also has to be done with care, but it is potentially more interesting and rewarding. The dangers of appearing to anthropomorphise the state make it tricky to describe a state as analogous to an individual, particularly when the theory being considered deals so explicitly with emotions and the unconscious. However, there is a body of psychoanalytic theory that explores how groups behave in ways that mirror the individual psyche. Wilfred Bion's work, for example, suggests that the unconscious dynamics in groups can lead to forms of group idealisation or denial in ways similar to those developed by individuals (Bion, 1974). Segal has explored these ideas in discussions of politics and war (Segal, 1997). Bion argued that 'the group is essential to the fulfilment of a man's mental life – quite as essential to that as it is to the more obvious activities of economics and war' (Bion, 1974: 53–5). This approach is familiar to political ideas, from Aristotle's argument that, as political creatures, people needed to belong to groups in order to realise a full life, to anti-Enlightenment thinkers like Rousseau and Hegel, who saw the state in its representation of collective political organisation as the route to or expression of ethical life and a source of individual affirmation. 'The state is not an instrument for the achievement of material satisfactions; it is a mode of relating which stresses shared values and common sacrifice at the expense of individual interests ... the individual is what he is only by virtue of his participation in some totality wider than himself' (Smith, 1989: 158).

Drawing now on Klein, we can point to the similar foundational bases of the state and the family in relationships. First, and most tangibly, within each forum individuals are mutually dependent – and thus dependent on the collectivity – for their survival and wellbeing. We depend physically on the state: on its ability to defend us and to provide goods we deem essential. Moreover, within the state individuals are shaped by and develop a shared history, culture and sense of the future. These intimate bonds of survival and identity lend relationships within the state – as in the family – particular intensity or thickness. Therefore, the ability to shape shared normative understandings within such core relationships forms the basis of the individual's ability to flourish, both physically and emotionally.

At the same time, the intensity and foundational nature of core relationships are fraught and often contentious. The thickness of relationships within the family, or between the individuals within and to the state, generates ambiguity, frustration and even hatred, as well as affection and love.

Let us look at core relationships a little more closely. Klein's work is preoccupied by object relations and the processes and interaction of the internalising and externalising of objects. She discusses the ways in which infants project their feelings onto close external objects and mentally internalise these objects which form their growing personality, shaping further encounters with and internalisations of external objects. The child is author of, and subject to, her internal objects, which are built on both positive and negative interactions with the world. Her unconscious life is dominated by them, and the ways she relates to them – including her intense feelings of hatred and love for them. The degree to which the internal objects equate positively to the external objects she experiences determines how successfully she adjusts to reality and her sense of containment and potential to flourish. Thus her ability to mend and contain good internal objects feeds her sense of fulfilment and capacity to interact positively with the world.

When we look at the relationship between individuals and the state, we might describe something similar. Following Rousseau, we see that the individuals in a community are at once the collective author of and subject to the state. The state is not just a tangible, external object: it is created, internalised and shaped by us, constituting part of our internally derived sense of wellbeing. It becomes something like a Kleinian internal object in the way we constitute and are constituted by it. At the same time, because the state is internalised, the external, or real, state's ability to provide psychological and physical underpinning becomes essential. If the state is weak and inadequate, if it fails to embody a sense of the collective identity, this undermines important psychological or ethical sources of affirmation, as well as the physical security we expect from it.[6]

In Klein's theory, relationships beyond the family do not have this essential foundational basis and can be used to test out more idealised or extreme versions of good and bad as a way of sorting out moral ambiguity. Such an opportunity is useful because it allows a more straightforward picture of moral questions to develop, one that reassures and enables vital processes of affirmation and repair to the damaged relationships within the family, and a reinforcement of the positive aspects of the developing internal objects – Klein's reparative processes. Kleinian ideas, when applied to the state and our relation to it, might see the thin ways in which the world beyond the state is depicted in stark moral terms as useful to the process of mending the state, an attempt to restore the state's function as a source of wellbeing, as a good internal object. Engagement based on such a depiction might lead to genuine repair, or it might, especially if it is manic, be destructive, superficial and in the end unfruitful.

Klein and the communitarians

Klein realises the importance to human wellbeing of a connection to a sense of the good. In this she echoes Taylor, who suggests: 'The aspiration to fullness can be met by building something into one's life, some pattern of higher action, or some meaning; or it can be met by connecting one's life up with some greater reality or story' (Taylor, 1989: 43). Klein writes:

> By a gradual process, anything that is felt to give out goodness and beauty, and that calls forth pleasure and satisfaction, in the physical or in the wider sense, can in the unconscious mind take the place of this ever-bountiful

> breast, and that of the whole mother. Thus we speak of our own country as the 'motherland' because in the unconscious mind our country may come to stand for our mother, and then it can be loved with feelings which borrow their nature from the relation to her. (Klein, 1998a: 43)

Klein's work explains why there is this thirst for a pure good, the desire for a connection to it. In the constant search for a reconnection with the good, external objects, people and causes are idealised and connected with in a process that strengthens the good internal object. Through this process – akin to Hegel's idea that individuals need to pass through the relatively thin realm of civil society, in transit from the family to the state, in order to 'see themselves' better – Klein suggests that people develop a capacity to realise more mature forms of love in which they can hold the good and the bad together without good being overwhelmed by bad.

Klein is dealing with two key questions which are central in communitarian approaches to morality in IR. First, how do we distinguish between the way norms are viewed in the intimate, communal realm and in the looser realm beyond? Second, how are these sets of norms related to, or dependent on, each other? Walzer and Frost have both contributed to this discussion about the qualitative difference between the moral frames of reference in the two realms; and both have suggested ways in which they are related.

For Walzer: 'In moral discourse, thinness and intensity go together, whereas with thickness comes qualification, compromise, complexity and disagreement' (Walzer, 1994: 6). Thin norms are broad, simple ideas like 'justice' and 'truth' – perhaps more apparently than actually universal, but resonant enough to allow brief (and superficial) moments of solidarity with people in situations far away, particularly in times of crisis. Such intensity is only possible in the absence of deeper scrutiny and contentious distributive questions, which are inescapable in the domestic realm. Here, complex, culturally embedded norms evolve slowly and are shaped by immanent conflicts of interest. Frost, in attempting to define a set of 'settled norms' existing between states, is also seeking a normative framework that can exist within the thinner international realm. His list of such 'goods', far more prosaic than Walzer's ethereal values, prioritises the preservation of the society of states and the principle of state sovereignty, and is primarily concerned with attempts to protect and promote the state system (Frost, 1986).

Both Frost and Walzer argue that thinner normative frameworks are made possible by thicker domestic norms. They start from the assumption that morality is a construction of communities. Since morality and the language of morality are developed within communities, the individual's sense of her place in a good community is intimately tied to her conception of herself as a good person. As Taylor puts it, the community defines the framework within which what is good can be found, and the individual seeks a connection to that good within it, or in relation to it (Taylor, 1989: 28). Without such a reference framework, any moral understanding is impossible.

Thus, Walzer argues that minimalist norms are always derived from maximalist ones: 'If we did not have our own parade, we could not march vicariously in Prague. We would have no understanding at all of "truth" and "justice"' (Walzer, 1994: 19). For him, thicker domestic norms are the basis for thinner international understanding, without the latter necessarily playing a role in supporting the former. They are, rather, a socially useful by-product of morality within communities. Frost, on the other hand, argues that the norms held within the community of states are derived from the need to preserve the state itself. In other words, the thicker normative framework of the community relies on the existence of the thinner international normative framework. In suggesting this, of course, he takes us back to the Hegelian conception of the state as the basis of self-actualisation for its members. Frost argues that individuals are not able to live a fully ethical life if the state is not recognised by other states as autonomous: there is a vital connection between the wellbeing of the state and the wellbeing of the individual (Frost, 1986: 177–9). The content and shape of the international normative framework directly supports the ethical basis of the state.

Klein's contribution to this, I believe, lies in her understanding of the dynamic between the two sets of norms. As we have seen, she argues that thinner conceptions of good and bad are generated within the relationships of the family and projected onto the outside world. But it is the grasping onto these purer norms of the thinner realm that makes it possible to deal with the more challenging thicker realm – they are reabsorbed to make sense of, and ultimately repair, the thick inner realm. Her depiction of the projection of pure forms of good and bad as a mechanism to deny or to help resolve moral ambiguity at home – to repair internal objects and relationships – helps underline Frost's description of international 'settled norms' as requisite for supporting the central role of the state and through it the individuals and relationships within it. Thus, the relationship between the two becomes more circular: one deriving from and in turn supporting the other.

It is this thicker form of the ideal, of the immanent ambiguities within it, that particularly resonates with Klein's work. Her ideas on the damage done by ambiguity to internal objects enables a fuller exploration of the feelings of frustration and aggression towards the state's imperfections and inadequacies; to see it – the loved and vital object – as a cause of guilt and in need of repair. Flowing from this is Klein's suggestion that a coming to terms with the moral ambiguity of intimate relationships demands a process of reconnecting with a sense of pure good in the wider world, where, as Walzer describes it, 'truth' and 'justice' appear universal and unblemished. By doing this, the internal objects – the ultimate source of wellbeing – can be repaired. Klein's ideas support Frost in his shaping of an international moral order which explicitly, even mechanistically, protects and repairs the state. But perhaps his 'settled norms' are a little too straightforwardly utilitarian in this context. Walzer's description of far looser values sums up aspirations to a universal good, a utopia, an ideal, which Klein argues is so important in this process of repair.

Africa: a damaged object?

Since the 1990s, particular dominant ideas have developed about the ways in which states might engage positively in the wider world. 'Good projects' might include identifying with universalising structures and ideas which transcend the state. These include international legal and normative frameworks such as the International Criminal Court, the UN Declaration of Human Rights and the ideas of political and economic liberalism; and activities in which states collectively involve themselves in order to pursue good – for example, the Millennium Development Goals. These structures and ideas, by virtue of their transcendence of the thick and morally ambiguous domestic realm, appear far more ideal than home-grown varieties. Further, and guided by the assumption of universal goods, is state involvement in causes: states take a stand or even engage against acts of barbarism, 'humanitarian disasters' or defiance of democratic processes. Almost inevitably, such causes appear flattened: they are characterised by innocent victims, subject to immoral forces, rather than being part of a politically and morally complex story.[7]

In particular, Africa has appeared to provide such causes. In the next two chapters, I am going to explore how Britain has viewed Africa as a site of reparation and attempted to 'do good' there. I want to explore how far Klein's ideas about guilt and reparation provide a framework for understanding what drove this policy. And I want also to come back to this question of how far such a policy might be seen as part of a reaction to ambiguous feelings towards the state, and how far it might present elements of manic reparation.

Notes

1 See Hugo Slim's discussion on 'moral dilemmas'. Slim makes the point that a moral dilemma is a choice not between the right and the wrong option but between several right options. Morality is no more clear-cut than politics (Slim, 1997).

2 Attachment theorists, to whose work internal objects are integral, describe them as 'internal working models'. 'Each individual builds working models of the world and of himself in it, with the aid of which he perceives events, forecasts the future, and constructs his plans. In the working models of the world that anyone builds a key feature is his notion of who his attachment figures are, where they may be found, and how they may be expected to respond. Similarly, in the working model of the self that anyone builds a key feature is his notion of how acceptable or unacceptable he himself is in the eyes of his attachment figures' (Bowlby, 1973: 203).

3 'In each individual there is a coherent organisation of mental processes; and we call this his *ego*. It is to this ego that consciousness is attached; the ego controls the approaches to motility – that is, to the discharge of excitations into the external world; it is the mental agency which supervises all its own constituent processes, and which goes to sleep at night, though even then it exercises the censorship on dreams' (Freud, 1960: 8).

4 Klein uses 'positions' rather than Freudian 'stages' to emphasise that the phenomena she was describing were not simply passing 'stages' or 'phases' such as, for example, Freud's oral phase. Klein's term implies a specific configuration of object relations, anxieties and defences which persist throughout life. Although there is a definite sense of development in Klein's description of the ways in which children increasingly grasp the reality of the world, she doesn't ascribe specific stages to particular ages, or a definitive order to development. Rather, the various 'positions' she describes, and the mechanisms used to avoid or resolve them, can recur throughout life (Segal, 2006: ix).

5 Segal explores this in her discussion of work with manic patients (Segal, 1986: 147–58).

6 Stephen Chan discusses similar themes as explored through Zimbabwean fiction from the perspective of what happens when the state fails to provide physical and psychological underpinning (Chan, 2005a).

7 Walzer argues they can only resonate in such ways, as moral thickness precludes less extreme causes from being universally understood. 'Our common humanity will never make us members of a universal tribe. The crucial commonality of the human race is particularism: we participate, all of us, in thick cultures that are our own' (Walzer, 1994: 83).

5

Healing the scar?

This chapter examines what Africa means to actors clustered around the state: MPs, officials and those working with them during the Blair era. I start out with some basic questions: How is British policy in Africa different from policy in other parts of the world? Why does Britain engage in it? What do the actors involved get out of it? Public sources gave clues: speeches, papers and initiatives from the government, and MPs directly interested or engaged in work in Africa suggested a number of themes which were pursued in interviews.

First, British engagement in Africa is represented as being driven by moral compulsion, in contrast to other parts of foreign policy which are discussed more in terms of British interests or political questions. As discussed in Chapter 1, under New Labour Africa gradually came to embody the ethical dimension of foreign policy, and speeches, statements and publications by Labour ministers reinforce this perspective. This suggests that Africa represents a purer realm, perhaps one that is less political: Blair's 'one noble cause worth fighting for' explicitly separates Africa from the 'difficult politics'[1] he has to deal with. I wanted to explore how deep this sense of a pure and moral cause went. How far was it rhetorical – a device, perhaps, to counter perceptions of government failure; how far of real importance to those concerned? Reinforcing this sense of purity is the fact that the approach and language across the political spectrum are remarkably uniform. Speeches from the Conservative and Liberal Democrat leaders and development spokespeople could as easily have been made by members of the Government. I wanted to pursue this – was there a consciousness that the three main parties were broadly in line over Africa? Was this something they found difficult or that they enjoyed?

Second, Africa's huge problems are revised frequently and with great energy. Tony Lloyd, a junior minister in the FCO, outlined four causes of Africa's malaise which reflect the common perception. First, he detailed the many armed conflicts which 'fuel instability, feed off the misery of civilian populations…devastate the country's resources and infrastructure' and 'damage the image of the whole continent'. Second, he described the poverty which 'creates misery and contributes to instability,' detailing the need for 'sound economic management' as a way to secure debt forgiveness and private investment. Third was the problem of poor governance, typified by 'corruption and abuses of human rights', and of weak institutions lacking accountability and transparency. Finally, came the lack of African cooperation, which hampers African countries' ability to 'resolve their own problems peacefully and independently of outside intervention' (Lloyd, 1999). I wanted to explore what Africa looked like to the British politicians involved there. How far does this picture reinforce or belong to the depiction of Africa as a moral cause? How far does it provide scope for an idealisation of British intervention? In what ways was such an idealisation maintained?

Third, although politicians like to project certainty, I wanted to investigate how far Africa was able to provide a particularly suitable site for clarity and directability – both in what needed to be done and in developing a sense that British action would be able to achieve success. The most dramatic example of the confidence and certainty that frequently appears to characterise the British approach to Africa is provided in Blair's speech to the Labour Party conference in 2001, when he famously said: 'The state of Africa is a scar on the conscience of the world. But if the world as a community focused on it, we could heal it. And if we don't, it will become deeper and angrier' (Blair, 2001). Does Africa lend itself particularly to notions of British capacity and potency? How far can this be seen as generating feelings of omnipotence? Of what significance is this?

The actors I interviewed belonged to various circles of interest and involvement, all centred on the state. In the middle was the Government itself; subsequent, slightly wider layers comprised Labour MPs who might be expected to most closely support or identify with government policy; further out were layers containing MPs from other political parties; weaving in and out of all of these were the officials who, in one sense, were at the heart of the state, while at the same time removing themselves from a too-close identification with the Labour Government. The final, widest layer was the political community beyond Westminster, which I wanted to examine from the perspective of the MPs themselves.

My thesis is that Africa policy can be viewed as representing a sense of the good state. In some way, British projects and activities in Africa could be separated from other state activity and conceived of as pure or ideal. Therefore, key questions will deal with how far the ideals of Africa, of British policy in Africa and of the relationship between Britain and Africa were conceived and maintained; how far these could lay the groundwork for building or restoring a sense of a good state. A further ambition is to try to establish how far and how strongly the Africa policy radiated beyond its government core, and how important it was to those involved near the core that it did so. Was this ideal state a shared project, something that united people in Britain, binding them into the idea of the state in constructive ways?

This chapter is based on a series of 30 interviews with politicians and officials involved in work on Africa. They included members of the Labour Government who had worked on Africa and development issues as ministers in either the FCO or DfID; opposition spokespeople on international development; backbench MPs involved in all-party groups on African countries;[2] supporters and observers of these groups; and officials from the FCO and DfID. Subsequent interviews in Nigeria and Sierra Leone with British officials and local actors will be brought into the discussion in Chapter 6.

In the first of four sections, I discuss how interviewees describe Britain's work in Africa. This is done in a highly idealised way: their work, and the work of the state, is separated from more 'political' projects, chiefly through the removal of interests and political division, and crafted into a sacred space. In the second section, I look at the ways in which those involved in work in Africa project purer forms of good and bad onto Africa, denying moral ambiguity there. In doing this, they create – and then protect – an idealised Africa with which Britain forms an idealised relationship. In the third section, I outline the ways in which the creation of an idealised Africa enables an assertion of omnipotence. Omnipotence here is the sense of completely knowing and understanding the object, and so being empowered to repair it, to make it right. In the concluding section, I return to Britain in a discussion of the ways in which my interviewees regard wider British attitudes to Africa and their attempts to do good there.

Idealised Britain: a sacred space

The trick to creating a sacred space is to keep it uncontaminated by politics – in other words, away from division and ambiguity. It must be something where ideas and actions are kept pure and unsullied by baser human activities and passions. Hegel, as I have already discussed, suggested that the good state could represent an ideal, although it could never fully realise it, shaped as it must be, by politics. Durkheim, on the other hand, develops a notion of a sacred space separated from the profane (and mundane), formerly realised through the realm of religious life. Durkheim's sacred space, like Hegel's good state, is an essential ingredient to moral wellbeing – of the community, but through the community, of the individual too. Both, as I suggested in Chapter 4, resonate strongly also with Klein's suggestion about the ways in which individuals build and protect good internal objects by projecting and identifying with notions of good. All three deal in different ways with the difficulty of living with imperfection – a strong common theme is the way in which the ideal has to be protected from more morally complex reality.

All the people I interviewed are steeped in politics. Their day to day work is about political conflict – between what they want to do and what others want to do; between what is believed to be right and what is seen to be expedient; between an ideal and reality. There is constant division involved between actors pursuing different agendas and interests. There is also internal ambiguity, concerned with moral and political choices which in the real political world are not clear-cut. But in the creation of policy in Africa as sacred, these conflicts are removed: these actors have carved out for themselves a little bit of public life that is connected to a morally pure space. Jenny Tonge, spokesperson for the Liberal Democrats on international development from 1997 to 2003, expressed the common view: 'Of course it's a moral issue: it's doing to others as you would have them do to you. That's not contentious ... something has to be done because you can't live with yourself if you don't. And I think all the parties agree on that, and I think we're closer than we've ever been.'[3]

Chris Mullin, who was a junior minister at DfID and then minister for Africa at the FCO between 2001 and 2005, also describes his pleasure in the jobs he did there as suiting 'someone who comes from the more idealistic ... wing of politics'. He felt that 'Africa offers an opportunity to occupy some moral high-ground, that other parts of the world don't'.[4]

How is this done? How does this corner of foreign policy come to occupy a moral space? First is the lack of tangible interests in the work – the key way in which Africa policy is differentiated from policy in other parts of the world; and second is that the lack of contention around African issues has erased differences between the parties. I will illustrate the significance of both dimensions.

Interests

The question of interests is key in being able to differentiate foreign policy towards Africa from conventional *realpolitik*. Since the time that Britain began to shake off its African colonies in the late 1950s, Africa has featured as a relatively unimportant part of foreign policy (Clapham, 2002: 87) – economic or political interests have not been reckoned as substantial, an approach that reached its peak during the 1980s.[5] What engagement there was tended to follow a mixture of Cold War logic and the view of Africa as marginal recipient of rather half-hearted aid policies (Cumming, 2001; Bose and Burnell, 1991).

The foundational maxim of realist foreign policy is that states will pursue their own interests regardless of wider good. The New Labour government's policies in Africa very deliberately rejected that approach, but how far did they relinquish interests altogether? There are three possible approaches. First, a straightforwardly altruistic approach, in which real self-interest is ignored in the pursuit of doing what is ethical. Second, what is self-interested and what is ethical pull in the same direction – Carr's harmonies of interest argument, which posits that a rational examination will reveal that, over the long term, interests work in common. And third, there are negligible issues of self-interest apparent in Africa, leaving the field clear for a purely ethical approach.

Evaluating the relative significance of these approaches requires that we establish what kinds of interest Britain has in Africa. Conventional interests would centre on the importance of developing political influence and allies, and promoting economic opportunities. With the exception of South Africa, Africa remains politically and economically unimportant to Britain.[6] Evidence of this can be found in the fact that the FCO has never placed a high rank on African posts, instead concentrating its best minds on Europe, the USA and the Middle East.

> Generally speaking, political ambitions or objectives in developing countries aren't important. If you talk to colleagues in the FCO, they're never really clamouring to get out to Kinshasa. It's not like they feel they've made it when they get to Freetown ... They're always looking at the G8 countries, and the major European countries. That's where the politics is.[7]

In economic terms, trade with Africa is not a significant contributor to Britain's economy[8] and the FCO economic wing puts few resources into developing it. 'There clearly aren't the huge identifiable British interests in Africa there once were, in the sense that the international mining companies are no longer national companies.'[9] Africa's mineral wealth – which recently has become such an attraction to the Chinese – apparently fails to get British pulses racing.

Instead, new kinds of interests are discussed in the context of Africa. These include: the desire to limit migration to Europe; concerns about the spread of instability into geographical areas of more importance; and fears about ways in which international terrorism might be nurtured in failing states. As Labour MP John Austin puts it:

> I think there is a general consensus that failing states lead to instability, whether it's because of the Islamic threat, or a terrorist thing, or instability is bad for business. And it causes refugees as well: I think there is a recognition now that if you allow states to fail and if you allow tyrannical regimes to come, people will present themselves on the doorstep of Europe.[10]

These interests can be nurtured through the promotion of stability and development in Africa – which makes life a lot easier for those who wish to pursue a robust development policy in Africa, as Clare Short explained:

> Whether it was the case in the past, and it probably was in the heyday of empire, that what was morally right and what was in Britain's self-interest were probably contradictory, it is no longer the case. And I mean that, I'm not just rationalising it. And that's a delight because you don't have any confusion, you can just get on with what's right: it's in Africa's interest, it's in Europe's interest, it's in the world's interest.[11]

Enlightened self-interest – a harmony of interests – is an attractive position, 'a delight'. Perhaps the real delight is the way in which this approach can take in all sides of the political spectrum, building an irrefutable case to please everyone. Conservative MP John Bercow describes this harmony of interests in more overtly instrumentalist terms. For Bercow, perhaps, the idea of self-interest is not as discomfiting as it might be for a politician like Short, who is more at ease talking about doing things because they are morally right. Bercow needs to demonstrate something more – that foreign policy is not leaving behind a realist flavour altogether – although he too is keen to distinguish the new forms this takes from traditional *realpolitik*:

> [We need] a wider definition of what constitutes interests. For example, if there's going to be an expansion ... in conflict, and in the causes of poverty, and the grievances are left unaddressed, then the consequences are there, in an increase of violence, the scale of the arms trade, an increase in terrorism, an increase in refugees, an increase in disease – HIV, malaria, TB ... So in that sense we do have an interest. You're right that not just a British but a Tory approach to foreign policy has tended to revolve around concepts of national interest. I simply think that, though that concept remains valid, it needs to be redefined ... You can take the Alan Clark view of the world ... I think Alan Clark pretty much would have said that if we don't sell arms to this regime, somebody else will – and there is that law of the jungle view – but I think that's very short-sighted. Apart from the fact that it's a very inhuman view.[12]

And Jenny Tonge, from the left wing of the Liberal Democrats, sees the harnessing of self-interest as a vital tool in building support for policies which should be pursued in any case:

> [Self-interest] is not incidental. Of course it's not, because that is the means by which you convince people that it's worth doing. But even if it wasn't, you still ought to be doing something about it if you're a decent human being ... Whatever the good reasons are, whatever the economic reasons, whatever the prevention of conflict reasons, even if they didn't exist, you've still got to do something about it, because it's just not fair.[13]

Returning to our original three approaches to interests, it appears fairly clear that the first – the over-ruling of self-interest by the need to do good – barely features in the public rhetoric. It is not needed since the perception is that any interests there are in Africa are geared towards the same ends as the interests of Africans themselves. But the question remains, how substantial are these interests; or how much do they instead form a rationalising narrative for British policy in Africa? One close observer of political initiatives on Africa suggested that the enlightened self-interest line was developed to garner possibly more sceptical British support for a more straightforwardly disinterested policy. 'In the nineteenth century, it would be argued, and probably well into the twentieth century, the British Government's line was to dress up its venal interests in moral claims. But we've flipped. So now what we do is we dress up moral direction, which I think is mostly what Tony Blair is interested in, as sort of in our economic interests.'[14]

Myles Wickstead, the DfID official who worked with Blair on the Commission for Africa, reinforces this view. 'There was nothing. There was no sense of even enlightened self-interest, I believe, in his establishing the Commission ... I think he is driven genuinely by the sense that there was a moral duty to make a difference in Africa.'[15]

It is not only Blair who prefers the moral direction. Many interviewees expressed a personal approach guided by a purer concern to do good. Tony Lloyd, for example, said: 'In the end, I think people should do good things because it's the right thing to do. That's my own personal complex of values. So I've never wanted to be driven into doing the right thing just because there is a quite legitimate reason of self-interest.'[16]

One Commons researcher who has worked closely on Africa issues with MPs from all the parties, felt strongly that in Westminster, Africa was not viewed as an area of national interest.

> I honestly don't think that people who engage here think in those terms [of British interests] at all. I think it's purely about human rights and the welfare of the people in the countries ... Occasionally you get barking types who say, well you've got to find some connection with terrorism or al-Qaeda, and then they'll take it seriously ... [but] it wouldn't work here because that's not what motivates people.[17]

Of the three approaches to British interests in Africa, the first can be largely dismissed, as there is agreement that conventional interests – those which might conflict with what is best for Africa – are negligible. Instead, there is a mixture of harmonious interests and a relative absence of interests. The former suggest a painless overcoming of politics, and thus tend towards an idealised view of the world. However, in the relative thinness of these 'new interests', it could be viewed as amounting to little more than a post-hoc rationalisation. It is difficult to see how sufficient development and stability be achieved in very poor, very badly governed, or very unstable parts of Africa to prevent migration to Europe; or disaffection be overcome in these countries to the extent that terrorism can be stifled. The relatively small development efforts focused on Africa can do little more than signal an intention and an interest in making this so, while richer and more stable parts of the world yield migrants and terrorists in far more significant numbers. There is also a question mark over the degree to which Africa is seen as a site of the radicalised Islamism that might yield terrorists. Somalia, Western Sahel and northern Nigeria have been looked at by the FCO as being amongst the most likely candidates. But the impression amongst officials is that the actual threat is small. As one FCO official told me, 'Radicalisation of this kind is not really very African.'[18]

The suggestion that real interest arguments are a tool to bolster the case for what is essentially a more straightforwardly disinterested attempt to do good must carry some weight. New Labour development policy documents marshalled a series of self-interest arguments, each echoing the topical theme of the day. Thus, the 1997 DfID White Paper reflected environmental concerns; the 2000 DfID White Paper was about globalisation; and later DfID and FCO pronouncements linked the counter-terrorism agenda to development. While an array of arguments might help support the case for development assistance in Africa, it is difficult to see that most actors came to this from a starting point of British interests. The moral case, I suggest, was prior. However, whether interests are irrelevant or harmonious, politics appears to have been removed from the policy: interests, where they exist, are benign and constructive. In adding to the notion of a policy space which overcomes political difference, they reinforce the sense of Britain's Africa policies as constitutive of a sacred space in British politics.

Consensus

The removal of selfish interests leads to another aspect of Britain's policies in Africa, that of consensus. In contrast to every other domestic and international issue, there are virtually no divisions between and within Britain's political parties on Africa. Let us now look at this second dimension of Britain's depoliticised Africa policy.

When Tony Blair began to develop a philosophy for New Labour after his election as leader in 1994, he was keen to stress that his was a new form of politics which would unite previously divided constituencies (Blair, 1998c). There was an assumption that difference and argument were to be overcome, rather than accepted as an inevitable part of politics, and New Labour would be able to absorb of a range of different interests – not just those of its traditional constituency, but big business and finance – and develop a set of policies to suit all. Traditional forms of Labour thinking – trade unionism, libertarian leftism and social democracy – had used terms of struggle and conflicting interests between labour and capital. New Labour, by contrast, suggested it could transcend political difference through the power of reason. As David Marquand puts it, the New Labour philosophy suggested that: 'There is one modern condition, which all rational people would embrace if they knew what it was. The Blairites do know' (Marquand, 1999: 226).

There was great excitement when Labour was elected with a landslide majority in May 1997. Blair's appeal to a new consensual politics was attractive and proved relatively resilient in the first months of his Government. Inevitably, however, the consensus came unstuck as parts of his own party began to rebel against his too conservative social agenda, while the opposition parties found their feet, and opportunities to criticise the Government. Division and conflict in foreign policy took a little longer, but came dramatically over the Iraq war when Britain saw unprecedented numbers of people involved in public protests.

In the middle of this return to politics as usual, government policy on international development and Africa alone appeared to embody the ideal of consensus across the political spectrum. The degree of consensus between the parties, between different political wings of the Labour Party and between backbenchers and the Government is striking. Myles Wickstead, the DfID official charged with organising the Commission for Africa, argues that the Commission for Africa played a large part in bringing people together: 'One of the most remarkable things about 2004–5 is that we no longer have political division about the importance of all this in this country. There's been an extraordinary political shift where everybody agrees on the importance of reaching the 0.7 per cent target...that would have been inconceivable two or three years ago.'[19]

However Jenny Tonge felt the consensus was established long before 2004. She described what it was like being Liberal Democrat spokesperson on international development between 1999 and 2003:

> It was extraordinarily difficult because there was nothing to oppose. That was the problem, and I think people find it even more so with Hilary Benn. I don't think there is a fag paper between the [parties'] policies on international development...It's very difficult to oppose the Government on international development. And in a way, why should we, what's the point? Surely it's better to get the parties to work together?[20]

The Conservatives, too, argued that they could unite around the Africa policies. Malcolm Moss, MP, said: 'I don't see a great difference between the political parties...I think that there is a genuine interest in Africa and African affairs, and a genuine desire to make it better somehow.'[21] The view is echoed by John Bercow who, as the Conservative Party spokesman on international development from 2003 to 2005, is credited with beginning to move his party's position much closer to the Government's, something that David Cameron subsequently attempted to reinforce.[22] 'I think there is quite a lot in common between the Government and ourselves in relation to Africa...the attitude certainly on the Conservative side has changed for the better...I have significant respect for Blair on his international record: I think it's his domestic record which is rather more lamentable.'[23]

Across the Labour Party too, there is a high degree of consensus about how to approach Africa. 'If you take the Campaign Group[24] in the Labour Party, who very rarely support the Government on anything these days, they will support them on Africa projects and their Africa policy,' said John Robertson.[25]

Jeremy Corbyn, from the left wing of the Party, finds himself in agreement on this with the most unlikely people. 'Eric [Joyce – chair of the All-Party Parliamentary Group (APPG) on the Great Lakes and Genocide Prevention] and I, for example, either meet to discuss things on Africa, where we usually agree, or we meet in radio stations debating the war in Iraq, where we fundamentally and totally disagree. There is a kind of coming together on this.'[26]

MPs who are critical of the Government on many aspects of foreign and domestic policy argue that on Africa, Blair was right. John Robertson, for example, says: 'Blair believes in what he does. I believe he believed in the case of Iraq, that he was doing the right thing. Even though some of us told him he shouldn't do it. But having said that, he believed he was right, and in the case of Africa, I believe he *is* right. I think he's spot-on there.'[27] And John Austin said: 'I'm not one of Mr Blair's fans, but I don't think the guy is all bad. I do think he has some sort of moral driving force ... I think setting up the Africa Commission was an ingenious and bold thing to do, and driving the thing forward at the G8 was, I think, all well motivated.' I asked Austin whether Africa was unique in its ability to unite people in this way. 'I think it is,' he replied. 'I get up in praise of Blair and Brown. Yes, it is. I don't think there's anybody that disagrees with it.'[28]

The fact that here is a policy area that transcends ordinary politics, and unites MPs and the Government in an important moral undertaking, provides a sense of excitement and enjoyment. It presents opportunities for those involved to feel connected to a project that restores and mends uncomfortable, or even broken, political processes.

> I sometimes think that if people outside could see people sitting down and putting their brains together and cooperating it would really restore their faith in parliament and politics. You know, when you see people from all sorts of different angles, someone like Chris Mullin working flat out with someone like Baroness Park of Monmouth, [when] you would have thought they had nothing in common.[29]

DfID itself most tangibly embodies the idea of the sacred space in the middle of the state. As Clare Short suggested:

> I've heard people say DfID is the ethical foreign policy, DfID's the good guys ... I personally set myself the ambition of getting as much cross-party support for the UK's commitment to development as I could ... I think they [the Conservatives] cottoned that it was popular with the public; that it's relatively inexpensive. You can play big with not much money compared with other areas of public expenditure and it's moral and kind and popular and actually underneath all that, it makes sense.[30]

Reinforcement came from abroad too, where DfID is held in high esteem and, suggests Short, became a flagship for British integrity. 'He [Blair] and Cherie, I can remember them saying to me a couple of times, wherever we travel, everyone's talking about DfID. So they got the message that good things were going on in DfID, that it was regarded in the international system as, you know, good.'[31]

DfID – and, because it most clearly represents DfID's perspective and ambitions, Africa – embodies a unique area of state action, appearing to fulfil the ideal of a transcendence of interests, politics and division. It created a sacred space at the heart of the state and restored a sense of connection with something good.

In the next section, I am going to look at the way in which a split-off idea of 'good' is projected onto an idealised Africa.

Idealising Africa: projecting good

V. Y. Mudimbe and Achille Mbembe both discuss in detail the ways in which Europeans have used Africa as a site of otherness against which to compare themselves more brightly (Mudimbe, 1994; Mbembe, 2001). Building on Edward Said's work on Orientalism (Said, 2003), Mudimbe argues that Africa provides the ultimate benchmark of 'otherness' for Europeans, a 'refused place', a place to project and deposit its own unacceptable facets (see Chapter 1). This idea of Africa as the place upon which to project nastiness, or, as Julia Kristeva puts it, the uncanniness within ourselves that we find difficult to acknowledge, (Kristeva, 1991: 182–92) is a familiar one. As Mudimbe suggests, it posits a purely relational role for Africa, a negative to our positive. As Said pointed out, otherness can involve romanticisation too; hence colonial ideas of the noble savage and views of European civilisation as being potentially emasculating or corrupting.

Mbembe describes Africa as some kind of a 'blank surface' on which Westerners can work. This allows the projection of pure good as well as bad: otherness can serve more than one purpose. This resonates with Klein's ideas about the splitting of good and bad feelings and the ability to project them into a more 'neutral' space. But, as Mudimbe suggests, this projection relies on a particular understanding of the interaction of European and African histories. Any mixing of history will muddy the dichotomy.

It is difficult to see how either historical involvement or the potentially richer understandings and relationships with Africa enabled by modern communications can fail to spoil the blank surface or undermine the idea of untouched otherness. Britain's historical role and relationships in Africa ought perhaps to implicate Britain in more ambiguous ways, something that might be expected to affect the MPs' views of their work; the large African diasporas living in some MPs' constituencies might thicken understandings of African political reality; the much vaunted effects of globalisation, which is supposed to bring shared problems and understandings to the fore, must necessitate deeper integration and shared understandings. However, as Klein suggests, the neat splitting of good and bad is really only possible *outside* the messy and more ambiguous relationships of the family. 'Out there', one has left behind interests and moral ambiguity; one also needs to be able to escape a sense of history and personal involvement which might erode the idealised picture.

In this section, I am going to describe the ways in which the politicians I spoke to manage to detach these potentially richer and more ambiguous influences from their work in Africa. I will first look at idealised conceptions of Africa and then deal with the way in which potentially more complex involvements are avoided. All this reinforces the view of Africa and Britain's role there as centred on a moral rather than a political project.

Ideal Africa

All the interviewees spoke with great affection for Africa and the people they met and dealt with there. There were strong currents of idealisation in this depiction. I will outline three types. The first, I would describe as 'Africa as fascinating primordial experience'. This was explained by Conservative

MP, Malcolm Moss:

> I haven't known anyone speak ill of Africa ... people say you're closer to nature there. I know it's a glib thing to say, but if you've been on a safari, or if you've been into the wilderness of Africa, you are going back in time in your own head to what it was like millennia ago, when the world was a new and exciting place to be. Probably frightening, too. I think it does give people a buzz.[32]

Here is an idea of a morally untouched, primordial place, where to arrive is to bring politics – perhaps even evil – for the first time. Moss's description is almost explicitly one of Eden. It expresses a longing for a return to something long lost, that time of moral certainty and omnipotence connected with very early infancy. As Klein describes it, exploration of strange and foreign places enables a sense of restoration: 'In the explorer's unconscious mind, a new territory stands for a new mother, one that will replace the loss of the real mother. He is seeking the "promised land" – the "land flowing with milk and honey"' (Klein, 1998a: 334).

The second type of idealisation, which recurred in discussion many times, is the charm and extraordinary resilience of people in Africa. MPs described the feel-good effect of dealing with them. Chris Mullin said: 'I always found in Africa that, despite all the poverty and problems, there is a basic optimism and cheerfulness among African people that I didn't always find elsewhere.'[33] Others spoke of how they 'fell in love' with 'the people' of Africa.[34] Within this was a tendency to idealise the nobility of ordinary people who have had to contend with so much, and specifically to see them as morally superior to Europeans. Claire Curtis-Thomas, who has been involved in a long-term development programme in Sierra Leone, describes her feelings about the people she works with.

> We are bowled over by the fact that you can suffer such terrible atrocities and forgive ... We were immensely moved by the reintegration of child soldiers ... and yet in our society we are so quick to blame children and so quick to label them and send them off to a horrible institution ... We realised that we were dealing with a group of people who had a capacity [for forgiveness] that we may never have possessed.[35]

Ordinary people in Africa are often presented as less complex, and morally superior to the materialism and selfishness that pervades European societies. Touching them connects us to something good.

Third, was the fascination with extreme political or conflict situations. This came in two brands: the horrified reaction to brutal, repressive regimes; and admiration for heroic leaders battling against the odds. There is a cherished history of politicians from the Labour Party finding heroes and villains in Africa. In the 1950s, many African nationalist leaders were lionised and idealised by the British left, and post-independence leaders such as Kwame Nkrumah, Julius Nyerere and Seretse Khama were seen as heroic ideological soul mates. Likewise, Africa has supplied a good number of outright villains – Idi Amin, Sani Abacha, Charles Taylor, Robert Mugabe and the South African apartheid regime. John Austin, for example, describes both in explaining his enduring interest and involvement in Ethiopia. On a visit to Ethiopia in 1993 – his first time in sub-Saharan Africa – he describes his fascination with the recent political turmoil experienced under the Derg, 'the most vicious and, apart from Saddam, one of the most repressive regimes', and his admiration for the new prime minister, Meles Zanawi. 'I thought he was doing all the right things. He had a fragile country, been fighting a war of liberation … in a tribal society where you've got all sorts of different factions and different groups … It wasn't a democracy but I thought it was moving in the right direction.'[36]

Problems arise with more morally complex figures. The most common manifestation of this approach to politics in Africa – and the problems arising when it doesn't work – was expressed in interviewees' discussion of South Africa, where the saint-like Nelson Mandela was contrasted favourably with his successor, the more overtly political Thabo Mbeki.

> Apartheid did energise and galvanise everybody. Here is this saint, you know, who came out of years of imprisonment, loving everyone including those who'd been torturing and imprisoning him for years. There was a great sense of there [being] great hope for Africa if there are people of this man's calibre … But there was also a general let-down at the failings of Thabo Mbeki, and I think failure too, not only on the AIDS issue, but failure to deal with the Zimbabwe issue … Post Mandela, I think one expected a far greater sense of leadership on human rights. And for Mbeki to be almost a brother-in-arms of Zimbabwe is quite worrying.[37]

British politicians are more comfortable dealing with heroes and villains in Africa – a Mandela or a Mugabe – than more complex political figures. Chris Mullin talked of his disappointment in leaders who had once appeared heroic but turned out to 'have feet of clay':

> No sooner do you find a country where things seem to be getting dramatically better, Uganda, post Amin and Obote, for example, under Museveni, who talked a very good talk for a long time, and indeed achieved a very great deal too, put the country back together again for the most part, but, like so many of them, he didn't know when to leave office. So for a while he was a favourite son, and if you were looking for a place where your aid and assistance might do some good, Uganda was it. But now he appears to have appointed himself president for life … Ethiopia's another example. After years of turmoil and famine, they appeared to have a good government. It doesn't do all the things that we think they should be doing, but it did have people who at least cared about their people … headed by a brilliant man, one of the most impressive I ever met during my two years in office, Meles Zanawi … [who], faced with a bad election result, appears to have behaved very badly.[38]

The tendency to view African politics as driven by criminals and heroes finds itself bewildered by political complexity. Such ambiguity is a challenge to the clarity and certainty that characterises the ways in which the politicians describe the African canvas on which they are creating – this is an area that I will discuss in a later section. Before I do, I want to explore, a little more, some of the ways in which British MPs manage to maintain an idealised sense of the relationships they have established in Africa.

Colonial (dis)entanglements

The sense of a legacy from colonial entanglements wasn't missing from discussions about Britain's relationships in Africa, but there were few indications that it endowed current British attempts to do good in Africa with greater complexity. Shirley Williams, who is active in the APPG on Zimbabwe, said: 'The current interest in Africa is not because, as in the Netherlands, for example, people have a feeling of shame about the colonial record. Maybe they should be more than they are, but they really aren't.'[39]

There were three main approaches to this question. First, was an uncomplicated view of colonialism as basically benign, or a tendency to pick out the more favourable parts of British involvement. Malcolm Moss, for example, who is proud to point out that the abolitionist campaigner, Thomas Clarkson, lived in his constituency, was one of several interviewees to stress the abolition of the slave trade as exemplifying Britain's historical role in Africa, and to dwell on the morally grander ambitions of later British colonialism in Africa. Moss described his interest in Africa as springing in part from 'the British involvement through the Empire in the colonies over a long period of time. Many of the parliaments of these postcolonial countries are modelled on our system, pretty well, and I think there's a desire to finish unfinished work. It's not working terribly well [in] many of them.'[40] Here any sense of failure contained in the colonial project is restricted to its lack of completion or thoroughness.

Second was the tendency of the Labour MPs to mention the colonial legacy, and even to associate it with guilt, but then immediately dissociate themselves or the Labour Party from it. Chris Mullin conceded that 'there may be a bit of colonial guilt around', before immediately pointing out that Labour's historical role was one of opposition to colonialism: 'the Labour Party's record on decolonisation's quite good, actually. I'm not sure the Labour Party has that much to feel guilty about.'[41]

Tony Lloyd's take on it was to suggest that Labour's traditional support base reflected people who had not benefited from colonialism.

> There are some very odd motivations. I can give you some not very nice bits: guilt would be one, a European and particularly a British guilt about Africa, particularly from my party, although ironically we were the Party that gave the first impetus towards decolonisation... Colonialism in the past was about the use of power and abuse of power in order to pursue advantage for this nation – actually, it wasn't about the advantage of the whole nation because the truth is that people from backgrounds like mine never got much advantage out of colonialism, unlike the rich.[42]

Claire Curtis-Thomas argued that dwelling on the guilt of the slave trade was pointless in the face of immediate and pressing need: she uses time to create distance from guilt. 'We were pretty bad in the past, and we feel pretty rotten about it... [But] I think people feel that this isn't the time to patronise this community and to seek from them forgiveness for a crime that was committed centuries ago.'[43]

The third group were the MPs who were most severe in responding to European guilt for the slave trade and colonialism – these were Labour MPs on the left of the Party. However, they also distanced themselves from the guilt by making their personal commitment in a country that hadn't been colonised by Britain. Jeremy Corbyn, who asserts that there is 'a collective guilt... over exploitation of the slave trade and everything else', is chair of the APPG on Angola.[44] John Austin, who chairs the APPG on Ethiopia, says: 'We plundered Africa, we became rich on the backs of Africa and we didn't prepare them for independence, and I think some of us think we have an ongoing obligation'.[45]

This dissociation further simplifies the British role in Africa today; it removes any sense of history and depth from the relationship, enabling it to be viewed as straightforwardly good. Here we are straying into the area where denial perhaps takes precedence over what Hanna Segal calls 'genuine reparation' (Segal, 2006). If Africa represents a damaged object, reparation is manic in that personal association with that damage has been removed. The state has been cleansed of guilt either by time or, in particular, because of its stewardship by a guiltless class.[46] The subject can most safely proceed with attempts to make things better, because she sees herself as completely guiltless in having caused the damage in the first place. Genuine reparation, by contrast, involves a far thicker engagement and an acknowledgement of the subject's own responsibility for damage.

'Real Africans'

Another potential way in which the idealised view of Africa might be muddied is in the way in which African constituents are viewed by those MPs who have them. One might expect that constituents, who are a constant presence with their demands and frustrations, would be expected to provide some further sense of complexity, at least in their tendency to tarnish the idealised view of Africans. However, this apparently didn't happen. Jeremy Corbyn says:

> Those [of my constituents] that come from Africa are pleased and interested [in his work in Angola], but they're not demanding anything... The African community in Britain hasn't been very effective at pushing its political interests. The only ones that have ever acted politically were South Africans, but they were normally highly political people forced into exile. They weren't economic migrants.[47]

John Austin has large African communities in his constituency which provide him with plenty of casework on asylum applications and family reunions. In particular are the Nigerians who 'buy up property – so you get a new street appearing and about 60 per cent of the houses go to Nigerians'. These people are 'mostly in work ... the wife is often a teacher ... they've got kids, they demand higher standards in schools, they want more discipline, they drive their BMWs to church on Sunday.'[48] But they don't influence his work in Africa, which is focused on the other side of the continent in Ethiopia.

African 'economic migrants' living in Britain, many of whom appear to be driven by materialism and aspiration, fail to fit ideal-African types. They are, surprisingly, not constantly cheerful, have no extraordinary capacity for forgiveness; are in fact preoccupied with everyday things. But since they are not political – they are not interested in the bigger project – they don't appear to spoil it. Political African migrants – South Africans exiled during apartheid, or, looking even further back, nationalist leaders who came to London as students in the 1950s and developed close and idealised connections with the Labour Party – are remembered as presenting Africa's political imperatives as simple ones involving battles against a self-evident evil. This reflects pre-independence African politics, when diverse political positions were united behind a single, overwhelming political imperative and political complexity was to an extent stifled. This is the 'political Africa' that interviewees remember, and it is a form of politics that represents moral battles with clear distinctions between right and wrong; the kind of African politics that interviewees felt most comfortable with. Perhaps too, it is a good example of Walzer's 'thin' norms, where people from very different communities can feel intense sympathy with dramatic struggles far away (Walzer, 1994).

Omnipotence recovered

Idealisation – of self and object and the relationship between the two – nourishes feelings of powerfulness and the ability to control political processes, something that may be felt to have been lost in domestic policy, or in other areas of foreign policy. This is not quite the same as overt attempts to dominate, because it is not seen as a struggle between ideas or actions, but a realisation of what is obvious or somehow 'natural'. Thus many interviewees were anxious to contrast current policy with what they saw as aggressive moves to accrue power. How far there are such clear-cut differences is a question I explore in Chapter 6. However, idealisation and the creation of these flat objects does enable many of those involved in work on Africa to develop a role where they feel they can control events and direct policy in ways that might have been expected or hoped to have come from a political career. Thus attempts to do good may result in control and a feeling of powerfulness. But two questions arise. First, is there any value in attempting to differentiate these from more overt manifestations of power and control? Second, how can we understand what drives this need to gain control over the object? In classic examples of the search for power there may be material advantages, but in the case of Africa – with its limited political and economic assets – such advantages are few. The illuminating work of Abrahamsen and Doty (Abrahamsen, 2000; Doty, 1996), amongst others, on the ways in which Western donor governments control Africa through the means of aid and support remains uninterested in this question of why they should be bothered.

Approaching this from a Kleinian angle, such attempts may result from repressed or sublimated aggression; and a consequent need to repair and protect damaged internal objects. Imagined omnipotence is an attempt to recover a lost infantile idealisation. Thus the flexing of an ideal 'political' control might help recover some sense of the lost political mission or restore to the state a role of authority and capability. In this interpretation, the preoccupation with 'capacity building' in Africa reflects an anxiety about the lost capacity of the British state.

British capacity

I want to describe the ways in which idealisation has led to feelings of enhanced capacity and control over political processes among British MPs and the ways in which they express it. The enormous problems and apparently clear moral landscapes of Africa lend themselves well to the idea that priorities are uncontested and solutions straightforward. This bestows a sense of power: in Africa, things can be done. Claire Curtis-Thomas – who describes herself as an engineer rather than a politician – was clear about the ways in which her 'non-political' approach could be made to work in situations of overwhelming need, as she found in post-conflict Sierra Leone.

> It's like an enormous film running three inches from your eyes and it's just awesome and of course you're spending all your time just trying to process the noise and understand what could address each set of deficiencies and where the genesis to address these deficiencies comes from. All of that going on because that's an inescapable consequence of being an engineer and being someone who's very concerned with improving the quality of people's lives, which is the fundamental position of all engineers, that's our job – to improve the quality of people's lives, and we go about doing that. So ... of course I came back with an absolute confidence that it is perfectly possible to do things in a country of this kind.[49]

Massive problems appear to generate clear-cut solutions, 'things' that are 'perfectly possible' to realise. There is a sense here that the scale of what is needed sweeps away any remnant of ambiguity. Chris Mullin, who observed this for two years from his stance as a minister for Africa, might have been expected to have come to terms with more ambiguity. But his comments very clearly reinforce what Curtis-Thomas says: 'I think there is general agreement about what needs to be done and how to do it ... It's pretty clear. You could set down on one sheet of paper the four or five things that need to be addressed.'[50]

British capacity here means less an overt feeling of aggression or superior physical strength than a more Foucauldian power of competence, of knowing how to repair and make good things where others have failed continuously and catastrophically. We can see what the problems are, we know what to do:

> I always feel a little bit uncomfortable when I hear ministers talking about African solutions to African problems, because although there is a lot of cogency in that argument, we mustn't set them up to fail. There's no point in having a badly equipped, badly trained African Union force which can't actually do much good. Nor is it satisfactory that we should simply rest content that it is simply a matter for Africa, because often, as we know, African states are reluctant publicly or privately to criticise each other.[51]

In extreme forms such as these, reparation focuses powerfully on ideas of exaggerated and idealised potency. The potency reaches into different spheres of African life, from the family, and the way politics is organised, to the repair of a collapsed state, as the following three comments show.

First, Claire Curtis-Thomas describes the ways in which her work enables her to intervene in family and social life in intimate ways:

> My family, we've adopted a family in Sierra Leone and we look after them and we send them off to school. The two mothers were raped during the war, both with two children as a result of that. And we've adopted those two women and their children and we support them. But their children are quite young. There are two girls and two boys, and both the mums have been subjected to female genital circumcision. But we made it a condition of our support that neither of the girls would be subjected to that, that under no circumstances would they be subject to this act simply because – the health implications for one – but I just fundamentally couldn't ever sanction that sort of abuse of a woman.[52]

Curtis-Thomas appears to consider that the two mothers are not really up to the job – they were raped during the war; they cannot support themselves or their children. She, therefore, is in a position to make important moral decisions about how the children are brought up. This is partially based on her superior understanding of the 'health implications', but 'fundamentally' on her feeling that the mothers – both 'subjected to female circumcision' themselves – are either incapable of understanding that such practice is abusive or unable to prevent such abuse of their daughters. Curtis-Thomas becomes mother to them all.

Second, John Austin, a relatively unknown backbench MP in Britain, finds himself able to access the highest levels of politics in Ethiopia, and to play a mediating and guiding role there:

> We saw the Justice Minister and we said, well, we welcomed the fact that he'd allowed an international jurist to observe the trials [of arrested opposition activists]...But, you know, some of the charges are a bit ludicrous, like attempted genocide. So charge them with the right things, but

> charge them, and if you're not going to charge them, let them out. And if you're going to charge them, get the court hearings going and have them in the full gaze of international press and observers.

Austin went on to meet members of the opposition parties.

> One of the complaints of the opposition was that the Government controls the agenda. And we said, yes, well, like it does in Britain, you know ... What you have is the right to interrogate, to question, to challenge ministers ... They said there had been no progress towards democracy, and I said, well, if there had been no progress, you wouldn't be sitting here with us now, complaining about the regime ... By and large the international community, apart from some irregularities, thought the election was not Westminster standards, but reasonably fair, and you've gone from half a dozen members to a hundred and something, and that's a degree of progress and it's moving in the right direction.[53]

Austin, arriving as a representative of a well-established democracy, chivvies and preaches on the correct forms of legal and political process. The Justice Minister attempts to bring 'ludicrous' charges and then mucks around with the legal process. Meanwhile, opposition MPs don't appreciate the meanings and forms of democracy, behaving like sulky children. Austin here dispenses good sense and advice all round, attempting to reconcile the two sides to each other. His role is authoritative, his stature impressive: his advice is pregnant with the weight of the 'international community'.

Third, Chris Mullin expresses the ultimate form of potency when he suggests that former colonial powers – under the neutralising umbrella of the UN – could return to sort out small failed African states:

> People don't think colonialism was a terrible time in these countries because everything since has been worse. And in Sierra Leone, they don't want us to go. They tell you that in the street: don't go ... Liberia's not a poor country; Liberia's a rich country that has been grievously mismanaged. So you could manage it, you could take all your costs, you could train a new generation, not just over an electoral cycle but over a long period, because there is a distinct shortage of honest, capable Liberians in Liberia. There are a few you can bring back from abroad, and there are some still inside the country, but there aren't that many and you're going to need to train up more, certainly when it comes to soldiers and police.[54]

Liberia, 'grievously mismanaged', is empty of 'honest, capable Liberians'. The people themselves want a colonial authority – the benign, capable parents – who know how to 'manage it', and will re-populate the country with a 'new generation'.[55]

These parental forms of omnipotence – knowing and directive, intended to be supportive – are enabled by the perception that overwhelming crisis has emasculated local forms of authority. 'You just can't sit back and watch to see if these countries can do it on their own because they patently can't ... It's only the Western world, or the developed world, that can actually do anything to actually change the situation in Africa.'[56]

Africa's resonance in Britain

In this chapter I have attempted to sketch the ways in which state and political elite actors involved in work in Africa describe their work and relationships in Africa as ideal. By depoliticising this little corner of activity, they are, I have argued, preserving a sense of the sacred at the heart of the state. This enables them to reassert a sense of British capacity – omnipotence even – something that perhaps has been lost to the state, and enable feelings of control and protection of the state as a good object.

What I haven't yet addressed is the question of how far the consensus and sense of projecting the good state is felt to extend more widely in the UK, and this is what I want finally to return to. I began this study with the assumption that this wider involvement is important to state actors involved – that they assume widespread popularity for the Government's Africa work, and that the idea of it as an embodiment of the good state has important resonances with people in the UK. However, this was not a clear-cut case. A few MPs did suggest that their work was strongly supported: Clare Short, for example, and Jenny Tonge, both of whom represented their parties' work on international development. Short, who became so strongly identified with international development, felt that she was able to represent a vigorous constituency interested in Britain as a force for good in the world.

> I think there's a very big chunk of moral decent opinion that feels that the levels of poverty against our plenty are morally disgusting, and has a deep instinct that such a divided world is unsafe ... We used to do these regional meetings on a wet Tuesday in Bristol, and I'd go and speak – they were policy consultations with the public – there was a massive attendance of people across all ages ... There's something out there: people really did care a lot.[57]

Short goes so far as suggesting that international development issues have been directly used by the Government to curry popularity. 'It's something that Gordon Brown cottoned on to, and the Government has, sort of, slightly used to make itself popular. The public like things being done about development, helping poor countries.'[58] And Tonge suggested that her relatively affluent constituency was deeply involved in development issues.

> My constituency was Richmond, they were wonderful. They pushed me as much as I pushed them. They were thrilled to bits that I was international development spokesperson. They supported me in every way. They turned out dozens and hundreds for Jubilee 2000. They were a very good, highly educated, highly affluent population with a lot of knowledge.[59]

But others, particularly those representing poorer constituencies, felt very differently. There was a sense that their work in Africa was not a helpful part of normal politics – Sally Keeble, for instance, described it as a luxury for an MP defending a small majority. 'In terms of domestic politics, it's a low priority... Particularly if you're representing a marginal seat, you really need to be working on things which are core to your constituents.'[60]

There was certainly no sense here that doing good in Africa was a vote winner. Tony Worthington said: 'It's one of those areas, and there are not many of them, where if you're trying to persuade people how to vote, there might be a few hundred, a few score of single-issue people, and for them the fact that you are doing this would make them vote for you. But not most people. I used to keep a lot of it quiet.'[61]

Others described practically having to hide what they did: that concern for Africa – and certainly visits there – were viewed as extra-curricular or even demonstrating a lack of concern for proper domestic issues. Malcolm Moss, for example, said: 'I'm afraid people generally speaking are just focused on living day to day... Some of my constituents might say under their breaths, "Well, it's all very well him gallivanting off around the world. How nice! What about the problems we've got at home? Why is he bothering with the problems in Africa?"'[62] John Austin said: 'In general I don't advertise when I'm going to Ethiopia.'[63]

I draw two thoughts from this. First, is the sense that these MPs derive heightened moral authority from their work on Africa, given this lack of wider support and interest. They cannot be accused of following popular opinion in their work: Africa is not a vote winner. This removes a further potential area of self-interest from their work; and it places their work, and that of the state, above the *hoi polloi*.

> People try not to be interested. People don't like to have a conscience. If you tell them about things and they can't avoid it, then they'll tell you they care, but people avoid caring, they don't want to know anything about it. They switch off and turn over the TV channel because they don't want to watch it... But Government shouldn't work in that way. We can't turn the television over, we can't turn a blind eye, we have to contribute.[64]

However, it also cuts off what they are doing, and the creation of a sacred space for the state, from the wider community – and this brings me to my second thought, which comes back to this issue of a damaged object. How far is there a sense of the state as a damaged object created by feelings of ambiguity, or even hostility, to the British electorate? Africa, it might be imagined, acts unambiguously as a sort of glue for a wider British community. However, it might equally be the case that state actors' need to protect the state sprang from a sense of it being under attack from this wider community. This is the question to which I will return in Chapter 7.

Notes

1 Blair contrasted his work in Africa – the 'noble cause worth fighting for' with 'difficult politics' in a speech made on a visit to Ethiopia (Blair, 2004).

2 All Party Parliamentary Groups are set up by groups of backbench MPs with

a particular interest in a topic or part of the world. As the name suggests, their membership includes MPs from all the main political parties. At the time these interviews were conducted in 2007, there were fifteen All Party Groups on sub-Saharan African countries or regions (Africa, Angola, Botswana, Ethiopia, Ghana, Madagascar, Namibia, Nigeria, Somaliland, South Africa, Sudan, Tanzania, West Africa Mano River Region, Zimbabwe and the Great Lakes and Genocide Prevention) and they vary in how active they are and what they choose to focus on. Some – such as the influential APPG on Africa – publish reports into Government policy or particular political issues in Africa; others concern themselves with developing business links between the country and the UK; some attempt to raise awareness of political or development issues relating to the country. Source: Houses of Parliament website: www.publications.parliament.uk/pa/cm/cmallparty/register/memi02.htm#a1, [cited, 14 March 2008].

3 Interview with Baroness Jenny Tonge (Liberal Democrat), London, 17 May 2007.

4 Interview with Chris Mullin, MP (Labour), London, 21 March 2007.

5 A trawl through the indexes of the autobiographies of foreign secretaries and prime ministers from the 1980s and 1990s reveals no more than fleeting references to Africa. Southern Africa is the partial exception (see: Carrington, 1988; Howe, 2008; Hurd, 2004; Major, 1999; Thatcher, 1993).

6 The historical British indifference can be compared with a much more active, even exuberant, French engagement with its former colonies (Cruise O'Brien, 2003: 141–54).

7 Interview with a DfID official, London, 4 May 2007.

8 IMF figures show that UK trade with sub-Saharan Africa forms a tiny proportion of UK trade. Imports to the UK from sub-Saharan Africa in 2006 amounted to US$10.6 billion; British exports to sub-Saharan Africa, US$7.3 billion, just 1.79 per cent and 1.62 per cent of total imports and exports to and from the UK respectively. Taking South Africa out of the calculation, the figures drop to US$3.25 billion and US£3.25 billion, just 0.55 per cent and 0.72 per cent of total imports and exports. Sources: IMF, Direction of Trade Statistics (annual values): www.imf.org/external/np/sta/index.htm and Office of National Statistics, UK Trade Figures, tables F1, F13: www.statistics.gov.uk/downloads/theme_economy/Mm24Jan08.pdf [cited, 22 March 2008].

9 Interview with Jeremy Corbyn, MP (Labour), London, 31 January 2007.

10 Interview with John Austin, MP (Labour), London, 19 February 2007.

11 Interview with Clare Short, MP (Labour), London, 6 June 2007.

12 Interview with John Bercow, MP (Conservative), London, 23 April 2007.

13 Interview with Baroness Jenny Tonge (Liberal Democrat), London, 17 May 2007.

14 Interview with Owen Tudor, head of the International Department, Trades Union Congress, London, 8 May 2007.

15 Interview with Myles Wickstead, head of the Commission for Africa, London, 27 June 2007.

16 Interview with Tony Lloyd, MP (Labour), London, 10 July 2007.

17 Interview with a parliamentary researcher who works with British MPs involved in Africa, London, 23 January 2007.

18 Interview with an FCO official, London, 1 May 2007.

19 Interview with Myles Wickstead, London, 27 June 2007.

20 Interview with Baroness Jenny Tonge (Liberal Democrat), London, 17 May. 2007
21 Interview with Malcolm Moss, MP (Conservative), London, 6 February 2007.
22 Development was one of the eight policy priorities Cameron outlined on becoming leader; he recruited Bob Geldof to contribute to the Conservative Party's review of international development policy; he fully supported the Africa Commission; he led a group of Conservative MPs on a visit to Rwanda in 2007, in an attempt to demonstrate the practical side of caring Conservatism.
23 Interview with John Bercow, MP (Conservative), London, 23 April 2007.
24 The Campaign Group for Labour Party Democracy, established in the 1970s, was committed to returning the party to a more radical socialist agenda.
25 Interview with John Robertson, MP (Labour), London, 16 January 2007.
26 Interview with Jeremy Corbyn, MP (Labour), London, 31 January 2007.
27 Interview with John Robertson, MP (Labour), London, 16 January 2007.
28 Interview with John Austin, MP (Labour), London, 19 February 2007.
29 Interview with a Commons researcher who works with British MPs involved in Africa, London, 23 January 2007.
30 Interview with Clare Short, MP (Labour), London, 6 June 2007.
31 *Ibid.*
32 Interview with Malcolm Moss, MP (Conservative), London, 6 February 2007.
33 Interview with Chris Mullin, MP (Labour), London, 21 March 2007.
34 Interview with John Austin, MP (Labour), London, 19 February 2007.
35 Interview with Claire Curtis-Thomas, MP (Labour), London, 14 March 2007.
36 Interview with John Austin, MP (Labour), London, 19 February 2007.
37 *Ibid.*
38 Interview with Chris Mullin, MP (Labour), London, 21 March 2007.
39 Interview with Baroness Shirley Williams, London, 25 April 2007.
40 Interview with Malcolm Moss, MP (Conservative), London, 6 February 2007.
41 Interview with Chris Mullin, MP (Labour), London, 21 March 2007.
42 Interview with Tony Lloyd, MP (Labour), London, 10 July 2007.
43 Interview with Claire Curtis-Thomas, MP (Labour), London, 14 March 2007.
44 Interview with Jeremy Corbyn, MP (Labour), London, 31 January 2007.
45 Interview with John Austin, MP (Labour), London, 19 February 2007.
46 Many in the Party could not imagine taking any share of previous British administrations' grubby dealings, as was made apparent to Robert Mugabe when, on suggesting it was time for Britain to make good its promises to pay for land redistribution in Zimbabwe, Clare Short wrote that: 'I should make it clear that we do not accept that Britain has a special responsibility to meet the costs of land purchase in Zimbabwe. We are a new government from diverse backgrounds without links to former colonial interests. My own origins are Irish and as you know we were colonised not colonisers' (Greste, 2000).
47 Interview with Jeremy Corbyn, MP (Labour), London, 31 January 2007.
48 Interview with John Austin, MP (Labour), London, 19 February 2007.
49 Interview with Claire Curtis-Thomas, MP (Labour), London, 14 March 2007.
50 Interview with Chris Mullin, MP (Labour), London, 21 March 2007.
51 Interview with John Bercow, MP (Conservative), London, 23 April 2007
52 Interview with Claire Curtis-Thomas, MP (Labour), London, 14 March 2007
53 Interview with John Austin, MP (Labour), London, 19 February 2007.
54 Interview with Chris Mullin, MP (Labour), London, 21 March 2007.

55 Mullin was clear that this had a far better chance of success in Africa than it appeared to be having in Iraq and Afghanistan because: 'Iraq was functioning in a way, prior to the fall of the tyrant…It has to have the consent of the people, and I don't think it had proved it had the consent of the people even at the beginning, never mind the end. And of course Iraq is riven with ethnic tension; as with Tito in Yugoslavia, the dictator was keeping a lid on a cauldron of hatred, whereas I'm not certain that's the case in some of these other countries I've been talking about.' *Ibid.*
56 Interview with Malcolm Moss, MP (Conservative), London, 6 February 2007.
57 Interview with Clare Short, MP (Labour), London, 6 June, 2007.
58 *Ibid.*
59 Interview with Baroness Jenny Tonge (Liberal Democrat), London, 17 May 2007.
60 Interview with Sally Keeble, MP (Labour), London, 4 June 2007.
61 Interview with Tony Worthington (former Labour MP), London, 26 June 2007.
62 Interview with Malcolm Moss, MP (Conservative), London, 6 February 2007.
63 Interview with John Austin, MP (Labour), London, 19 February 2007.
64 Interview with John Robertson, MP (Labour), London, 16 January 2007.

6

Idealisation in Africa

I have suggested that being close to the good seems to mean extending out into a far away place where it is possible to draw an idealised picture of yourself. From Britain, the work in Africa looks very clearly good, along the lines I have drawn – it is disinterested, grand, unifying and differentiating. But if the work in Africa is to have lasting currency in these terms – if it is to continue to enable self-idealisation – there must be something about the way Britain engages in Africa that allows this idea to persist, and the ideal to remain more or less intact, despite increasing engagement which might have been expected to erode the idea of goodness.

This chapter looks at how the British Government engaged in Nigeria and Sierra Leone between 1997 and 2007. It is based on a series of interviews carried out with British officials who served in Nigeria and Sierra Leone, and with Nigerian and Sierra Leonean political activists and commentators who engage with or observe the British attempts to do good in Africa. I wanted to get a feel for how much the notion of connection to a pure 'good' could survive the experience of coming face to face with the inevitable messiness of implementing policy on the ground. My discussions aimed to get at answers to three key questions. First, how do British officials conceive of a sense of the ideal in their work? Second, do they feel that this sense of the ideal tallies with London's conception of British work in Africa? Third, how do officials maintain their sense of the ideal in the course of their engagement with political actors and processes in Nigeria and Sierra Leone?

I wanted to test two potential sources of disjuncture that might lead to more frustration or a more nuanced understanding of the messiness of diplomatic engagement in Africa than what I found in London. First, did the British officials discover that what they were trying to do met with resistance and difficulty in Africa? Did the idealised policy, developed in London, become tangled when it met political reality on the ground? Second, on the other hand, did these officials, working within political realities in Africa, become disconnected from the wider aims of the British Government? Had they 'gone native', and if so, was this a source of friction with London?

In effect, I wanted to see whether the ideal Africa policy, once pushed out into Africa, became eroded. Stretching Mamdani's analogy,[1] I saw the ideal as a spider with a large, robust body centred in London, its long spindly legs reaching out and planting themselves in African capital cities. My question is, to what extent do the legs actually root themselves in African reality? The degree to which they engage with reality will determine how much they then pump back complexity and difficulty to London, perhaps tending to erode the ideal from the edges; or to pump back affirmation and nourishment for the ideal.

This chapter is arranged in four sections. The first provides some context for the two case studies. I discuss why I chose them and how I conducted my fieldwork there. The second section deals with the way in which British officials in Nigeria and Sierra Leone conceive their role and its connection to 'the good'. I examine their personal motivations and sense of their position; and their understanding of the wider British project in Africa and how well this resonates with their own role and work. Closely woven into these ideas is the sense of Africa as a moral and significant project. My conclusion here, is that the sense of the ideal among British officials working in Nigeria and Sierra Leone is very close to that framed in London. The remainder of the chapter explores ways in which this ideal is maintained. The third section looks at the ways in which Britain imagines itself engaged in a non-ideological political arena in Africa. As discussed in Chapter 1, this attempt to explain politics in non-ideological terms places it closer to a sense of the moral or the good. British engagement in both countries is described in a similarly apolitical way by officials. However, I suggest that while this framing resonates reasonably well in Sierra Leone, it sits less happily in Nigeria. The fourth section explores an alternative strategy employed by British officials, which is an attempt at non-engaged engagement. This begins with the conception of Britain's historical role in West Africa as essentially benevolent or long-forgotten. It finds current expression in a British oppositionalist posture which attempts to reform from the outside. This enables, I will argue, a continued distance from messy politics and self-idealisation. I explore how well this approach has worked in Sierra Leone and Nigeria since 1997, and suggest that while it continues to hold up well in Nigeria, it is in danger of unravelling in Sierra Leone. Finally, I conclude with a suggestion as to how British experiences in Africa help to support a self-idealisation.

Nigeria and Sierra Leone: recent engagement

Historically, as we have seen in Chapter 3, West Africa has the closest connections to Britain's attempts to do good in Africa. Freetown, established in 1787 by a group of British abolitionists as a home for freed and recaptured slaves, and made a British protectorate in 1807, was at the heart of British attempts to end the slave trade – a defining moment in the development of a national sense of virtue. Expansion into the interior above Freetown, Lagos and other coastal towns at the turn of the nineteenth century was pursued for a number of reasons – including self-interest and philanthropy – and was projected by the British as part of their attempt to do good in the world.

West Africa is also particularly appropriate for studying British attempts to do good because it is less complicated by self-interest arguments than other parts of Africa which involved European settlement. Historically, this meant that the colonial authorities felt themselves more purely concerned with native welfare. In the modern era, it makes dealing with West Africa appear less complicated: there are no memories of bloody independence struggles as in Kenya, no remaining white populations with links to the motherland to remind Britain of the messier side of colonial relations, as in Zimbabwe. The colonial era appears more straightforward, its ending cleaner, and this colours perceptions of the current relationships between Britain and the countries of West Africa.

During the New Labour era Nigeria and Sierra Leone were almost immediately identified with the ethical approach to foreign policy, and both have, in different ways, continued to define the approach. Nigeria, which in 1997 was ruled by Sani Abacha, a particularly brutal military dictator, typified Robin Cook's description of the democratic and human rights abuses he wished to overcome. When Abacha died a year later, and multi-party elections followed, the new President Olusegun Obasanjo was felt to embody what Britain saw as a right-thinking, progressive African leader (see Chapter 1). After 1999, Britain, from being barely engaged, became increasingly involved in Nigeria, focusing on a good governance/debt cancellation package and slowly building up a sizable DfID programme there. Blair and Obasanjo had a good relationship and worked together setting up the Commission for Africa; and Obasanjo was a key player in the New Partnership for African Development (NEPAD), seen by international donors as the progressive face of African developmentalism.

Sierra Leone became part of the New Labour folklore of an ethical intervention. Although High Commissioner Peter Penfold's involvement with mercenary support for Ahmad Tejan Kabbah's government was embarrassing at the time, it was quickly overcome by direct British military involvement, and after the end of the war, Sierra Leone became the key site for British state-building in Africa, with substantial military and financial support committed over a ten-year period. Portrayed in Britain as a straightforward battle between a decently elected government and a criminally led rebel movement, Britain's role was largely accepted at home as unambiguously clean and right.

Nigeria and Sierra Leone make an interesting contrast in size, wealth and autonomy and have therefore between them received a range of types of British help. First, Sierra Leone, smaller, poorer and very damaged by a long civil war, saw Britain deeply involved in political and social direction. In Nigeria, the most the British could hope to do was to influence the course of politics from the sidelines. Second, Sierra Leone has virtually no self-interest arguments for Britain, and therefore involvement there can be more credibly portrayed as straightforwardly disinterested. Nigeria's oil wealth, higher levels of political capital, and regional economic and political importance make it less an object of development aid than one of diplomatic pressure (during the Abacha regime) and a potential partner (under Obasanjo) for Blair in his work in Africa. Britain does have some economic and political interests in Nigeria: one of the questions I was keen to pursue was how much the development programme there was seen to be working in tandem with these, and whether conflicts of interest were involved.

I visited Abuja and Freetown to conduct interviews in July and August 2007. Both countries were preoccupied by elections: Nigeria still coming to terms with presidential and state elections in April; Sierra Leone right in the middle of presidential and parliamentary elections.

Abuja is an affluent, middle-class city. Its poorer inhabitants are regularly swept off the streets, and the relatively inexpensive motorbike taxis that help commuters from the margins of the City get to work are periodically banned from the city. Modern and clean, Abuja contains many monuments to Nigeria's oil wealth, in public buildings like the huge cathedral and mosque, and the national stadium. There is a sense of disconnection here from the 'real Nigeria' – everyone I talked to explained that a visit to Abuja was not a visit to Nigeria.

The Nigerian elections in 2007 were widely condemned as flawed, and people I met in Abuja were still angry about them. Nevertheless, the new president, Umaru Yar'Adua formed his government during my visit and there was a lot of curiosity about what the various appointments would mean. Even those who were critical of Yar'Adua – interviewees from the Nigerian Labour Congress (NLC) and the *Daily Trust* newspaper, for example – were impressed by some of his first moves against corrupt former state governors. Political activists were prepared to get on with their engagement: 'We have to put the elections behind us now,' explained Olaitan Oyerinde of the NLC. 'It's pointless to go on contesting them, and we have some hopes of the new Government. Yar'Adua has been saying some useful things about the rule of law and corruption.'[2] There was little interest in what the British thought of the elections.

Freetown, in the week leading up to the elections, was both excited and nervy. Political confidence in Freetown in 2007 was still low after the shocks and traumas of political collapse and civil war. The people I met were anxious that a political contest might mean violence, and generally wary about the prospects for improvement under a new government. There was a sense of anxiety, too, to prove that Sierra Leoneans could run proper elections without external assistance: it mattered in terms of a sense of national pride as well as the importance of a healthy relationship with aid donors. Kissy, the east end of Freetown, is an area that had been ransacked by the departing rebel forces in 1999. Its residents had watched the government collapse and flee to Guinea and had seen their city captured and destroyed by rebel forces. On the night of the rebel retreat, they had cowered, terrified, in the local cemetery as the rebels marched past, burning houses and shooting civilians as they went. They – alongside thousands of refugees from the rural areas – now live in the ruins of their town, in half-destroyed houses and newer more flimsy shelters, with intermittent water supplies and no mains electricity. There remains a constant sense of stress. Fear of crime and violence, of the fragile state of the economy which causes occasional dramatic price rises (during the election period this was marked), dominates their lives. Many rely on remittances sent from family members in other parts of West Africa or the UK. Although many senses of routine and dependability in day to day life have returned – school, shopping in the market, visits to church – they remain fragile, and people are wary about trusting them too much. I stayed with a very religious family in Kissy. Every morning they would start the day with prayers, asking God to choose the right president for Sierra Leone. The prayers and hymns they sang were all about a God 'who never fails', a reliable, 'able' God – everything the state was not. They trusted neither the politicians nor themselves to be able to bring about a more containing state.

Because of the ongoing political dramas in both Nigeria and Sierra Leone, I was unable to interview anyone from either government. However, I interviewed British officials from the FCO and DfID and leaders from political NGOs, civil society organisations and political commentators in both countries. All the officials spoke to me off the record; the Nigerians and Sierra Leoneans spoke on the record. I was particularly interested to discover how the relationship between British officials and locals worked: did both sides view British engagement in the same way? Did Nigerians and Sierra Leoneans buy into the ideal, or did they put different interpretations on what the British were up to? These were short visits, and I was aware that it was going to be difficult to get deeply under the surface of the relationships. But I did have the advantage of being British and therefore I could at least begin to get an impression of the kinds of comments and reactions British officials might get, a sense of the way what they are doing is reflected back to them by the people they meet in the countries where they work, and how far these relationships might help to reinforce their sense of connection to a good project.

Connecting to the good

Broadly, in both countries, I found that officials felt comfortable in their work, and this comfort was derived from, first, their perception of being personally closely connected to something good and important, and second, their sense that their approach fitted well into the broader British approach to its work in Africa. The good was based on the ability to make a difference, to be taken seriously, to work in a disinterested way on a large moral project. All the officials spoke of the enormous personal satisfaction they got from doing a job which made tangible improvements in the lives of people in Africa. This personal closeness to a 'good project' was very important. Many of them contrasted it with other FCO jobs which they saw as boring or meaningless; as politically messy or self-serving. One said: 'It genuinely feels good to be able to make a positive contribution to political reform here. You're helping people here and back home. It's one of the major plusses that you don't get in other parts of the world.'[3]

Peter Penfold, who served in many African capitals during his time at the FCO, and finally as High Commissioner to Sierra Leone, made a comment that was reflected in many other interviews with officials:

> I felt that in places in Africa, certainly the ones I went to, as a result of your efforts you could actually make a difference. Now our great and good and clever guys who would go to Washington and Paris and Bonn would work extremely hard, but at the end of three or four years they would look back and say, 'well, what difference has it actually made to this country?' Whereas I felt, particularly later on in places like Sierra Leone and Uganda, I could look back and say, 'yes, I made a small difference there'.[4]

British officials feel particularly valued in Nigeria and Sierra Leone. Even junior officials found they could get access to government ministers and senior officials. One relatively junior official told me: 'You can meet anybody [in the Government] here. Where else is that true?'[5] There is a reasonable element of satisfied vanity here. As one London-based official sharply points out: 'The British like being in Africa because they are treated as big and important: little people can play at being kings. In Arab countries the British are resented or hated: in Africa, we are liked.'[6] For the officials in post, the high level of access demonstrates that their contribution is particularly valued and important.

> In Sierra Leone I get a huge level of access to ministers and senior civil servants compared to another foreign country. In terms of good will, it just means people are always ready to listen to you and we're coming from a shared position, which is a lot easier ... There's no other country in which I'd get as warm a welcome as I do here, I don't think ... And you can see that what you do has a direct impact on the lives of people in Sierra Leone ... It makes it a good place to work.[7]

It is also very important to officials that they are involved in an important project. Africa provides Britain with a grand project like nowhere else in the world. The problems are horrible and huge: poverty, conflict and AIDS appear on a scale beyond anywhere else. Moreover, at least in the parts of Africa which used to be part of the empire, Britain is the big player in terms of international intervention and help. Both these perspectives are reinforced by officials on the ground, through how they see Africa and how they experience their work there.

> All the big issues for them [the British government] are more starkly manifested in Africa. The scale is different: HIV, the environment – they need

> special attention. Plus there are weaknesses in African states which can lead to disaster. So we are addressing the same issues as elsewhere, but on a different scale. This scale forces the Government to put Africa up the agenda.[8]

Most agreed that although Africa's problems are not qualitatively different from those of other poor parts of the world, the size and concentration of the problems is much larger, which makes intervention more of a priority, and more likely to make a difference.

> The issues are so much more stark and so the contribution that we make is that much more powerful. So if you're thinking about Sierra Leone and the fact that we contributed something ridiculous in terms of the GDP of the country or government spending there, that enables DfID to be even more powerful and more influential and more controlling.[9]

Penfold provides the most dramatic example of a British official taking on a heroic role.

> Every single Sierra Leonean – *every single Sierra Leonean* – suffered a personal tragedy, whether it was the death of a loved one – a mother, father, son, daughter – the loss of a limb, the burning down of their house, having to flee to another part of the country or to another country, loss of jobs and so on. There's nobody in Sierra Leone who hasn't got a story to tell you: the whole population. And given the role that the British High Commission had, we had by far the inside track of any mission out there: far more important than the Americans, or the Europeans, or the United Nations ... At the gates of my residence or the gates of my office, I'd be confronted every day by people, some with their arms and legs chopped off, and there were countless, countless stories ... What did they do? They came to me. They didn't go to their government; they didn't go to the NGOs because the NGOs had fled; they didn't go to the United Nations. They came to the British High Commissioner. [10]

This is at the extreme end of the story of British support in Africa, but it contains elements that came up over and over again in discussions with officials: the enormous scale of the problems; the idea that Britain was in a key position of responsibility; Britain portrayed as active and able to step in and help. A more junior official who I met in Freetown described his feeling of what the British were able to contribute:

> I think possibly one of the most important things has been the intangible psychological support; the Sierra Leoneans really do feel that they have [what] some would say is a father figure in the UK. I prefer to think of it as a bigger brother who was willing to put their life on the line to end the war and who is now committed to sign a ten-year agreement saying, 'we will support you in the next ten years and almost certainly afterwards'. And that's important, I think, to the man on the street.[11]

Supportive London

The officials I interviewed felt that what they were doing was well reflected by the shifts in attitude towards Africa in London, where Blair, Brown and others' interest in Africa had made their work more valued. Whereas in the recent past Africa had been seen as peripheral, and ambitious people avoided postings there, now a cadre of Africanists was being groomed; political interest and certain financial backing were on offer. 'Credit to Tony Blair for whatever reasons, he really decided to put Africa way up on the agenda…I think he felt a commitment to it. And as a result Africa began to get the attention it deserved.'[12] Importantly, this interest and commitment was in the right direction. The tone of the Foreign Office – from the ethical element onwards – had been very favourable, largely supporting what many of the older officials felt they had been trying to do in Africa all along. 'I think when he first made it [the speech on the ethical dimension] there was a difference. People in the Foreign Office, generally, very much welcomed it. I think many of my colleagues interpreted it in the way I interpreted it.'[13] The growing importance of DfID, the priority of poverty reduction and the substantial financial commitment behind it were also thought to be right. The approach was given an even weightier and purer bent through its resonance with wider international ambitions: the Millennium Development Goals (MDGs) had been absorbed into the objectives of both DfID and the FCO and put their work way beyond British self-interest.

However, there was some difficulty in talking about this subject, particularly with FCO officials. When allowed to express it in their own terms, the officials all tended to talk in terms of FCO or DfID objectives, which could be easily combined with British interests. For example, two of the FCO 'strategic priorities' are to promote sustainable democracy and development, and to reduce conflict and support an international system based on the rule of law. The pursuit of these is in 'Britain's interests'. When I questioned how far these could be reduced to direct British self-interest – it was difficult to see how poverty and war in Sierra Leone directly impacted on the UK, for example – a grander more moral element did appear alongside self-interest.

> The UK is genuinely committed to a world which is free of war and free of poverty. And there are two reasons for that: one is that it's morally the right thing to do, and maybe we don't talk about morality in politics very much now, but we used to: there used to foreign policy with an ethical dimension. And the other is the self-interested argument that we can't live in an ivory tower for much longer if the rest of the world continues to grow in population and get poor. And conflicts which start here have a funny way of spreading throughout the region. It's all linked up.[14]

This approach was even echoed in Nigeria, where the British do feel they have more tangible economic and political interests. 'There is a big element of the ethical foreign policy here. That's not true everywhere (not the Gulf, for example), but yes, in Nigeria, we're genuinely trying because we can't afford to sit back. Here, there's a good balance between the ethical and self-interest, especially compared to other parts of the world.'[15]

Officials, like many of the MPs I spoke to, were quick to point out that a key element of British interest in Africa was that it worked in harmony with the wider issues of development and conflict resolution. This is a tradition which sees British interests as benign and in harmony with those of others, and it is particularly popular, whether because it is genuinely believed or because it sounds better or works better politically. One reason why it is so frequently pushed may be because of an old-school British dislike of sentiment.

> If you create the impression that you're on a moral crusade, then you immediately start losing support. Government feels uncomfortable, it's not the way you devise policy. It's a bit like Tony Blair having the effrontery to talk about his faith at one stage and Alastair [Campbell] saying, 'we don't do religion'. So I think one has to be a little careful about that. I think that just as strong an argument is that the world collectively needs to ensure that Africa is secure, is developed.[16]

Others were prepared to be more forthright in expressing their feeling that British interests have been largely abandoned in Africa. One DfID official claimed that, despite the rhetoric about development work in Nigeria being tied to the need to contain and dampen potential Islamic extremism in the north, in his experience there had never been any pressure to consider the Islamic element. 'I don't really believe that the threat is seen as real. It's more a sort of politically credible reason given to make the policy look more serious, harder, maybe for domestic consumption to justify why we're doing all this work.'[17]

On the other hand, others were able to describe moments of friction. Another DfID official in Abuja explained to me that his office had to repeatedly put the case to London that the north was a bigger priority than the oil-producing Delta in development terms.[18] This was a potential conflict of interests between British commercial interests in making the Delta region more secure and the policy of meeting the MDGs. As the official explained it, London hoped that the two could work in harmony – helping the Delta to become prosperous would bring stability. However, his argument was that the Delta states were significantly richer than those in the north. If the MDGs were to be met, DfID should be focusing on the poorer northern states. In this example of non-harmonious interests, the official felt that his argument prevailed – eventually London accepted that the MDGs should take priority over Britain's interest in stability in the Delta.

Broadly, then, the British officials working in Abuja and Freetown found that working at the coalface of a big and moral project was important to their sense of a personal connection to the good. They all felt that they could achieve this well in Africa – better than in other parts of the world – because they were taken seriously and respected for their contribution in

African countries. They also felt that their approach fitted well within wider British objectives. On the question of British interests, although uncomfortable about expressing this directly, they tended to see themselves as working primarily in the pursuit of Africa's interests; so it was fortunate that these dovetailed with British wider interests and objectives. The few officials who were prepared to admit that there might at times be conflicts between these have found that London generally let British interests take a backseat, and this was another important reinforcement to their idea of being involved in a pure and basically disinterested project, backed up by support from London where objectives and outlook were broadly commensurate. There was a strong sense that, in representing Britain, they were representing something good.

This support from London tells half the story of how well officials working in Nigeria and Sierra Leone were able to maintain their sense of connection to an ideal project. But what about the other half? How does engagement with the messy reality on the ground affect the ideal? How can it continue to remain intact? In the next two sections, I suggest two broad themes that enable the preservation of the ideal in the midst of messy reality.

The ideology gap

Mark Duffield has described how the current international aid regime has increasingly entered political and social realms in attempts to support development. 'Development assistance', he says, 'is no longer concerned with helping support an often conservative pro-western alliance of southern elites; it is now in the business of transforming whole societies' (Duffield, 2002: 39). It approaches the task in a specifically technical way. 'For the new humanitarianism, politics is confined to the policy choices of aid agencies. In other words, politics has been conflated with policy' (*Ibid*: 75). Duffield defines politics as 'policy decisions that aid agencies make when faced with hard ethical choices' (*Ibid*: 96). Thus politics is reduced to internal choices and decisions separated from local politics.

As discussed in Chapter 3, nowhere has this apparently been easier to do than in Africa, the continent that is imagined as ideologically and politically empty (Mbembe, 2001). The British officials I met in Nigeria and Sierra Leone tended to describe their work as political – it concentrated on engaging with governments to induce better behaviour from them, rather than older approaches which either supported ideologically congenial African elites or attempted to by-pass government to provide services through international aid agencies or work with local civil society. To do this they need to engage with politicians and officials, to support reforms in governance, largely concentrated on developing more robust state institutions, particularly bureaucracies, and ending corruption. According to British officials, the work is political because they need to be aware of the political relationships and the nature of the political leadership they are dealing with.

But it is not ideological, because it is not in the business of dealing with an array of political approaches or wading into ideological debates. It is Duffield's description of a policy-oriented approach to politics – a technical, non-political politics.

Historically, Africa has never been seen as an area of geopolitical importance by the Foreign Office. During the 1990s, the problems of Africa's instability and economic failures were increasingly seen as due either to some sort of irrational primordialism (Kaplan, 1994) or, in backlash to this, as driven by greed or grievance (Berdal and Malone, 2000). Both approaches suggest that politics is not a significant driver in African history, and in this they reinforce older descriptions of Africa's political culture as tending to work towards consensus within a paradigm of deferment towards authority.[19] In unstable post-colonial states, this tendency has been reinforced, as political difference can be potentially explosive, occurring without the containing institutions of a formal state (Zolberg, 1968). Then, lack of political or ideological difference becomes an important guarantor of stability. Moreover, as many have argued, most African states, impoverished, indebted and dependent on the international aid regime, don't necessarily have the luxury of control: they are constrained by the political and economic rules of the international financial institutions and other donors (Williams, 2000). Reinforced by these perspectives, the donor view of political struggle in Africa as limited can appear to have found a comfortable fit.

When donors began to take an interest in governance issues, fingering them as the problem with Africa, this was done in technical fashion (World Bank, 1997). Governance, which might have been seen as an FCO area, sat quite easily with DfID, which could define it as 'about applying methods rather than politics'.[20] Officials describe African politics as about improving transparency and accountability, stamping out corruption. They don't define it as being about political debates or choices.

Sierra Leone and Nigeria provide rather different contexts within which to practise this approach. In Sierra Leone, the acuteness of the political collapse enabled very close direction by the British and a tendency to see the Sierra Leonean Government as without political ideas of its own. The starkness of Sierra Leone's problems generates apparently obvious and uncontested priorities, turning political argument into a distracting irrelevance. The scale of the problems tends to obscure both the political complexities behind them, and notions that there may be more than one approach to solving them.

> It's a lot easier in Sierra Leone reaching a common position, or having shared interests, than in other countries, because everyone is focused on development – it's kind of the priority. Underpinning development has to be security reform and good government, but underneath it's really all about how do we develop Sierra Leone. And that's what the people of Sierra Leone want, that's what the Government wants and that's what the international community wants...in Sierra Leone it's quite easy to focus

> everyone's minds on what will develop Sierra Leone and get agreement on all that.[21]

The officials say they do not come across alternative political ideas, and so their conception of Africa as devoid of these is largely reinforced. Within this framework, problems arise because of lack of capacity or corruption, not political alternatives. For example, in a discussion about the 2007 presidential elections, one British official said: 'I don't think there are two camps here, no. I think there is a variation between politicians, but it's more between their capabilities rather than their ideological positions.'[22]

Up to this point, interviewees largely confirmed the Duffield view – that problems in Africa were about ideologically neutral governance issues and that 'political' engagement could be a technical exercise. I explored with Sierra Leonean and Nigerian interviewees how far this view coincided with local accounts of political problems. The two countries offered rather different perspectives.

In Sierra Leone there appeared a stronger resonance of the idea of a lack of political difference. For example, one NGO activist virtually echoed the British line on the competing political parties: 'They [the political parties] are all the same. The only thing is which of them has the mature people of high calibre.'[23] This wasn't necessarily seen as a bad thing. Sierra Leoneans are still wary of political differences. The NGO activists I spoke to were grappling with questions as to how the political system could be made more robust in the context of a real fear of political difference which is seen as destabilising and dangerous. Their approaches tended to focus on what they described as an apolitical engagement with politics: a politically neutral approach to developing essentially non-ideological political virtues such as accountability, transparency and responsiveness. They felt, for a number of reasons, a long way away from being able to frame a system that could contain ideological difference.

> We are not mature enough in terms of tolerance in promoting the ideas of good governance and democracy. And the one most important quality in politics is tolerance, accommodating each other. This is difficult now because politics in Sierra Leone is based on tribe or region. These are the political factors. They are the unwritten conventions of politics in Sierra Leone. Sometimes, by your tribe, you owe your vote to a particular party, sometimes by your region.[24]

First, all the NGOs are reliant on foreign financial support. This means that they cannot be seen to be politically-engaged. All describe themselves as non-political, but engaged in attempting to strengthen the political structures and processes, often in an explicitly technical, ideologically neutral way. Valnora Edwin, director of the Campaign for Good Governance, a largely British-funded organisation, said: 'It is a political thing. But it's not political in the sense that you do not become partisan, and it's a matter of ensuring a healthy political system.'[25] Second, for an organisation trying to win wider credibility, being identified with a political party ties you to a region or ethnic group – not the way to build a nation-wide support base. Third, within Sierra Leone politics is so discredited that NGOs that want to be taken on good faith cannot afford to be seen as partisan or political. Fourth, politicians fail: an over-close relationship with a party or political figure can mean a share in their downfall.

Therefore, when people talk about building institutions, they mean institutions to enforce accountability and transparency, to prevent abuses of office and enable solid legitimacy of the state. They aren't looking for a structure to contain ideological difference.

> We need to challenge some of the non-progressive elements in our culture, some of those blockers that are preventing us from achieving. We need to question ourselves, to ask, do we want to perpetuate this kind of system? We need to reshape it ... Yes, Africans have a sense of communal living; Africans have a tradition of not challenging their elders; Africans have a tradition of keeping quiet.[26]

Nigeria is more difficult because there are more explicit tensions within the political system. However, here British officials describe political struggles in terms of (good) reformers battling with (bad) obstructive elements: the British officials depict their role as one of wading in to lend muscle to the 'good guys', typically in attempts to stamp out corruption: 'A lot of it is about encouraging them in ways they would like to go, but may be wary. We want to embolden them even more to enforce anti-corruption measures.'[27]

In Nigeria, it was suggested to me, the president and some ministers are basically right-minded but weak, and are constantly having to battle against a series of state governors, many of whom are very corrupt. British officials express a desire to help Nigerian ministers, but also wariness as to how much they are really able to resist corrupt elements and do the right kinds of things. One DfID official described British policy as about searching for 'reform-minded' individuals and organisations which could be supported and helped to develop public accountability.[28] An FCO official said:

> Political work is guided by the extent to which we can work with the Government ... Obasanjo was mostly engaged in fire-fighting in his first term, particularly in mixing up the military. There was no one he could really trust; he was in a difficult position and reforms were slow. But we always thought that this was a guy we could work with. We had to at least try.[29]

Among Nigerians, politics is political and ideological – none that I spoke to imagined that there was a fixer from the outside who could sort them out. The view that came closest to welcoming foreign support expressed the idea that it was possible to transplant some sort of ideologically neutral political framework to contain the contentious political process within Nigeria. In fact, foreign-funded organisations were viewed from this perspective as better able to hold the Government to account, because the Nigerian system made locally-funded organisations biased or corrupt and, therefore, unable to do so. Foreign funding insulated an organisation from local corruption and enabled it to stand up for ordinary Nigerians. This view, taken to its logical conclusion, has Britain and British organisations motivated by good intentions, playing a politically neutral role. Self-interest basically doesn't get in the way.[30]

Many Nigerian intellectuals did not see it this way. They argued that there are and should be real ideological differences within Nigerian politics. They see the British as inappropriately wading in on the side of a neo-liberal ideology and its advocates. For example, Peter Ozo-Eson, director of the Labour Centre for Social and Economic Research, told me: 'They strengthen the neo-liberal arguments within Nigeria, and skew the debate. It helps suffocate policy choices for development and it's very damaging for the country at this stage.'[31]

Arguments as to whether and why the British should desist from this involvement vary: some didn't mind the idea of foreign political engagement per se, but objected to the colour of the British neo-liberal politics. Some of these people hoped that Nigeria could develop a more directly commanding economy: they might see Chinese involvement as at least historically more favourable. Generally, this group did believe it was possible to develop big political progressive ideas that could transcend national politics. Others felt that in principle it wasn't healthy for Nigeria to have foreign involvement in political discourse. Nigerian political life mixes the 'universal' with thicker domestic norms and ideas. For example, a radio reporter I met described her work on child abuse, in which she draws explicitly on a human rights discourse which lends her power to make public interventions in police abuse or inactivity in ways that local law and precedent do not: 'Yes, it's rooted in Western norms, but as long as it's useful in terms of creating good changes, that doesn't matter.'[32] At the same time, the newspaper the *Daily Trust*, also dealing with a story about child rape, and considering how it wanted to intervene in an issue that confronts the culture of silence around rape, asked: 'If a girl is raped at six, how will she marry at twenty?'[33] For members of the *Daily Trust* Board, this was a question of how far a culture of tolerance should be allowed to continue, and whether the paper should play a part in attempting to change the tendency to tolerance, both by encouraging tougher rule of law, and influencing perceptions of child rape. This issue reflects the choices Nigerians face as to the degree to which they reach for a universal set of ideas or political solutions, and underlines the relative irrelevance of British interventions.

Here is one final reflection on the political process in Nigeria, which is about as far from idealisable as any. Although I found a sense of weariness with the political process and its easy capture by the ruling party, and although people were still furious about what they viewed as stolen elections, they were still engaging actively. Even the most vociferous of Yar' Adua's critics were watching his movements with interest. Here there was intense and energetic engagement within an imperfect political system; and little sense that an external deliverer was needed.

British experiences in Sierra Leone and Nigeria suggest that a more damaged political system is much easier to view as politically empty and enables a more straightforward self-idealisation. One of the Sierra Leonean interviewees, a former employee of the British High Commission, put it very clearly.

> I compare the Sierra Leone situation during the war to a ship on the ocean. All the other things are hanging there, hanging forgotten because there is only one need and that is staying alive. And when there is peace, suddenly all these other things become important and how do you prioritise, how do you achieve them, how do you sequence them?[34]

Disengaged engagement

Staying out of messy politics is essential for preserving the purity of the British contribution to good in Africa. Politics is necessarily about failure, compromise and contests – which is why the prophet-like role which transcends it is so much more attractive. Yet officials engage in Africa explicitly in an attempt to effect reform, to improve policy and governance. Even if these are seen in technical, ideologically neutral ways – as discussed above – they are still likely to hit obstacles or be forced into compromise when implemented in the real world. So how do British officials manage to engage with attempts at political reform and retain this sense of a connection to purity?

It has been important for British officials to maintain a sense of distance and disengagement, as a way of managing to avoid the messy engagement of a deeper relationship that would erode the ideal. It has always been easier to do this in West Africa than elsewhere. This point was brought home rather literally by a comment made by Muhamed A. Deen, president of the Sierra Leone Labour Congress, who started his working life under the colonial regime. 'Sierra Leoneans would prefer the British to come back and run our administration than our own brothers and sisters. Some of us were privileged to work under the British system. They don't have brothers and sisters here: they gave you promotion based on merit. You deserve it, you get it; you don't deserve it, no way.'[35]

'Brothers' and 'sisters' interfere with objective, good governance. Contrast this with other parts of Africa where at least 'cousins' did settle – Zimbabwe and South Africa – and see how their presence introduces all sorts of extra complexity and a deeper miring in the real. This complexity continues to make doing good much harder in southern Africa.

In Sierra Leone and Nigeria, a far more individualised engagement is possible – the British official represents an abstract ideal and is unencumbered by complex affective ties. Their sense of what the historical colonial ties mean is particularly interesting. Generally, it was striking that the British officials are much less affected by any sense of historical implication in Africa than the Nigerians and Sierra Leoneans I interviewed. Reflecting the views of the politicians I interviewed (see Chapter 5), colonial relationships are either long-forgotten or remembered in a benign and helpful way by British officials. This sense of a largely resolved historical relationship was summed up by Myles Wickstead, a senior DfID official who has worked in several African posts:

> We've got these very strong historical and cultural ties and links. Legal and judicial systems are built on the British model, in very large parts of Africa, particularly in the east and south and parts of western Africa too. I think there's an interesting shift. I think the relationship between Africa and the UK went through a fairly difficult patch in the 1960s and 1970s – the right to be free of the colonial yoke and all that sort of stuff – but all that's long behind us. Whereas I think the French are still going through that process because they didn't perhaps let go in the same way that the UK did. It does come back to how the UK is perceived in a pretty positive way.[36]

Another official, based in Abuja, described how the British, on attempting to re-engage with the north of Nigeria when the High Commission moved to Abuja in 2003, were delighted to find that they were remembered and remembered warmly. 'We found we were pushing at an open door,' he explained.[37] The residual ties there appeared to work to make engagement more straightforward, as well as reinforcing the sense of Britain as a disinterested and well-meaning friend.

Most of the Africans I spoke to saw it rather differently. In their view, the British are not neutral, but co-creators and shapers of Nigerian or Sierra Leonean political history. Garba Abari, a retired academic and member of the editorial board of the *Daily Trust*, said: 'As the former colonial power, its history and the history of its economic prosperity intricately tie it to Africa.'[38] In looking for reasons for British engagement and interest in Africa, most Africans I spoke to raised the colonial link. For some it was driven by a continuing sense of responsibility or affection: 'The British were our colonial administrators. They trained us, they granted independence; so they will not neglect us.'[39] For others, by a sense of guilt for wrongs done:

> Sierra Leone and Africa more generally have lost the basic manpower and resources as a result of colonialism and the slave trade ... I think that morally, they must assist us, one, because of slavery, and, two, because of colonisation and their time in control of our wealth. On the whole African leaders have not been pushing for reparations, but if I was one of them, I would push it.[40]

There was a sharp mismatch between African and British senses of the significance of the legacy of colonialism. Peter Ozo-Eson from Nigeria's Labour Centre for Social and Economic Research, suggested that: '[Blair's] work on Africa has been like a balm on the conscience of the UK for the colonial past.'[41] This is not a description that any British officials could recognise. The British official feels able to approach business from a position of relative purity.

Thus, floating free of difficult historical implication, British officials fashion their relationship with Africans as if virtually from scratch. Historical engagement in Africa brings a sense of affinity and understanding but not complexity. However, idealisation of the relationship might still be in danger if subjected to regular contact. The solution to this problem lies in which relationship is to be idealised, and the answer lies in a largely imagined relationship with the African poor. British officials present their role as one of representing this group and attempting to induce the (far less idealisable) political representatives and officials to do the right thing by them.

> In a number of countries you don't or you haven't had the systems whereby governments can be electorally accountable with strong parliaments and whatever. So in a way I think the donor community has historically acted as a little bit of a proxy for the electorate in those countries and tried to stand up for the ordinary person, saying these sugar prices are penalising your people and shouldn't you do something about that? So I think in a way, for perfectly honourable motives, the international community has acted as a proxy and an advocate of people.[42]

This idealisation of the ordinary person is relatively easy to maintain, especially when officials admit they feel rather cut off from the lives of most Africans. Officials in Abuja make the joke that they live 'three miles from Africa', and the daily round of engagement with officials and ministers in the capital is a long way from the lives of the people they are there to help. One DfID official said: 'I think it would be a very good exercise for people from the office to get out more and live and work alongside ordinary people in Nigeria. But it's very difficult to organise.'[43] In Freetown too, the city is divided into the centre and east, where the 'ordinary Africans' live and work, and up on the western hills, the government offices and residences, the embassies and large NGO compounds, and the expatriate walled and gated residences. In these situations, officials must assume that there is a close affinity between their conception of progress, and how it should be realised, and that of Africa's poor. This is ideationally reinforced by basic cosmopolitan assumptions about human nature that have long informed Britain's relations with Africa.

> They want what all people want. They want security and they want to be one government, they want education for their children and they want to live longer and have a general sense of prosperity. I think these are all human aspirations, and it's quite easy to see when these aren't being met in their most extreme forms. And in that case it's quite easy to act as an advocate for them.[44]

The position of an advocate is essentially one of constructive opposition to the state. It allows a critical engagement with the state on behalf of the people, but a distancing from implication in the actual business of governing.

It also needs to resonate in some sense with the African poor for it to be sustainable.

I want to argue that it has been easier to make this work in some circumstances than in others, and to use recent experiences in Nigeria and Sierra Leone to illustrate them. British activity in Sierra Leone and Nigeria since 1997 gives us four rather different types of engagement: in Sierra Leone, a heroic rescue during a crisis followed by close political direction of the Government; in Nigeria, sanctions, withdrawal and condemnation, followed by reformist attempts from the margins. These have met with different levels of success, in terms of maintaining this position of disengaged engagement.

In Sierra Leone, the British were greeted as saviours by many people in Freetown. The British High Commissioner, Peter Penfold, in particular was lionised. In fact, the British were fortunate in that most of the rougher military action was carried out by Nigerian troops who effectively drove the rebel troops out of Freetown.[45] The British arrived at the end, almost falling from the sky in a daring rescue-bid.[46] Penfold himself had long been viewed by many people in Freetown as a protective, paternal figure, in a climate where little protection was to be had from the state. He describes his role as being about standing up for ordinary Sierra Leoneans, as he did when the 1997 coup took place:

> I summoned Johnny Koroma and his people to my residence the next day, along with the Nigerian High Commissioner and the UN special representative, and we told them that we weren't going to accept this. Not because we were the international community telling them this, but because the people themselves were not accepting it. We could see the reaction in the streets: people didn't want it.[47]

His attempts to represent the views of the people of Sierra Leone did resonate. His confidence that he, as a British official, could step into the situation and take responsibility, was in the mould of a colonial official. Michael Kargbo, a Sierra Leonean academic who has written about the British role during the civil war, described his first meeting with Penfold: 'I didn't know him before I went to London. So he walked through the door and what I saw was this colonial officer. And I said, okay, straight away, that's what we're dealing with ... He would say there's a substantial part of the population that would want to be re-colonised by Britain. So he had a sort of confidence that what he did was very powerful.'[48] During that time of acute crisis in Sierra Leone, it was possible to do this credibly. Penfold was and remains overwhelmingly popular in Freetown: 'He's not an ordinary human being. I don't really care what people in the UK said about him. When he came here, he saw that the people of Sierra Leone were crying, and he did something about it. He'll always be welcome in this country.'[49] Penfold became an embodiment of the British aspiration to heroically represent and support ordinary Africans, something that Blair and others saw and developed in their picture of the modern British role in African crises, although nowhere quite so literally as in Sierra Leone.

However, by the time of my visit in 2007, the British weren't viewed in quite such a positive light. Their very close involvement with the Kabbah regime since the end of the war was beginning to be compromising. 'The kind of level of support in a country with so little capacity and resources, it was almost too much. It was easy, I think, to get senior politicians, ministers, officials to take decisions because DfID suggested them. So it was almost like we were part of Government, rather than supporting Government.'[50]

This deep involvement of the British High Commission and DfID in Government policy meant they were directly implicated in its failures. Five years after the end of the war, with much trumpeted levels of aid and support going in, Freetown looked not very different from how it had immediately after the war. People were angry that there was still no mains electricity supply, that there were few jobs and that state services were rudimentary. The motivations and effectiveness of the British, as well as the Sierra Leonean Government, were beginning to be questioned. Mistrust in the good intentions of the British had begun to surface. For example, a common gripe I came across was the luxurious standard of living provided for the British soldiers who were there to train the new Sierra Leonean army – 'concrete houses' for the British; 'mud houses' for the Sierra Leoneans. Some criticised the British for continuing to provide direct budget support to a corrupt regime; others for suspending it in the run-up to the elections, an act that was perceived as showing favouritism towards the opposition. British officials patiently explain that many of the advances are invisible because they have been about building the capacity of the state – establishing a robust bureaucracy and other institutions which are gradually reaching a position to effect the material changes that Sierra Leoneans want to see. But many Sierra Leoneans don't see it this way: they argue that the British have been too close to the Government and that they don't understand what ordinary people need. This, indeed, is a reversal of the British self-conception and suggests that the more ambitious approach taken in Sierra Leone – focusing as it has on a very close involvement in governance – is in danger of undermining the British ideal of itself in Africa.

In Nigeria, the experience was at first one of dramatic moral posturing on the international stage; and then gradual re-engagement after the restoration of multi-party rule in 1999. In the first years of non-engagement, the British were able to maintain a strictly ethical tone. Tony Lloyd, who was the minister for Africa at the time, told me that the British Government's line of disengagement from Nigeria during Abacha's regime was:

> one of the things [he] was most pleased about ... Frankly, if a Labour Government had come into power when apartheid was still in existence, it would have been incredible for [us] to say, well, we're a bit uncomfortable about this apartheid stuff, but actually, we're going to nuance the policies a bit because we've got to get on with these people ... We would have had to

> carry through whatever that meant with the apartheid regime. The parallel between Nigeria and the apartheid regime is not exact of course, but it was similar.[51]

Afterwards, the establishment of a DfID office and the move of the political section of the High Commission to Abuja in 2003 were both part of an attempt to become involved in political and material development in Nigeria, but very much from the margins, with nothing like the levels of control and influence found in Sierra Leone. This left officials more credibly on the side of ordinary Africans: they described their jobs as being about looking for alternative ways of enabling people to hold their government to account.

> A couple of years ago we supported an exercise of the Federal Government which benchmarked all the states against a set of governance indicators that we helped them design to try and measure performance on financial management and service delivery systems and policy making across all the states. What we found was that [it] was quite a useful way to concentrate minds in state governments about what they were doing. As soon as they realised that they were going to be looked at, and they were going to be compared against all the other states, in a reasonably robust exercise, and that those comparisons were going to be published, that did actually concentrate minds quite a lot in some states. It's a different route to accountability.[52]

I asked him whether this meant that he saw the British role as one of holding the Nigerian state to account on behalf of Nigerians. 'I would see our role as being to get the information out there; that can help people put pressure on Government through the media, through other channels, and ask the right questions.'[53] The British officials in Nigeria were generally much more sanguine about their role and felt less under siege than those in Sierra Leone. It was feasible to maintain an idealised role in the limited context of relative disengagement.

Conclusion

Separating the good and the political works relatively well in West Africa. The proportions of the problems appear to unify the actors around clear, technical approaches; an apparent lack of politics resonates with this idea. Added to this, the British actors are able to feel that they have left family and history behind them, and entered a normatively pure and politically neutral zone. Finally, the British find that, on the whole, their views are taken seriously. This returns us to the importance of the sense of capability that working in Africa seems to endow.

Both the transcendental and the transformative approaches to connecting to the good can be found here. The common cause made with universal norms such as human rights and good governance can be grasped without contest within the apparently empty Africa. At the same time, as representatives of the capable state, British officials embody the good state. In playing out its logic within the thinner relationships they make in Africa, they reaffirm its existence and health. In realising these ways of connecting to the good, modern British officials are in many ways playing out the idealisations and fantasies of their Victorian predecessors.

The theme of reparation is evident. Again, the idea of Africa as a damaged object is constantly evoked, and the British role there is defined in relation to an Africa that needs to be mended. The Britain in Africa case carries several elements of Segal's description of manic reparation (see Chapter 4). Her description of the object of manic reparation as 'felt as inferior, dependent and, at depth, contemptible' is compelling in the Africa case. The perception that the damage has been done by others is evident in both the apparent insignificance of a colonial legacy (other than a benign one) and the argument that British interests are relatively few and, where they do exist, work in harmony with African interests. Considering the depth of British engagement in much of Africa, this might appear difficult to sustain. It is sustained, however, through the highly idealised ways in which many British politicians and officials perceive Africa and Britain's relationship with it.

Notes

1 Mamdani described British rule in Africa as a 'spidery beast', the body representing more formal direct rule in African capitals and the legs extending little bits of British influence into the rural areas, ruled indirectly (Mamdani, 1996: 28).
2 Interview with Olaitan Oyerinde, head, international department, National Labour Congress, Abuja, 30 July 2007.
3 Interview with an FCO official, Abuja, 1 August 2007.
4 Interview with Peter Penfold, London, 3 July 2007.
5 Discussion with an FCO official, Abuja, 28 July 2007.
6 Interview with an FCO official, London, 1 May 2007.
7 Interview with an FCO official, Freetown, 6 August 2007.
8 Interview with an FCO official, Abuja, 1 August 2007.
9 Discussion with a London-based official at DfID, London, 4 May 2007.
10 Interview with Peter Penfold, London, 3 July 2007.
11 Interview with an FCO official, Freetown, 6 August 2007.
12 Interview with an FCO official, London, 3 July 2007.
13 *Ibid.*
14 Interview with an FCO official, Freetown, 6 August 2007.
15 Interview with an FCO official, Abuja, 1 August 2007.
16 Interview with an FCO official, London, 3 July 2007.
17 Discussion with a DfID official, Abuja, 29 August 2007.
18 Interview with a DfID official, Abuja, 30 July 2007.
19 These were promoted by independence leaders like Julius Nyerere and Kwame Nkrumah, who argued for an African form of politics based on consensus rather than competition. This, it was argued, was more in tune with African political

culture and served the practical need for stability and development (Nkrumah, 1998; Nyerere, 1967).

20 Interview with an FCO official, London, 27 April 2007.
21 Interview with an FCO official, Freetown, 6 August 2007.
22 *Ibid.*
23 Mohamed A. Deen, president, Sierra Leone Labour Congress, Freetown, 7 August 2007.
24 Interview with Max Conteh, director of education, Sierra Leone Labour Congress, Freetown, 7 August 2007.
25 Interview with Valnora Edwin, Campaign for Good Governance, Freetown, 11 August 2007.
26 Interview with Morlai Kamara, governance programme manager, Network Movement for Justice and Development, Freetown, 8 August 2007.
27 Interview with an FCO official, Abuja, 1 August 2007.
28 Interview with DfID official, Abuja, 30 July 2007.
29 Interview with an FCO official, Abuja, 1 August 2007.
30 This line was taken by Onamusi Onadeko, an NGO activist who runs an organisation called JLERO, which attempts to strengthen the rule of law in Nigeria. He takes the approach that there is a politically neutral model, compatible with democracy, which can be imported (interview, London, 13 July 2007).
31 Interview with Peter Ozo-Eson, director of the Labour Centre for Social and Economic Research, Abuja, 30 July 2007.
32 Interview with Henrietta Ibrahim, Radio Nigeria, Abuja, 1 August 2007.
33 Discussion at the weekly Editorial Board meeting of the *Daily Trust*, Abuja, 2 August 2007.
34 Interview with a former locally engaged FCO official, Freetown, 11 August 2007.
35 Interview with Mohamed A. Deen, President, Sierra Leone Labour Congress, Freetown, 7 August 2007.
36 Interview with Myles Wickstead, London, 27 June 2007.
37 Interview with an FCO official, Abuja, 1 August 2007.
38 Interview with Garba Abari, executive director, Abuja Policy Consulting, Abuja, 2 August 2007.
39 Interview with Mohamed A. Deen, president, Sierra Leone Labour Congress, Freetown, 7 August 2007.
40 Interview with Max Conteh, director of education, Sierra Leone Labour Congress, 7 August 2007.
41 Interview with Peter Ozo-Eson, director, Labour Centre for Social and Economic Research, 30 July 2007, Abuja.
42 Interview with Myles Wickstead, London, 27 June 2007.
43 Discussion with a Nigerian-based British DfID official, London, 27 July 2007.
44 Interview with Myles Wickstead, London, 27 June 2007.
45 The Nigerians are remembered without affection. One Kissy resident who had lived in Freetown throughout the war told me that people have not forgotten how the Nigerians, in fighting the rebels, killed and injured many civilians too, and how they bombed the retreating rebels as they fled into the hills above Freetown, destroying many villages (discussion with Mr Cole, Freetown, 7 August 2007).
46 Video copies of a documentary entitled *SAS: Mission Impossible* were still

doing the rounds in Freetown on my visit in 2007. The film is a heroic account of the SAS rescue of a group of British soldiers who had been captured and held captive by a rebel group – the trigger to broader British troop involvement in Sierra Leone. On my arrival I was shown the film by the family I was staying with and told it was about 'how the British came to save us'.

47 Interview with Peter Penfold, 3 July 2007, London.

48 Interview with Michael Kargbo, 4 August 2007, Freetown.

49 Interview with a former locally engaged official, Freetown, 11 August 2007.

50 Interview with a DfID official, London, 4 May 2007.

51 Interview, London, 10 July 2007.

52 Interview with a DfID official, Abuja, 30 July 2007.

53 *Ibid.*

7

The good state

This book has been about the way in which Britain under New Labour 'did good' in Africa as a way of creating a central core of ideal activity for the state. The themes and approaches contained within this trend were not new, but drew on eighteenth- and nineteenth-century ideas about the continent and Britain's role there. I have suggested that the creation of a good project formed an important part of protecting the state from internal ambiguity and decay, by creating a utopian core at the heart of what it does.

In this chapter, I am going to look at the wider, international context, and at recent history, to explore the important question of why this approach began to resurface in 1997. It is clear from historical accounts that Africa mattered relatively little to Britain from the period of independence in the 1960s up until the mid-1990s (see Chapter 1). South Africa was an exception: continuing British interests there, combined with revulsion at the apartheid regime, made South Africa an object of heated ideological division in Britain. However, limited reaction to other momentous events on the continent underlined the relatively marginalised interest it held for Britain. The Rhodesian Universal Declaration of Independence in 1965 provoked disquiet but not the British reaction campaigners hoped for. The Nigeria–Biafra war (1967–70) stirred up discussion as to what Britain should do, but elicited a broadly realist approach from Harold Wilson's Labour government, which supported the Nigerian Federal Government.[1] Ethiopian famine in the 1980s stirred popular sympathy and support, but reluctant state interest. Wars in Ethiopia, Somalia, Mozambique and Angola; military coups, human rights abuses, state corruption on a massive scale; deepening poverty in much of the continent – none of these gave rise to a particular feeling that the British state should make sorting out Africa its particular business. The Rwandan genocide in 1994, and the relative lack of Western intervention, drew horrified responses and provoked questions as to the role of Britain in helping to prevent such atrocities (Melvern and Williams, 2004) – something which later fed into New Labour thinking on foreign policy. There had always been variations in approach – Labour governments tended to give a higher profile to international development and spend more on it than did Conservative governments. But on the whole, Britain did not view Africa as politically or economically interesting. The

1980s, under Margaret Thatcher's premiership, saw the nadir of interest in Africa (Bose and Burnell, 1991).

What changed from 1997? Drawing on the discussion so far, it was not the case that Africa came to be viewed as more political, or more economically worth engaging with. Africa remained 'empty'. If anything, it had become emptier than before. The neo-liberal experiments of the IFIs had further eroded weakened states; and the end of the Cold War had seen the withdrawal of the few pockets of superpower patronage that had been extended to the continent (Villalon, 1998: 3–26). Both of these trends had contributed to the collapse of a number of states, and to entrenched poverty in many others. More generally, African states appeared weakened and impotent – 'zombified', as Mbembe described them (Mbembe, 2001: 104), by economic decline and crises of legitimacy. AIDS, increasingly affecting large parts of the continent, became a symbol of African decay and state impotence. If there was a part of the world that could apparently exemplify damaged and declining states, it was Africa.

It could be argued that it was this perception of the prostration of Africa that evoked a British response: that the situation became one that could no longer be tolerated. The Rwandan genocide and the end of apartheid – both in 1994 – might have been tipping points: one providing a shocking indictment of international neglect which stirred consciences and provoked the feeling that the richer states must help Africa; the other, by ending Western arguments about how or whether to attempt to end a corrupt racist regime, allowing a unification of purpose and ideas about the continent.

These events were significant, but I believe that they most importantly provided traction in the way they appeared to meet a need, emerging among British political elites – particularly in the Labour Party – for an arena of ideal activity in which the state could operate. This need arose from a coalescing of ideas about what the state was for, and what it increasingly was not for, and the ways in which state actors responded. These ideas came broadly from two sources. The first emerged from recent international events and trends – particularly the end of the Cold War and the growth of globalisation – which had brought about the apparent end of balance of power politics, the flowering of optimism about possibilities for the end of ideological division, grand new international challenges and narratives and the creation of 'international harmony'. They at once undermined the position of the state as the hub of power, limiting its capacity to frame and participate in ethical issues; and offered potential sources of a more transcendent – because apparently universal and disinterested – good beyond the state with which it might identify. Unifying political and economic ideas offered suggestions of the end of ideology and an era of reaching for technical solutions along political directions which had been settled (Fukuyama, 1992). The second source of ideas came from recent British history and concerned the alienation of the state from moral debate and engagement. This particularly preoccupied the Labour Party as it contemplated office for the first time in nearly twenty years. The 1980s had shifted British conceptions of state, class and society, and, in embracing key elements of the neo-liberal state remit of Thatcherism, Blair and New Labour had to relinquish the grander liberalism traditionally articulated by the Party and central to its conception of itself.[2] The sense of uneasiness about what the state could and should do both fed ideas generated by the post-Cold War order and was further reinforced by it. From both sources – international and domestic history – came the erosion of the post-war consensus on the traditional role of the state as central to key moral and organisational functions of British society. Labour felt itself to be inheriting a damaged state.

In this chapter I want to explore how this damage to the state has been expressed, and two potential ways it might be mended. The first involves the embrace of more transcendent or romantic conceptions of a higher good – in the expression of universal values like human rights and democracy – which might enable the state to create a link for itself with a new authority of the good. The second sees a state attempt to transform politics – by making and identifying itself with the good. Both draw on Kleinian ideas of the export of and identification with pure good in an attempt to repair damaged internal objects. Both resonate with traditional British ways of conceiving a 'good' other, or the creation of a good project beyond the state where it can be idealised and remain pure. And in both, an external, distant, foreign object – Africa – represents a proxy damage that can be restored in the pursuit of a repaired state.

International (transcendent) goodness

Two significant international trends formed a backdrop to Labour's response to the triumph of neo-liberalism: the end of the Cold War and the perception of deepening globalisation. Together these appeared to undermine the idea of state capacity, while at the same time holding forth possibilities of a connection to more spiritual forms of good.

The end of the Cold War eroded the idea of the state as the centre of politics by overturning the traditional conception of interacting state units. Realist approaches to IR, which dominated during the Cold War, are predicated on the idea of the ubiquitous clash of interests between states. But without the Soviet Union, these appeared to be gone, and new ideas about international cooperation burst forth in a rush of enthusiasm in the early 1990s. President George Bush senior, speaking in 1992 at the end of the Gulf War, put this in terms of a new world order:

> Until now, the world we've known has been a world divided – a world of barbed wire and concrete block, conflict and cold war. Now, we can see a new world coming into view. A world in which there is the very real prospect of a new world order. In the words of Winston Churchill, a 'world order' in which 'the principles of justice and fair play... protect the weak against the strong...' A world where the United Nations, freed from

> cold war stalemate, is poised to fulfill the historic vision of its founders. A world in which freedom and respect for human rights find a home among all nations. (Bush, 1991)

But if the Hegelian 'other' had gone, removing an important source of negation for the good state, the end of history appeared to present new opportunities for connection to a far grander universal good: ideological difference, politics, were gone, leaving an era of human rights, international law, democracy and new, enlightened objectives such as the MDGs. These represented a transcendent source of good, attainable by relinquishing state activity and politics.

Benign views of globalisation reinforce these notions, playing into traditional liberal ideas of a natural order and an invisible hand which will distribute wealth and stimulate growth in ways that inter-state rivalries have inhibited. This could not be an unalloyed abdication of human responsibility – globalisation also presents challenges which human agency will be called upon to overcome. Thus, more active liberal approaches are stimulated by new global problems such as migration, environmental decay and contagious new wars. However, these further erode the power of the state, as, being global problems, they demand global authority to overcome them. Thus Peter Hain could write about 'The End of Foreign Policy' and Clare Short could talk enthusiastically about the new shared objectives shaped in response to these problems (Hain, 2001; Short, 2004). This still plays into a more transcendent form of the good, as it demands responses by supernational bodies and norms that are beloved of the more libertarian wing of the Labour Party for their apparent capacity to rise above politics and interests. It allows for idealisation of international 'togetherness' and capacity, something very clearly expressed by Blair in his 1999 Chicago speech and again in his 2001 speech to the Labour Party conference.

All this represented a dramatic swing away from the idea of state-centred goodness towards a universal, spiritual goodness. This did not appear to represent a disaster for Labour – it resonated with ideas and causes that helped shape the Party. Tony Benn, a solid representative of 'old Labour', summed up the approach: 'I'm a UN guy: I believe in justice, I think justice is the key. I believe in right and wrong, not profit and loss. And these are the tools I bring to any issue that comes up.'[3] Cook and Short, key players in international issues, were both from the Party's more idealist wing, more libertarian, inclined towards pacifism, keen internationalists. Together, they shaped an approach to foreign policy that tapped into this cosmopolitan tradition. Cook's ethical dimension relied heavily on the notion of universal human rights, the supremacy of democracy and international law. Short, through DfID, also plugged into universal goods, such as the human rights framework, the MDGs and the UN aid target of 0.7 per cent of GNI.

I will describe this in three stages. First, the ways in which Cook sought to differentiate his foreign policy from that of his Conservative predecessors; second, the ways in which he and Short built up a more cosmopolitan view of the world; and third, briefly, the ways in which Labour and British exceptionalism continued to shape the apparently new internationalism.

Plugging the state and political activity into a universal good represents significant ways in which the state can be repaired. Let me suggest a rather tangible way this might be done. Cook and Short, and increasingly Blair and Brown, were strongly propelled by a vehement rejection of the Conservative Party's tendency to put national interest over higher principles.[4] This tendency was typified by a series of foreign policy decisions which represented for Labour a moral failure. They included the rejection of sanctions on South Africa in the 1980s and the continuing relationship with the apartheid regime; the failure to intervene in the Rwandan genocide in 1994; the lack of response to violent conflict in the Balkans in the early 1990s; and the way the Government had tacitly allowed the export of arms to Iraq and then attempted to cover up the scandal in 1992. Since I am interested in policy in Africa, I will elaborate on the two African examples.

The Conservative Government's attitude towards South Africa – exemplified for its critics by its refusal to enter a sanctions regime – represented one of the clearest cases of national self-interest trumping wider ethics, and provided a 'real, substantive dividing line' between the parties.[5] Foreign Secretary Geoffrey Howe had argued in the 1980s that sanctions would damage substantial British interests, and that apartheid was 'more than a moral question', one that could not 'be seen in isolation from a whole range of complex and intractable political, economic and social problems'. He criticised 'some nearer home, who cling to an over-simplified and unrealistic view of the situation in South Africa and what outsiders can do to help' (Howe, 1988: 5). Statements like this provoked an indignation that was crucial in shaping New Labour's foreign policy. It reaffirmed in the minds of Labour politicians the idea that some values and principles should be more important than national self-interest, and that the state itself had a duty to uphold them. Labour's sense of identification with the anti-apartheid struggle has been an important part of its sense of its 'purer' self.[6] Cook's ethical element is an explicit endorsement of this approach: 'The Labour Government does not accept that political values can be left behind when we check in our passports to travel on diplomatic business' (Cook, 1997b).

The failure to intervene in Rwanda in 1994, an apparently clear case of genocide, which international systems and norms had been crafted to prevent, represented a dramatic failure of the international ideal, and presented a case of apathy and lack of concern with the wider international good and norms which appeared acutely reprehensible. This event cemented the importance of international norms, and the duty of individual states to protect and promote them. Both Short and Blair claim to have been motivated by memories of Rwanda in their decision to intervene in Sierra Leone (Kampfner, 2004: 62–77).

The tone changed dramatically. New Labour ministers did not talk in terms of political and moral complexity or texture as Howe had done.

Instead, the focus was on universal challenges, approaches and harmonious interests. And New Labour showed itself far more ready to engage and intervene in cases where it saw moral failure and an international duty to protect and promote universal values. The post-Cold War era of globalisation provided the context in which to do this: it made ideas of internationalism real. As Cook put it in 2000: 'It was fashionable in the past decade to debate whether this century would be America's century, or Japan's century, or maybe even Europe's century. In reality, it is going to be the internationalist century' (Cook, 2000).

Short, too, described the 'internationalist century' in explicitly universalising ways. In its first three years, DfID produced two white papers, which framed Britain's approach to development policy around two prevailing international themes: the challenges of environmental crisis in 1997; and the effects of globalisation on the poor in 2000. First, there were striking allusions to the excitement of the international realm – the grandeur of the global historical narrative being engaged with, the opportunities it presented for progress and hints of the degradation that might result from neglecting it.

> We are living at a time of profound historical change. Great wealth and great squalor exist side by side. We could move forward to a period of massive progress and the removal of abject poverty from the human condition. Or we could see growing poverty, marginalisation, conflict and environmental degradation. Neither prospect is inevitable. The future is a matter of political will and change. Cynicism and negativism are the enemies of progress. It is when people see that progress is possible that the demand for reform and advance is energised. (DfID, 2000: 7)

Second, universal themes extend from such challenges towards an implicit understanding of the needs they produce and the responses they demand. The DfID White Paper of 1997 set forth a 'Statement of Purpose' for a set of policies and actions that it aimed to contribute to in developing countries around the world. It listed 'lower child and maternal mortality, basic health care for all, including reproductive services, effective universal primary education, literacy, access to information and life skills, safe drinking water and food security [and] emergency and humanitarian needs' as the particular contributions it aimed to make (DfID, 1997: 19).

The 2000 DfID White Paper claimed that:

> Making political institutions work for poor people means helping to strengthen the voices of the poor and helping them to realise their human rights. It means empowering them to take their own decisions, rather than being the passive objects of choices made on their behalf. And it means removing forms of discrimination – in legislation and government policies – that prevent poor people from having control over their own lives and over the policies of governments. Government must be willing to let

> people speak, and to develop mechanisms to ensure that they are heard. This is central to what we mean by a rights based approach to development. (DfID, 2000: 27)

Such 'basic human requirements', and the human rights framework and mechanisms for understanding and providing them, were again self-evident because universal. The moral authority gained from sacrificing national self-interest provided a basis to comment on the way other governments and political systems worked, and to intervene when necessary. Labour also drew on its assumptions of 'understanding' the poor which, we saw, informed a key stream within the Party from its inception (Chapter 3), and on its idealisation of international organisations which apparently transcended politics.

However, despite the grander rhetoric about universalism, elements of exceptionalism – Labour and British – remained. Britain could take charge of the universal objectives.

> This is a White Paper which reflects Britain's unique place in the world and our opportunity to adopt a new international role. No other country combines membership of the Group of Seven Industrialised countries, membership of the European Union, a permanent seat on the Security Council of the United Nations (UN) and membership of the Commonwealth. Our particular history places us on the fulcrum of global influence... Helping to lead the world in a commitment to poverty elimination and sustainable development is an international role in which all the people of Britain could take pride. (DfID, 1997: 20)

Moreover, it was a Labour government that had the authority to lead Britain on development. The 1997 White Paper discuses the history of international development in Britain, pointing out the seminal white papers produced under Labour governments in the 1960s and 1970s, and contrasting this with the 'lost decade' of the 1980s (*Ibid*: 8). Labour had always prioritised development in this way, unlike Conservative regimes under which 'development policy was subordinated to commercial and short-term political interests' (DfID, 2000: 12). By the time of the 2000 DfID White Paper, Short could demonstrate the ways in which Britain under Labour had become author of an international good. 'We have spent the last three years working to achieve these objectives. We now have unprecedented consensus – across the UN system, the IMF and World Bank, most Regional Development Banks, leaders of developing countries, the G8 and the OECD – that the achievement of the Targets should be the focus of our joint endeavours' (*Ibid*: 7).

Labour latched into this idealised international realm. It gave the key actors an international role they enjoyed. It fitted with strands of Labour ideology that looked towards internationalism as transcendent of state *realpolitik*. It provided a good point of differentiation from the Conservative regimes of the 1980s and 1990s. And at the same time it carried the image of 'good Britain' into the world, reinforcing the idea of British specialness. As one DfID official put it: 'We don't do development or support development in the way that other governments do it. We're prepared to take risks. We're prepared to say what needs to be said…If you're thinking about negotiations in international arenas…people look to the UK to take the progressive line.'[7]

However, it also masked an underlying and profound sense of uneasiness. The end of the Cold War and hastening globalisation brought a sense of loss with them too. The transcendence of the national realm undermines a crucial aspect of the idea of the good state, particularly as it has been conceived in parts of the Labour Party which saw an active state as intrinsic to a moral project. This is reinforced by globalisation which further reduces the state's capacity to deal with the uncontrollable trends and forces that shape the world. As Andrew Williams argues, 'displaced allegiance for many people from their state and even their "people" to an abstract entity, global capitalism…is perhaps the greatest dilemma facing liberal thought after the end of the nineteenth century, one that has not been fully resolved today' (Williams, 2006: 37).

New Labour and the missing state

Anxiety induced by the apparent erosion of the state was expressed through more omnipotent conceptions of the British role in Africa and these have to do with a resurrection of the state and its capacity. To examine what this means we need first to return to this idea of an ideal state. Conceptions of what is ideal vary, and it is useful in this context to revisit Isaiah Berlin's two liberties which describe alternative roles for a liberal state (Berlin, 1969). When the state's role is defined around the concept of negative liberty, its role is reduced to providing a normatively neutral enabling framework within which individuals pursue their own versions of the good life. A positive liberty approach involves a much more involved role for the state, in directing a collective moral agenda. Positive liberty, as Berlin points out, carries the dangers of totalitarianism and has largely been rejected in favour of a morally neutral role for the state. This was a struggle for many in the Labour Party, dominant elements of which have historically favoured a more positive role for the state. Blair himself, and the whole New Labour project, appeared explicitly to accept that this conception of the state must be relinquished if the Party was to be made electable.[8] It was also a tacit acknowledgement of the changing demographic of Labour's traditional support base, much of which had responded well to the individualising culture of aspiration promoted in the 1980s. After the Thatcher years, there appeared to be little popular appetite for a return to the idea of a more proactive state. There is an underlying feeling of betrayal, or at least of disappointment that Labour's once-idealised working class supporters should so eagerly have bought into Thatcher's materialistic vision.[9]

Therefore, the Labour Party as it came to power was in the midst of an identity crisis, having lost its ethos and confidence in its traditional constituency. Any ambitions to create a positive and active state programme for Britain had been curbed. If members of the Party's core were particularly anxious or angry about this, the leadership was not without its own misgivings.

David Chandler argues that Blair's interest in Africa was a deliberate and instrumental means to quiet the elements in his Party who were most dissatisfied with his conservative policy agenda (Chandler, 2003). There may be some validity in this: it did, arguably, provide Blair with a rare unifying achievement. But Chandler's approach cedes too much to the Labour leadership's capacity for organisation and planning; and it underestimates Blair's own zealous commitment to a more positive idea of doing good and the ambiguity about New Labour's neo-liberalism within the leadership itself. This was not simply a story of New Labour coercing or persuading old Labour to adapt to reality: there was anxiety within New Labour itself about what the role of the Party and the state should now be. Many of the intellectual contributors to New Labour expressed this unease with the limited vision of the state they were inheriting, and made efforts to establish a new way to define a politics of the left, and a basis for state action in the new climate. The period in the run up to the 1997 election was a particularly creative one for think tanks on the left of British politics, and Demos, the Fabian Society and the Institute of Public Policy Research (IPPR) produced a menu of ideas about how a new politics of the left would look and work.

The Demos book, *Tomorrow's Politics*, described the way in which the erosion of the state, which should play a crucial role in representing collective ideals, had damaged a sense of the community. This damage to the state as focus of a collective project occurred in the twentieth century because of the ways progress was equated with warfare, rising inequality and environmental decay (Hargreaves and Christie, 1998: 9–10).

> Losing a sense of progress can have a serious and direct cost. Societies with a strong sense of the future bring out the best in people. In traditional societies, this sense was achieved through religion and ritual that situated the individual in an unbroken chain linking ancestors and descendants. Today the idea of progress is our nearest equivalent for encouraging more caring, more responsible, more moral and less selfish behaviour. Yet many of today's pressures make it appear as if we live in an eternal present. Our two dominant decision-making structures – the consumer market and representative democracy – are particularly oriented to the present. (*Ibid*: 10)

In this account, modernity had damaged the state by focusing it on the pursuit of objectives that were ultimately destructive, emptying it of moral purpose and thus of collective meaning. This anxious flavour, alongside an excitement and optimism of the new ideas that might be realised through governing again, fed a plethora of left-inclined thinking within the intellectual parts of the Party.[10] Particularly notable about them is the way in which so many of them reach out, beyond Britain, for answers.

Geoff Mulgan, a significant contributor, articulated the intellectual end of New Labour, first as founder and director of Demos, a think tank close to the Labour leadership, and then in his roles as advisor to Gordon Brown and head of Blair's policy unit in Downing Street. In his book, *Politics in an Antipolitical Age*, published in 1994, the year Blair was elected leader of the Labour Party, Mulgan described the gloomy political scene that Labour was about to inherit. Key to his description was the increasing emasculation of the state as a realm of politics that connects with people, and that has a contribution to make to ethical social life. Meaningful national politics had been eroded, suggested Mulgan, by globalisation, localism, increasingly incoherent national identities and the inability of national politics to solve problems or to inspire. The national narrative, he argued, had lost its moral purchase, leaving the state apparently predatory and self-serving, rather than capable of embodying some sense of collective meaning. Grand stories and political heroes had gone, something supported by the wider 'end of history' idea. 'The world is stagnant, exhausted, locked into closed loops of bureaucracy and culture that excludes new energies' (Mulgan, 1994: 22). Politicians, disconnected and morally exhausted, 'cannot inspire or convince' (*Ibid*: 8). Civic virtue, political participation, community – once important parts of public life – had been eroded by 'acquisitiveness and the substitution of state for community, a general characteristic of modern societies' (*Ibid*: 22). Mulgan described the bleak outcome of this increasing meaninglessness of the state and, because it clung on as the key site of politics, an 'erosion of virtue', as politics became 'little more than a balancing of interests, devoid either of any mission or of any overarching criteria of judgement, leaving no reason for anyone to care or to take part' (*Ibid*: 25). For national politicians, this represented a crisis of identity and legitimacy.

The question then arose as to how moral purpose and collective meaning were to be restored. Was there still room for the state, or had it been compromised beyond repair? Mulgan's answer was to reach out beyond the state. His analysis provided access to new forms of political engagement which connected the autonomous liberal individual to a higher rationality. Mulgan's 'anti-political age' was really about the evolution of politics, and its extension into new arenas. Politics would not be lost, but would shift to 'become less part of the definition of the collective, the nation, class or republic, and more part of the armoury of the self-defining, self-creating individual' (*Ibid*: 18). Mulgan advocated a new political actor, the 'politician as social creator' (*Ibid*: 31). This person would reject the national state, ideology, class and interest-based constituencies in favour of a relationship with new constituencies which share 'mores and values', deriving a 'transcendental' ethos 'from the interests of the species as a whole'. As this happened, 'the politician is forced into the role of articulating right and wrong' (*Ibid*: 33), thus filling the gap left by the decline of religion. Mulgan's diagnosis suggested that 'the long-term trend is unmistakably towards the sovereignty of an embryonic world public' (*Ibid*: 188). Globalisation would chip away at state sovereignty by enabling the spread of universal values and democratising global relationships. States would have neither particular interests to defend nor the monopoly of representation and action. There is a lot of Woolf in here (see Chapter 3). Woolf, who also saw the national project as corrupted and damaged, looked to a purer form of authority to represent a source of good. Like Woolf, Mulgan argues that the state has corrupted itself. The solution is to reach out to something higher and purer. The thinner norms and values he now sees as attractive to individualised social actors can be reached through dispersed, delocalised impersonalised relationships.

Mulgan's 'politician as social creator' who transcends interest and ideology is a distinctly super-character, a Weberian ideal-type who shakes off the moral complexity of the politician. He is an idealised parent-figure, a 'prophet' rather than a morally complex 'priest' (Weber, 1963). Mulgan's new communities connect people through ideas, values and causes, rather than locality and history. His vision of the political organisation and ideas of the future is inherently cosmopolitan. 'Communities' of shared values or interests are based on the coherence and compatibility of their members, which rest on liberal conceptions of choice and self-defined identity. These characteristics – sameness and choice – represent thin and idealised relationships. Conflict is banished because values and ideas are uncontested, or, if consensus fails, alignments and groupings break up and reform in more compatible ways. Thus Mulgan's ideas represent an escape from the idea of community rooted in the history, proximity and lack of choice that are essential to thickness. Relationships based on compatibility and sameness are already thin; the assumption that they are chosen and can be relinquished adds transience and superficiality. The point about communities centred on the state, or the family, is that you don't choose; you can't leave; you have to learn to live with disagreement and compromise. In his reaching out for transcendence, Mulgan gets rid of them.

Robert Cooper, another policy adviser to Blair, provided an alternative which gives less room for idealisation – perhaps because Cooper was a professional diplomat rather than a party political advisor. Like Mulgan, Cooper saw the erosion of traditional state-based community as an inevitable legacy of the Enlightenment, of rationality, the growing assertiveness of the individual and the erosion of personal ties in favour of anonymous commercial dealings. He suggested that the extreme ideologies of the twentieth century – fascism and communism – were attempts to save the state from this modernising trend. But, inevitably, newly post-modern states will succumb to this logic. 'The individual has won and foreign policy is the continuation of domestic concerns beyond national boundaries and not vice versa. Individual consumption replaces collective glory as the dominant theme of national life' (Cooper, 2003: 53).

The logic of enlightenment is one driver of state decay: the other is its inability to respond to the new demands of globalisation which, along with the creation of opportunity, brings dangers: 'Emancipation, diversity, global communication – all the things that promise an age of riches, creativity – could also bring a nightmare in which states lose control of the means of violence and people lose control of their futures' (*Ibid*: ix). National sovereignty, the system of balance of power between autonomous states, cannot contain new threats because it buys internal stability at the cost of international anarchy: its view on the world is essentially amoral (*Ibid*: 8). This loss of control can be countered best by a post-modern form of pooled sovereignty which would establish a 'post-modern peace'. 'In the post-modern world, *raison d'état* and the amorality of Machiavelli's theories of statecraft have been replaced by a moral consciousness that applies to international relations as well as to domestic affairs' (*Ibid*: 31).

Cooper's description is a lot less glamorous than Mulgan's. There is no heroic social actor to fill the gap left by religion. Instead, Cooper is using the European Union (EU) as the model for the future of political organisation, and the British have tended to view the EU as a forum for grubby, trade-off politics, rather than the grander ideals of internationalism pursued by many on the left. Relations between European countries are too thick to sustain such idealisations – the EU represents more of a traditional community than Mulgan's. However, there is some mileage here for notions along Hegelian lines, provided by the existence of an alternative, disordered world. The new unbounded international arena is exciting and creative, but it contains sources of destruction too. As we gain control of our world, we capture and embody the good, so our potency creates envy and destructiveness in the world beyond. It is this image of the 'pre-modern' world that haunts Cooper's analysis. His vision of the new world, even with the erosion of the state, continues the Hegelian theme of negation contained in the dangers posed by the 'pre-modern' world.

The Fabian Society's pamphlet *Progressive Globalisation* provided a superficial, but typically Fabian, answer to the demands of globalisation (Jacobs, Lent and Watkins, 2003). The globalisation of liberalism of the late nineteenth century, its authors argued, caused the new assertiveness of states and specifically the creation by them of social democracy to control capitalism and serve the public interest. What was needed now, they argued, was not a return to the state as the location of social democracy, but an international social democracy; the development of pooled sovereignty and international bodies to meet the world's public interest (*Ibid*: 6). This is a modern manifestation of the Fabian approach of rather grandly – and glibly – extending national ideas to the international realm (see Chapter 3). It is also typical in its assertion of the creative powers of organisation and control to meet problems.

Foreign Office minister Peter Hain argued along these lines. He suggested that power had been sucked away from governments and states – by the voluntary ceding of sovereignty in international cooperation, by the increasing financial clout of multi-national companies, and by the increasing monopolisation of moral sovereignty by the NGOs. States still have teeth, but they must now work with these new powerful players to tackle global problems. Hain contrasts the new 'foreign policy' with traditional diplomacy, a game of internally driven national interests in which 'there is little shared vision among all the players' (Hain, 2001: 5). He argues that world leaders must 'align the way their nations see their own interests with the new global imperatives' of the problems of environmental decay, poverty, HIV, drugs and terrorism, and the opportunities of trade' (*Ibid*: 7). In this way, foreign policy is eradicated.

Where does this get us? It is clear that there is excitement and anxiety about politics and the state. Much of the writing focuses on the increasing lack of opportunity for the state to realise either a programme of action or a moral directive role. It has lost capacity; it has lost moral resonance. Crucially, it has probably lost the one because it has lost the other. All in different ways reach out beyond the complexities of the immediate community towards a more cosmopolitan ideal.

Blair himself contributed to the intellectual shaping of a new politics of the left. His 'third way', building on a theme proposed by Anthony Giddens (Giddens, 1998), was an attempt to grapple with the same problem. Like the other ideas explored above, the third way recognised the failures of neoliberalism but refused to accept a reassertion of the state as an answer. What was the essence of the third way? It was not a strong agenda in itself: its 'values' were vague and woolly, difficult to pin down. It attempted to create a sense of the good within the heart of politics, by refusing to accept division and difference. Blair's approach was an attempt to design a universalising tent, domestically and internationally, to keep everyone happy (see Chapter 1). His critics accused him of failing to come up with a galvanising ethos, but he was essentially for unity.[11]

Blair was reaching for what Pierre Manent argues is state purpose lost to modernity. Manent suggests that 'pre-modern' societies are obsessed with unity, and tend to repel or conceal division. He contrasts this with modern societies whose political systems are rooted in ideas of division – of the powers of state, of religion and state, of society and state – which make them stable but essentially frustrate and limit the exercise of power, leaving society with a sense of its own impotence and the impotence of the state. It is the downside of negative liberty: it erodes any sense of a collective project or connection to source of good (Manent, 2006). Blair tried to encapsulate some of this sense of unity which would restore to the national narrative a sense of potency. Yet this broke down in issues that really matter – where thicker interests and competing ideologies squabble. In domestic politics it happened over questions of distribution very readily. Key programmes such as the one on reducing child poverty were very difficult to realise. In the international realm, too, consensus over al-Qaeda evaporated and dissipated in Afghanistan and Iraq. Because Blair's aspiration to unity and good and its intellectual underlay tried – as we have seen – to survive on far thinner conceptions of the good, they were unable to deal with political thickness and the ambiguity that came with it.

Saving the state – in Africa

In Africa, which I have argued is seen as ideologically neutral and interest-free, embodying the 'pre-modern', New Labour did much better in its quest for the good state. For Labour MPs, Africa offered important ways to contribute to its repair. It did this in a number of ways. First was the explicit way in which Africa represented the Labour values which had been jettisoned in so many other areas. As Tony Lloyd said:

> At a time when my own party was quite hard-nosed about quite a lot of things – or had at least given the impression that it was in retreat from its values-base in matters domestic, or even in matters international in some parts – the ability to say, 'but we are going to [make] and we have made real progress around the whole swathe of issues around development', was about [a reassertion of] that fundamental canon that anybody in the Labour Party ought to have about internationalism, about our socialism. Amongst those things are equality, and the struggle for dignity for every person on the planet. In that way, if in nothing else, the most cynical interpretation is that this could be at least one area where we can be pure and noble and I can hold my head up high and others can hold their heads up high.[12]

Lloyd depicts an area in which 'we have made real progress around the whole swathe of issues', and reasserted a 'fundamental canon' of socialism. Here is the state once again able to do good things. Clare Short, famously bitter about Blair after the invasion of Iraq, made the same point. 'It [the policy on Africa] speaks to the heart of that social justice, doing decent things ... It's a thing that makes the members of the Labour Party who've had to bite lots of bullets happy ... [It's] New Labour tries to speak to unhappy Labour-as-a-moral-crusade-or-it's-nothing-Labour.'[13] The Government, pursuing policies in Africa that reasserted the state's role as a provider and doer of good, was able to reconnect to Labour's conception of itself as a moral crusader. It did this in ways that domestic and other parts of foreign policy could not, either because of its espousal of conservative policies, or because of the uncomfortable compromises of governing.

The second way in which policy in Africa helped to rehabilitate a sense of a good state was the degree to which it could evade compromising or unpalatable policy choices. Chris Mullin described his unhappy feelings during his time as a junior minister in a domestic department where doing the right thing always appears to be constrained and ambiguous.

> There are many jobs in government you could get where you might be doing the right things but you wouldn't be entirely happy. I mean, if you were

> immigration minister, for example, that's a very tough job; you've got to do some very tough things, and you're subject to political constraints that you might not approve of... I had had eighteen months at the Department of the Environment, Transport and the Regions, where life was a vast cascade of all the many things one's superiors wished one to do. And I got out of that – it seemed to me to be a waste of everybody's time.[14]

Mullin, who described himself as being 'from the idealistic wing' of the Labour Party, disliked the political shenanigans of domestic policy. But as minister for Africa, he was able to feel a reconnection with his idea of what government should be. This reconnection was far more plausible in Africa, at once both further away and, as we have seen, more idealisable and presenting much more stark and dramatic needs than domestic constituencies.

The third element of Africa policy that fulfilled a Labour need was the way it provided more tangible opportunities for doing good – tackling injustice, fighting poverty – than Britain did. John Robertson evoked a sense of the need to extend out into the world to find moral fulfilment; a positive role for the state.

> The Labour Party has always thought of itself as being the party that looked after everybody... We've always looked after people who are the poorest and it's just been a natural progression into something like Africa... Tell me where poverty is compared to where it was in 1997 and you'll find the wealth has gone up... Nobody should starve in this country, nobody should be homeless. There are rules in this country that should catch these people, whether they want to be caught or not. In Africa, they don't have these rules. They don't collect taxes, therefore there's nobody answerable and they have to live on very little, on what they can scavenge during the day. Now our people don't have to do that.[15]

The party which 'looked after everybody' now operated in a country in which 'rules' that should 'catch' people in trouble undermined possibilities for a positive role domestically. 'Naturally' it looked further afield to find new objects and realise this ambition. Africa's larger problems made helping far less contentious.

There was a suggestion too of ingratitude. This was rooted in a distaste of materialism and greed, something that the Labour Party perhaps felt forced to embrace in order to become electable. But it is a theme echoed by MPs from the other parties too. It was apparently now impossible to idealise the British working poor in quite the ways that it might have been in the past. They were not as poor as they had been; and their rising wealth had exposed their vulgarity and materialism. Africa could be very clearly contrasted with domestic politics and demands which were often fraught and irritating. At home, political projects were more mundane and people less grateful. Claire Curtis-Thomas, for example, summed up the frustrations of dealing with domestic issues in her constituency, contrasting them with her work in Sierra Leone where starker priorities left far less room for contention.

> You get into politics because you wish to serve others, you wish to do well by others... [But in the UK] you're further up the food chain, aren't you? You're not dealing with people who are dying of starvation, you're not dealing with people who are dying of malnutrition, you're not dealing with people who will never work in their entire life and will be dead by the time they're thirty-five... That's why it's much easier to help in these countries and have an equivalence of view about how you tackle these things, because there isn't an either/or. If you went to a community here and said to people, what are your priorities, they wouldn't start by saying abandoned children, they'd say I want someone to come and clean my litter three times a week, or a new bobby, or why isn't the library open longer hours? ... I was very lucky to secure £9 million in my own community to build a library and a new cinema and a new civic hall. The whole project collapsed because the community cinema said, 'I don't think we want to be part of this anymore.' They just walked away from £9 million. And you just think, we should be so lucky that we've got so much money for a facility like this, and so rich that we can just walk away from it. How in Sierra Leone they just say yes, we'll have this and we'll have that. There's none of, 'well, is it the right colour?'[16]

In a sense, if Britain can somehow 'float free' of interests in Africa, the continent also allows the politicians who are involved to 'float free' of all the ambiguity of more problematic relationships and demands made on them. For Curtis-Thomas, this was about the difficulties she faced in dealing with the demands of her constituents and local business interests. In a similar vein, Malcolm Moss expressed the frustration that politicians aren't appreciated at home: 'You don't do it [pursue a political career] to make money, despite what some newspapers seem to think these days. You do it partly out of altruism, partly out of a desire to make a difference, and an extension of that can go into foreign affairs.'[17] Africa allowed these politicians – and their conception of the state – to escape the messiness of more dependent and complex relationships. Importantly, it did this through a conflation of the idea of universality and the idea of the transformation of politics. This denial of dependence and moral complexity provided opportunities to float free in an arena where omnipotence can be retrieved, the 'good state' recreated. Tony Lloyd summed up how it worked:

> Where in the world do people make you feel easy about yourself? I remember once going into a very remote community in northern Tanzania and I went to listen to a women's group talking about domestic violence, and I was just an observer and said a few words to them at the end, all this sort of bullshit stuff politicians can churn out every day of the week: how good it was that they were entitled to their own dignity; no man had the right to use strength or power to abuse women; they should as sisters protect each other and empower each other – all easy stuff to say, really. But they were just so lovingly grateful and I was almost massaged to death by twenty-seven women coming to embrace me just because they wanted to show how grateful they were that this strange guy from a country they knew

> little about, in some position of power that they probably wouldn't have made any sense of, had taken the trouble to come along to say a few words that were reasonably kind. And those kinds of things are quite humbling, but also quite ennobling – or 'en-dutying' – because they send you away with that sense of moral purpose ... And you get that in Africa.[18]

The Commission for Africa, coming towards the end of Blair's time in office, managed to bring together the strands of an ideal state activity: it created unity within Britain – political, moral and popular – and it put the British state at the centre of an international good cause. The Commissioners themselves, according to the head of the secretariat, Myles Wickstead, embodied the sense of unity by creating 'an incredible sense of community ... Everybody wanted this to work; everybody understood that this was a real opportunity to get it right and went out of their way to make it work'.[19] According to Wickstead, the commissioners were able to reach a consensus on the outcomes. 'It wasn't a compromise, no no no, not at all. It was the way it turned out and I think everyone was very happy with it.'[20]

Conclusion: the eroded state

I do not want to exaggerate Africa's importance, either to the British Government or, even, to the actors who take a particular interest in it. Rather, I am attempting to explain how a re-engagement with Africa on particular terms in the period under discussion might have been shaped and driven by domestic anxiety and concerns. This chapter has argued that for Labour politicians in particular, the British state appeared damaged in the late 1990s, and that foreign policy was one way in which both intellectuals and state actors attempted to reach beyond the difficulties of the state towards a purer, idealised realm as a basis for repair. The book has attempted to show how a significant number of state actors approached their work in Africa in such a manner, and the ways in which they found that the continent provided a proxy damaged object. For these actors, their work in Africa lent them a sense of the good state repaired, both by fostering a sense of connection to a transcendent good and by enabling them to feel that the state could reassert itself in a powerful and good way.

Klein has written explicitly about the way in which foreign adventures can feed a sense of domestic repair.

> In the explorer's unconscious mind, a new territory stands for a new mother, one that will replace the loss of the real mother. He is seeking the 'promised land' – the 'land flowing with milk and honey' ... We can see that through the interest in exploring ... various impulses and emotions – aggression, feelings of guilt, love and the drive to reparation – can be transferred to another sphere, far away from the original person. (Klein, 1998a: 334)

Klein explicitly returns us to biblical or utopian accounts in her description of the common need to resolve the great difficulties experienced in trying to integrate good and bad. Klein's theory rests on the ways in which people simplify deeply complex and ambiguous human reality in order to contain it.

Africa is a tangibly 'damaged object'; it is 'the scar on the conscience of the world'. Blair's fascinating and powerful description resonated keenly and he used it more than once. In it, Africa appears to exist not as a distinct, external, real object, but as something painful and disturbing inside us, disrupting our sense of internal comfort and connection to the good. Blair said: 'But if the world as a community focused on it, we could heal it. And if we don't, it will become deeper and angrier' (Blair, 2001). A sense of unease, even guilt, haunts Blair's account of Africa. Although he suggests that we have the capacity to repair it, at the same time, the analogy is unsettling. You cannot, after all, heal a scar: at best, it might be concealed. The unease underlying Blair's bravado and potent expression of capacity to heal carries the flavour of a more manic attempt at reparation.

Africa is presented as pitiable, helpless, fragile, broken, needy and incapable. Moreover, African states themselves are suggestive of the ultimate picture of impotence – or occasionally of a predatory, destructive potency – which provided the perfect foil for what Britain was not. At the same time, Africa appears remote in terms of our minimal attachment to its history and culture; yet it feels familiar in its language, institutions and particular sense of cultural connection. It is thin and simplified: we know where we are with Africa. For the politicians and officials I spoke to in relation to their work in Africa, the sense of guilt – either in relation to the colonial conquest and rule or in relation to the vigorous British involvement in the slave trade – hardly featured in relation to their attempts to support Africa's repair (see Chapters 5 and 6). Instead, a constant feature of the current British involvement in Africa is its virtual lack of interests there. This lack of interests expresses a further detachment from messy reality and helps to purify the engagement, fitting well with Segal's description of reparation 'done without acknowledgement of guilt…in relation to more remote objects…[which] must never be experienced as having been damaged by oneself…[and] be felt as inferior, dependent and, at depth, contemptible' (Segal, 2006: 95–6).

Damaged Africa represents a highly controllable object with which to restore infantile feelings of omnipotence through splitting and projecting. British attempts to 'do good' there thus appear to be 'based on an omnipotent control of the object', aim to deny guilt and responsibility for damage, while 'love and concern for the object – the hallmark of genuine reparation – are relatively weak' (*Ibid*: 147). There is in Africa, both a strong flavour of idealisation – of 'ordinary Africans', for example, or virtuous political leaders – and the sense of ingratitude and fear that the controlled object might one day rise up and retaliate, that Segal refers to.

In addition, the sense of anxiety about the damaged state, and the ability of the political classes to really mend it, are supportive of a manic approach to reparation in Africa. Behind the bravado there was, under New Labour in

Britain, an element of despair at the impossibility of mending the damaged state. Without the sense that real reparation can be effected, reparative attempts are likely to be manic, incapable of delivering the hoped for reparation of a damaged internal object, and, quite possibly, incapable of doing much good to a damaged external object either.

Notes

1 British companies supplied the bulk of the Federal Government's weapons during the civil war, rising from 36 per cent in 1966 to 97 per cent in 1969 (Aluko, 1977: 312).

2 This is not to deny that there had always been a gap between Labour rhetoric and Labour performance in government. The shift now, though, was to give up on the ideal, the idea of the good state. It was most dramatically demonstrated when Blair re-wrote the Party's constitution, omitting the commitment to public ownership. Tudor Jones traces the role and significance of Clause Four, and the effects of its demise on the Party (Jones, 1996).

3 Interview with Tony Benn, London, 9 May 2007.

4 Michael Gordon, in his history of Labour's foreign policy, argues that the Party from the very first defined its foreign policy in repudiation of that of the Conservatives. Ramsay McDonald argued of foreign policy that 'the whole corrupting system should be swept away' (quoted in Gordon, 1969: 5).

5 Interview with Sally Keeble, MP (Labour), London, 4 June 2007.

6 Nelson Mandela, a toweringly heroic figure for the Labour Party addressed the Labour Party conference in 2000, praising the party for contributing 'significantly to our freedom'. He went on to talk about the fight against inequality as 'one of the major political and moral tasks of the Labour Party in the twenty-first century' (Mandela, 2000).

7 Interview with DfID official, London, 4 May 2007.

8 Although Blair struggled too, and made explicit attempts to frame a more positive role along Berlinesque lines, going as far as to write to Berlin for guidance (Swift, 2008: ix).

9 A *New Statesman* survey in 1994 established Robert Tressell's *The Ragged Trousered Philanthropists*, an idealised account of class warfare, as the book that most influenced the political outlook of Labour MPs (Gallagher and Platt, 1994: 22–5). At the same time, the Party's leadership was increasingly reflecting the far more materialist concerns of the modern voter. Blair described the moment when, meeting a self-employed electrician polishing his Ford Sierra, he realised what had happened to Labour's traditional voter. 'His Dad voted Labour, he said. He used to vote Labour, too. But he'd bought his own house now. He'd set up his own business. He was doing very nicely. "So I've become a Tory," he said. In that moment, he crystalised for me the basis of our failure…His instincts were to get on in life. And he thought our instincts were to stop him' (quoted, Mail Online, 2007).

10 The cosmopolitan approach developed by Labour's intellectuals does not represent the whole Party, of course. The mainstream membership has been more inclined to adhere to a more communitarian approach. I am grateful to Andrew Williams for this point.

11 David Owen tartly pointed out that Blair's belief in moral unity was a result of his lack of experience of office: he hadn't had to deal with conflict and compromise. Interview with David Owen, London, 26 June 2007.
12 Interview with Tony Lloyd, MP (Labour), London, 10 July 2007.
13 Interview with Clare Short, MP (Labour), London, 6 June 2007.
14 Interview with Chris Mullin, MP (Labour), London, 21 March 2007.
15 Interview with John Robertson, MP (Labour), London, 16 January 2007.
16 Interview with Claire Curtis-Thomas, MP (Labour), London, 14 March 2007.
17 Interview with Malcolm Moss, MP (Conservative), London, 6 February 2007.
18 Interview with Tony Lloyd, MP (Labour), London, 10 July 2007.
19 Interview with Myles Wickstead, London, 27 June 2007.
20 *Ibid.*

8

Conclusion

I began this book with the idea that New Labour's approach to Africa represented something different from foreign policy as usual. This position has often appeared difficult to defend: realist interpretations, those who pointed out the self-promotion or self-justification of politicians, and the sometimes justifiable charges of hypocrisy, all throw up compelling alternative explanations. None of these can be totally dismissed. There have been occasions on which British interests have been put before African welfare: the sale of a military air traffic system to Tanzania, and the tacit support for Ethiopian incursions into Somalia, for example. More common are examples of where action failed to keep pace with rhetoric, seen in failures to back up condemnation of human rights abuses in the Democratic Republic of Congo and Sudan, or even Zimbabwe, in all of which the most ardent proponents of liberal intervention have argued for more stringent sanctions regimes or even Western military engagement. And the perennial argument that aid levels could be higher can be difficult to counter, given the explicit commitment to tackling the disparity of wealth between Africa and the West. The creep towards what some would see as a modest ambition of 0.7 per cent of GNI has been slower than many in the INGO sector would have liked and a world away from the cosmopolitan ideal as presented with compelling logic by Peter Singer (Singer, 2002).

These events and arguments are undeniable, and they do tarnish the ideal of an ethical policy in Africa. But they present a somewhat motley collection of lapses of commitment rather than a compelling case that Britain's Africa policy can be explained within a more conventional foreign policy framework. They suggest imperfections rather than the need for a complete debunking. As David Chandler has acknowledged, the approach is a puzzle. He has virtually thrown in the towel in his conclusion that the West has pursued its quasi-imperialist project out of a sense of embarrassment at its own excess of power (Chandler, 2006).

My ambition with this work has been to take seriously the idea that under New Labour, British policy in Africa was 'different from politics as usual', and to investigate how and why this was so. I have been keen therefore to distinguish between the way in which Africa policy fits into wider foreign policy – and the compromises and problems it encounters – and the ideal it represents. I have argued for a much more active sense of a British role in Africa, built on the traditional perception that Africa is apart from the rest of the world in its poverty, its chaotic violence and its passivity. I have attempted to explore what an engagement with Africa on these terms might mean, how it is imagined and described by state actors, and how it helps constitute their conceptions of their own political work and their sense of the work and identity of the British state.

The argument

Most important has been the way in which British activity in Africa represents a sphere apart in which 'the good' can be established as uncontested and unambiguous. This brings together cosmopolitan conceptions which eradicate moral thickness and ambiguity, with a religious, or quasi-religious, conception of a disinterested good. Because of this escape from affective and morally fraught ties, the story of Britain in Africa comes to represent the story of the Good Samaritan, the Christian benchmark of what it means to be a 'good neighbour'. Africa, for Wilberforce a key means to re-establishing proper Christianity in Britain, became for Chamberlain and Lugard a replacement for religion through its ability to create and sustain a common moral core. Such an idea was appropriated in its different ways by Brockway and the anti-colonialists; and it has resonated more recently in the quasi-religious language of Blair and Brown.

In my attempt to understand this creation of a sphere apart, I have drawn on a number of political theories and ideas. What these have in common are, first, an assumption that the good is not necessarily actually transcendent of the human community but is contained within and compromised by it; and second, an attempt to understand why and how the conception of a purer, uncontaminated form of good appears to be necessary to human communities. Durkheim's theory on the role of religion within communities provided a first, useful way to help construct an idea of the ways in which a sacred or pure activity is a vital component of the ethical health of the community. I have suggested that British engagement in Africa – far away, emotional, rooted in action (ritual, even), transcendent of profane politics – resonates with the idea of a sacred core of state activity. I have also suggested that Durkheim's ideas have an affinity with Hegel's depiction of the idea of the good state – interpreting Hegel's good state as an aspiration, or an ideal, separate from, and reinforcement of, the more complex real state. Throughout, the idea of utopia has constantly arisen – utopia as a representation of unhappiness with political reality and as an aspiration to perfection, either through an escape from politics altogether or in the construction of politics itself as author of the good.

Durkheim and Hegel, alongside many of those writing about the nature of utopianism, build up a picture of the ways in which communities create or reach out for an ideal good as a way of contending with ambiguous reality within which the good – or at least goods – are eternally contested. Within these ideas are already hints of a psychological approach. Durkheim and Hegel's juxtaposition of the ideal and the real are suggestive of a human need for containment and security. Anxiety and unhappiness with moral complexity, and the creation of collective fantasies of perfection are, as Manuel has pointed out, the hallmarks of utopias (Manuel, 1973). But reaching even deeper, to the underlying assumptions of the approach and ideas I have pursued, lie communitarian conceptions of the ways in which subjectivity is created through relationships between individuals. Klein explores all these themes, and I have used her work to see if it is possible to enrich the ways we can think about relationships within and between political communities.

Klein's work most immediately appeared to resonate with Walzer's ideas in the way she contrasted 'thick' emotionally intense and difficult relationships within families with the 'thinner', more idealisable relationships beyond them. Her exploration of the ways in which thinner relationships sustain and enable the development of thick relationships, and through them of the development of subjectivity, also echoed Hegel's idea that mutual recognition between states brings about individual state subjectivity. Most interesting of all was Klein's discussion of damaged internal objects and attempts made at reparation through connection to an idealised external good. This very clearly appeared to help an understanding of the ways in which moral ambiguity within close relationships undermines wellbeing; and it points to ways in which a thinner, external realm might provide opportunities for idealisation – a clear representation of what I have argued we see in New Labour's engagement in Africa. Moreover, Klein's ideas about the reparation of an external damaged object – a proxy for the damaged internal object, the 'scar on the conscience of the world' – provided a basis for exploring not only how, but why, Africa policy had the meaning it appeared to have.

The empirical side of the book explored these ideas in relation to the thoughts of a number of state actors as they reflected on their work in Africa. The language they used expressed strongly cosmopolitan themes: they idealised 'ordinary Africans' and the ability of international norms and institutions to transcend politics, and they appeared to conjure up a sense of a transcendent good which they found in Africa and in British work there. But the ways they talked particularly of their work in Africa also carried a strong flavour of potency and a tendency to idealise the state itself and its ability to express a sense of the good. In this, they were describing a more transformative approach in which the state itself becomes author or expression of the good. Perhaps this is not surprising. It seems unlikely that state actors themselves would take the transcendent approach to the good which we saw in explicitly oppositionalist abolition and anti-colonial movements. This turned out to be something of a balancing act, particularly in FCO and DfID posts in Africa where the ideal was sometimes most successfully realised within less intense, more peripheral relationships.

However, as explored in Chapter 7, an explicitly transformative approach was not something that appeared available to New Labour in 1997. Within the prevailing international norms, and the demographic and political changes in Britain itself, more positive versions of state activity appeared unviable and were rejected as too 'modernist' or 'antagonistic' by New Labour's intellectuals and politicians. But these very ideas and changes had appeared to erode and perhaps even fatally undermine the state, leaving it damaged. As I argued in Chapter 4, such damage corrodes communal wellbeing, undermining as it appears to do the state's ability to provide both physical and psychological security. Manent describes the fatal flaws of modern political communities: 'The public square', he argues, 'risks becoming an absolutely empty, naked space' (Manent, 2006: 23). In Kleinian terms, the state as a vital internal object appears fatally damaged. Perhaps it cannot be mended?

In this context of a damaged state, I argued that New Labour's attempts to repair the state by transcending it were insubstantial. It is in this light that Britain's turn to Africa should be considered. Although expressed in the terms of universalism and the context of internationalism, Britain's role in Africa resonates keenly in terms of the way it projects an ideal and potent British state. In doing this, it represents an idealised transformation of the state as author and owner of the good. The dramatic way in which Britain in the first flush of New Labour's ascendancy can be compared with Sierra Leone as a collapsed state in 1997 underlines the way in which Africa can help to construct and maintain this idealisation.

Difficulties with methodology

There are three main areas that have continually troubled the writing of this book. The first clear difficulty has been how to treat what interview subjects said. How far were politicians justifying or glorifying their work or the work of the Government? To what degree were officials repeating government lines and policy objectives? In my attempts to grasp what was said, what it meant, and how far to believe it, I have necessarily taken a subjective approach, based on my own belonging to, or understanding of, the communities I am writing about. I have reached for truth or judgement only in the sense that these are 'rooted in the theorist's own relative identity with the object of his or her analysis and validated solely in terms of the reader's recognition of that identity as in some sense the reader's own' (Hutchings, 1999: 117–18). The effectiveness of the conclusions I draw, therefore, depends heavily on how far this identity does resonate with the reader – a precarious position.

Second, this approach also informs the way I have used the interviewees' ideas to implicitly depict wider conceptions of the state and the idea of the good state. The bulk of the empirical part of this study deals with state actors' feelings about their individual contribution to politics or public life, and about the role and health of the state. Given more time and resources, I would have liked to explore how widely such a conception of politics and the state's engagement in Africa does resonate more widely. Clearly there have been moments of intense identification with the project – most notably during the Make Poverty History campaign in 2005 – and there are more steadfastly interested constituencies for whom it does matter, but these almost certainly comprise small elites. Most of the politicians I interviewed felt that such connections were ephemeral or of minority interest. I discovered very little feeling, from politicians of any hue, that Africa was an electoral asset. Indeed, as I suggested at the end of Chapter 5, in some sense the wider public's indifference or even antagonism towards doing good in Africa lent some politicians a further sense that what they were engaged in was disinterested; as well as adding to the sense that part of the damage done to the state came from the electorate itself.

What I have argued, though, is that for a significant number of state actors, what they do, and what the state does in Africa, represents a particular relationship for Britain with a good project. And more widely, that this particular project best distils the aspiration to something good that first made New Labour resonate so successfully with the British electorate. One question I have not had time to address, but which is potentially interesting, concerns the rationale behind development education programmes in British schools introduced by the Government. It would be interesting to explore the degree to which these are seen as a way of engaging the wider population in this sense of the good state.

The use of Klein throws up a third methodological question: is it viable to use work on the internal psyche of individuals to explore political questions? I have discussed this in Chapter 4, where I suggested that Klein's work might be a useful way to think about how foreign policy is constituted; and, more interestingly through analogy, of the ways in which relationships within and between states entrench state subjectivity. The first, which deals with the motivations of state actors, is an area that has already been examined in a large body of literature, although overwhelmingly in relation to the projection of aggression. The best of these do not attempt to explore the psyches of individual politicians, but rather to draw on inherent and universal psychological processes that can help an understanding of the ways in which individuals and groups relate to each other. The second, analogical approach is more problematic, particularly in the context of this study which builds on interviews with elite actors. With that caveat in mind, I suggest that the ideas and motivations of this group of state actors are closely tied to a wider (if less intense) need to view the state as engaged in good, reparative acts. As I argued in Chapter 4, the ways in which the state is a source of physical and emotional wellbeing, and subjectivity, is a theme that has been explored by political theorists from Aristotle to Rousseau. An examination of state actors' motivations and perceptions provides a distillation of how the state is shaped and geared towards an ideal activity and, as the 'keepers and protectors' of the state, politicians and officials reflect the constructed norms and ideas of the wider community. State actors are articulating a wider imagination of Africa and British work there, which views Africa as damaged and Britain as both disinterested and competent to mend it. The ability of state actors to project the idea of the ideal state, and wider acceptance of this, help constitute a sense of an ideal community, even if only superficially. In a sense, the shared belief in itself is constitutive of the ideal state and provides echoes of what Chris Brown has termed 'we-feeling' in relation to national moments of crisis (Brown, 1992: 70).

Four further questions

The charge of hypocrisy is often levelled at government policy on Africa. How much really did change once New Labour came to power? The answer is, quite a lot, although probably not as much as was claimed. I have explored this question only partially, in the introduction, and only in order to establish some basis for treating New Labour's interest in Africa as more than mere spin. A detailed analysis of the ways in which New Labour's idealisation of its role in Africa has fed into British policy there, and the effects this has had in Africa – particularly on the shape and extent of development efforts – has been beyond this study.

Moving beyond tangible effects, a second important question that I have been unable to develop is the way in which treatment of Africa as a 'damaged object' might affect Africans. How far does it play into existing self-conceptions? To what extent is it utilised by African leaders to extract further aid or other types of assistance? What in the longer term might be the effects of such an approach on the ways in which Africans operate their own domestic and international politics?

Third, there is the question of how far the approach of this study can be turned around to enable an exploration of the degree to which Africans might imagine, depict and relate to a former colonial power as a way of shaping conceptions of the African state. How might Sierra Leoneans, for example, view their state through the prism of its positive and possibly idealised relationship with Britain? In contrast, might it be possible to view Zimbabwe's much more hostile relationship with Britain as also constitutive of a particular conception of the state? In this case the projection of aggression might be viewed even as an explicit attempt by Zimbabwe's government to keep safe conceptions of the Zimbabwean good state. This question clearly demands an exploration of how far the conceptual model developed in this study – which draws so heavily on European political ideas – would be useful. The degree to which a psychoanalytical approach is helpful in an African context is fascinating in itself. But it might also complement the questions raised above about the effects of British idealisation on Africa – through a comparison of two African states, one of which complied with the idealisation, and the other of which rejected it.

Finally, in Chapter 7, I discussed the ways in which the rise of New Labour, and the particular configuration of its political history and ethos, interacted with the wider international climate to deliver a sense in the mid-1990s that the state was damaged and in need of repair, generating particular responses. How far then, this analysis can be extended to wider foreign policy trends – in Britain at other times, or in other countries – is a further question only very partially explored. My discussion of the historical context of Britain's engagement with Africa dealt with the idea that the domestic context might generate particular responses. What is missing, perhaps, is any sense of what it is about state activity or feelings about the state that operates when projection of idealisation does not apply. Why, for example, might Africa not have figured as an object of British good in the 1970s, a period of economic and political crisis? Does this have something to do with the way in which the state itself was viewed as still central to questions of reparation? In other words, was it that the state was inadequate, but the idea of the good state – the focus of political and social demands – remained healthy? This demands a more historical approach to tease out the extent to which the health of the state has fluctuated, and the degree to which an external damaged object has been demanded and imagined.

Bibliography

Primary written sources

Political and government speeches

Blair, Tony (1997), 'The principles of a modern British foreign policy – speech at the Lord Mayor's Banquet, London, 10 November 1997', Downing Street website: www.number-10.gov.uk [cited 16 March 2006].

—— (1998a), 'Speech at the State Department, Washington, 6 February 1998', Downing Street website: www.number-10.gov.uk/output/Page1155.asp [cited 16 March 2006].

—— (1998b), 'Speech on foreign affairs, London, 15 December 1998', Downing Street website: www.number-10.gov.uk [cited 16 March 2006].

—— (1999), 'Doctrine of the international community – speech to the Economic Club, Chicago, 24 April 1999', Downing Street website: www.number-10.gov.uk/output/Page1297.asp [cited 16 March 2006].

—— (2000), 'Statement on Sierra Leone, 19 May 2000', Downing Street website: www.pm.gov.uk/output/Page328.asp [cited 20 May 2006].

—— (2001), 'Speech to the Labour Party Conference, 2 October 2001', Guardian Unlimited: http://politics.guardian.co.uk/speeches/story/0,11126,590775,00.html [cited 13 July 2004].

—— (2002a), 'Speech to Ghana's Parliament, 2 February 2002', Downing Street website: www.number-10.gov.uk/output/page3451.asp [cited 26 November 2003].

—— (2002b), 'Speech to the World Summit on Sustainable Development, Johannesburg, 2 September 2002', Downing Street website: www.number-10.gov.uk/output/Page1724.asp [cited 16 March 2006].

—— (2004), 'Speech on Africa, Addis Ababa, 7 October 2004', Downing Street website: www.number-10.gov.uk/output/Page6452.asp [cited 16 March 2006].

—— (2005), 'Remarks on the launch of the Commission for Africa Report, 11 March 2005', Downing Street website: www.number-10.gov.uk/output/Page7314.asp [cited 16 March 2006].

Brown, Gordon (2005), 'International development in 2005: the challenge and the opportunity – speech at the National Gallery of Scotland, Edinburgh, 6 January 2005', HM Treasury website: www.hm-treasury.gov.uk/newsroom_and_speeches/press/2005/press_03_05.cfm [cited 6 January 2005].

Bush, George (1991), 'Speech to Congress, 6 March 1991', www.al-bab.com/arab/docs/pal/pal10.htm [cited 30 March 2009].

Cameron, David (2006), 'Fighting global poverty: speech in Oxford to a group of Oxfam supporters, 29 June 2006', Conservative Party website: http://conservativehome.blogs.com/frontpage/files/david_cameron_global_poverty_speech.pdf [cited 5 May 2009].

—— (2007), 'Speech to the Rwandan Parliament, 24 July 2007', ePolitix website: www.epolitix.com/latestnews/article-detail/newsarticle/david-cameron-rwanda-speech-in-full/ [cited 5 May 2009].

Chamberlain, Joseph (1898), 'Speech to the Liverpool Chamber of Commerce', *The Times*, 19 January 1898, p. 7.

Cook, Robin (1997a), 'Foreign policy mission statement – speech at the Foreign and Commonwealth Office, London, 12 May 1997', Guardian Unlimited: www.guardian.co.uk/world/1997/may/12/indonesia.ethicalforeignpolicy [cited 14 December].

—— (1997b), 'Human rights into a new century – speech at the Foreign and Commonwealth Office, London, 17 July 1997', Foreign and Commonwealth Office website: www.fco.gov.uk [cited 20 December 2005].

—— (1998), 'Human rights: making the difference – speech at Amnesty International's human rights festival, London, 16 October 1998', Foreign and Commonwealth Office website: www.fco.gov.uk [cited 7 February 2006].

—— (1999), 'Cook congratulates Nigeria on a successful transition programme, joint interview with President Obasanjo, Abuja, 10 March 1999', Foreign and Commonwealth website, www.fco.gov.uk/en/newsroom/latest-news/?view=News&id=2243618 [cited 10 June 2004].

—— (2000), 'Foreign policy and national interest – speech to the Royal Institute of International Affairs, Chatham House, London, Friday, 28 January 2000', www.foc.gov.uk/servlet/Front?pagename=OpenMarket/Xcelerate/ShowPage&c [cited 7 February 2006].

—— (2001), 'Human rights, a priority of Britain's foreign policy – speech at a meeting of human rights NGOs, Foreign and Commonwealth Office, London, 2001', Foreign and Commonwealth Office website: www.fco.gov.uk [cited 7 February 2006].

—— (2003), 'Resignation speech to the House of Commons, 18 March 2003', http://news.bbc.co.uk/1/hi/uk_politics/2859431.stm [cited 11 November 2008].

Kennedy, Charles (2005), 'Speech to the Centre of Reform on aid and trade: accountability and responsibility, 12 July 2005', ePolitix website, www.epolitix.com/mpwebsites/mpspeeches/mpspeechdetails/newsarticle/global-visions-liberal-democrats-and-internationalism///mpsite/charles-kennedy/ [cited 5 May 2009].

Lloyd, Tony (1999), 'Britain in Africa: a policy overview – speech to the Africa Day Conference, London, 25 May 1999', FCO website, www.fco.gov.uk/en/newsroom/latest-news/?view=Speech&id=2149321 [cited 5 May 2009].

—— (2002), 'Supporting positive change in Africa: the UK's role – speech to the British-African Business Association, 19 February 2002', FCO website, www.fco.gov.uk/en/newsroom/latest-news/?view=Speech&id=2149366 [cited 5 May 2009].

Mandela, Nelson (2000), 'Speech to the Labour Party Conference, 28 September 2000', Guardian Online, www.guardian.co.uk/politics/2000/sep/28/labourconference.labour7 [cited 4 April 2006].

Short, Clare (2003), 'Resignation speech to the House of Commons, 12 May 2003', ePolitix.com, www.epolitix.com/mpwebsites/mpspeeches/mpspeechdetails/newsarticle/resignation-speech///mpsite/clare-short/?no_cache=1 [cited 11 November 2008].

Government and official publications

Commission for Africa (2005), *Our Common Interest: Report of the Commission for Africa* (London: Commission for Africa).

Department for International Development (1997), 'Eliminating world poverty: a challenge for the twenty-first century – White Paper on International Development' (London: Department for International Development).

—— (2000), 'Eliminating world poverty: making globalisation work for the poor – White Paper on International Development' (London: Department for International Development).

Howe, Geoffrey (1988), 'South Africa: no easy answers', in *Perspectives for Africa* (London: Central Office of Information).

Trades Union Congress (2005), 'Congress 2005: General Council report' (London: Trades Union Congress).

UNDP (2000), *Human Development Report 2000: Human Rights and Human Development* (Oxford: Oxford University Press).

—— (2002), *Human Development Report 2002: Deepening Democracy in a Fragmented World* (Oxford: Oxford University Press).

World Bank (1998), *Development and Human Rights: The Role of the World Bank* (Washington: World Bank).

—— (1997), 'The state in a changing world', *World Development Report.*

Parliamentary debates (by date)

Debate on Mr Wilberforce's Resolutions Respecting the Slave Trade, 12 May. Vol. 28, *Parliamentary History* (London: Hansard, 1789).

Debate in the Commons on the Abolition of the Slave Trade, 26 February. Vol. 31, *Parliamentary History* (London: Hansard, 1795).

Debate on Mr Wilberforce's Motion of the Abolition of the Slave Trade, 18 February. Vol. 32, *Parliamentary Debates* (London: Hansard, 1796).

Debate on Mr Wilberforce's Motion for the Abolition of the Slave Trade, 15 May. Vol. 33, *Parliamentary History* (London: Hansard, 1797).

Queen's Speech Debate, 13 February. Vol. 36, *The Parliamentary Debates (Authorised Edition), Fourth Series* (London: Waterlow and Sons Limited, 1895).

Supply Debate, 22 August. Vol. 36, *The Parliamentary Debates (Authorised Edition), Fourth Series* (London: Waterlow and Sons Limited, 1895).

Supply Debate, Colonial Services, 8–24 February. Vol. 53, *The Parliamentary Debates (Authorised Edition), Fourth Series* (London: Waterlow and Sons Limited, 1898).

Royal Niger Company Bill (Second Reading), 6–21 July. Vol. 74, *The Parliamentary Debates (Authorised Edition), Fourth Series* (London: Waterlow and Sons Limited, 1899).

Appropriation Bill, 7 August. Vol. 76, *Parliamentary Debates (Fourth Series)* (London: Hansard, 1899).

Newspaper, journal and website articles

Assinder, Nick (2002), 'Blair's missionary zeal confounds critics' (10 February 2002) BBC News online: http://news.bbc.co.uk/1/hi/uk_politics/1812905.stm [cited 9 February 2006].

BBC Website (2004), 'UK Kenya envoy "regrets insult" (15 July 2004) http://news.bbc.co.uk/1/hi/world/africa/3896971.stm [cited 30 April 2009]

BBC Website (2005), 'Robin Cook's obituary' (6 August 2005), http://news.bbc.co.uk/1/hi/uk_politics/4127676.stm [cited 29 February 2009].

Cook, Robin (1999), 'Interview' (5 July 1999), *New Statesman*.

Ferguson, Euan (2003), 'One million. And still they came' (16 February 2003), Observer Online: www.guardian.co.uk/uk/2003/feb/16/voterapathy.iraq [cited, 5 October 2006].

Gallagher, Julia, and Steve Platt (1994), 'From Bevan to Bible', *New Statesman and Society*, 7:322, 22–5.

Garton Ash, T. (2006), 'How will the ventriloquist's dummy of history judge Blair's foreign policy? *Guardian* (30 March 2006).

Greste, Peter (2000), 'Why Mugabe is deaf to the West' (15 April 2000), http://news.bbc.co.uk/1/hi/world/africa/7349166.stm [cited 20 April 2009].

Hain, Peter (1999), 'Only money will set Africa free', *New Statesman* (11 October 1999).

Mail Online (2007), 'Mondeo Man? Now Tories chase Miss Classroom' (26 April 2007), www.dailymail.co.uk/news/article-450806/Mondeo-Man-Now-Tories-chase-Miss-Staff-Room.html [cited, 30 March 2009].

Pall Mall Gazette (1895), Leader, 'Josephus Africanus', *Pall Mall Gazette* (22 August 1895), p. 1.

Pall Mall Gazette (1898), 'Review: "*A Short History of British Colonial Policy*" by Hugh Edward Egerton', *Pall Mall Gazette* (8 January 1898), p. 4.

Star (1895), Leader, 'Mr Chamberlain', *The Star* (24 August, 1895), p. 1.

Times (1895), Leader, 'The Colonies', *The Times* (26 August, 1895), p. 4.

Times (1897), Leader, 'The Colonies', *The Times* (19 January, 1897), p. 4.

References

Abrahamsen, Rita (2000), *Disciplining Democracy: Development Discourse and Good Governance in Africa* (London: Zed Books).

Abrahamsen, Rita, and Paul Williams (2001), 'Ethics and foreign policy: the antinomies of New Labour's "Third Way" in sub-Saharan Africa', *Political Studies*, 49(2): 249–64.

Achebe, Chinua (1958), *Things Fall Apart* (Oxford: Heinemann).

—— (1986), *Arrow of God* (Oxford: Heinemann).

Adler, Emanuel (2005), *Communitarian International Relations: The Epistemic Foundations of International Relations* (London: Routledge).

Allen, Charles (1979), *Tales from the Dark Continent* (London: Andre Deutsch).

Aluko, Olajide (1977), 'Nigeria and Britain after Gowan', *African Affairs*, 76 (304): 303–20.

Beilharz, Peter (1992), *Labour's Utopias: Bolshevism, Fabianism, Social Democracy* (London: Routledge).

Berdal, Mats R., and David Malone (2000), *Greed and Grievance: Economic Agendas in Civil Wars* (London: Lynne Rienner).

Berlin, Isaiah (1969), *Four Essays on Liberty* (Oxford: Oxford University Press).

Berman, Bruce (1990), *Control and Crisis in Colonial Kenya: The Dialectic of Domination*. (London: James Currey).

Bion, W. R. (1974), *Experiences in Groups and Other Papers* (London: Tavistock Publications).

Blair, Tony (1998c), *The Third Way: New Politics for the New Century* (London:

Fabian Society).

Boehmer, Elleke (2005), *Colonial and Postcolonial Literature* (Oxford: Oxford University Press).

Boff, Leonardo (1988), *Trinity and Society* (Tunbridge Wells: Burns and Oates).

Bose, Anuradah, and Peter Burnell (1991), *Britain's Overseas Aid Since 1979: Between Idealism and Self-interest* (Manchester: Manchester University Press).

Bower, Tom (2004), *Gordon Brown* (London: Harper Collins).

Bowlby, J. (1973), *Attachment and Loss (Volume Two) Separation: Anxiety and Anger* (New York: Basic Books).

Boyle, M. (2004), 'Utopianism and the Bush foreign policy', *Cambridge Review of International Affairs,* 17(1): 81–103.

Brogan, Hugh (2006), *Alexis de Tocqueville: A Life* (New Haven and London: Yale University Press).

Brown, Chris (1992), *International Relations Theory: New Normative Approaches* (New York and London: Harvester Wheatsheaf).

Buber, Martin (1996), *Paths in Utopia* (Syracuse University Press).

Bull, Hedley (1995), *The Anarchical Society: A Study of Order in World Politics* (Basingstoke: Macmillan, 2nd edn).

Bullock, Alan (1983), *Ernest Bevin: Foreign Secretary 1945–1951* (London: Heinemann).

Butler, Jeffrey (1968), *The Liberal Party and the Jameson Raid* (Oxford: Clarendon Press).

Buxton, Thomas (1968), *The African Slave Trade and its Remedy* (London: Dawson's).

Byrd, P. (1988), *British Foreign Policy Under Thatcher* (Oxford, New York: Philip Allan).

Cain, P. J., and A. G. Hopkins (1993), *British Imperialism: Innovation and Expansion, 1688–1914* (London: Longman).

Callaghan, John (2007), *The Labour Party and Foreign Policy: A History* (London: Routledge).

Cammack, Paul (2006), 'Global governance, state agency and competitiveness: the political economy of the Commission for Africa', *British Journal of Politics and International Relations,* 8(3): 331–50.

Carr, Edward Hallett (2001), *The Twenty Years' Crisis, 1919–1939: An Introduction to the Study of International Relations* (Basingstoke: Palgrave).

Carrington, Peter (1988), *Reflecting on Things Past: The Memoirs of Peter Lord Carrington* (New York: Harper and Row).

Chabbott, C. (1999), 'Development INGOs', in Thomas Boli (ed.), *Constructing World Culture: International Non-Governmental Organisations Since 1875* (Stanford: Standford University Press).

Chan, Stephen (2003a), 'A new triptych for international relations in the twenty-first century: beyond Waltz and beyond Lacan's Antigone, with a note on the Falun Gong of China', *Global Society* 17(2): 187–208.

—— (2003b), *Robert Mugabe: A Life of Power and Violence* (London: I. B. Tauris).

—— (2005a) 'Trauma and the idea of unreconciled citizenship in Zimbabwe: the novels of Vera and Kanengoni', *Third World Quarterly,* 26(2): 369–82.

—— (2005b), *Out of Evil: New International Politics and Old Doctrines of War* (London: I. B. Tauris).

Chandler, David (2003), 'Rhetoric without responsibility: the attraction of "ethical" foreign policy', *British Journal of Politics and International Relations,* 5(3): 295–316.

—— (2006), *Empire in Denial: The Politics of State-Building* (London: Pluto Press).

Clapham, Christopher (2002), *Africa and the International System: The Politics of State Survival* (Cambridge: Cambridge University Press).

Cochran, Molly (1999), *Normative Theory in International Relations: A Pragmatic Approach* (Cambridge: Cambridge University Press).

Coleman, J., and C. Rosberg (eds) (1964), *Political Parties and National Integration in Tropical Africa* (Berkley, CA, and London: University of California Press).

Colley, Linda (2005), *Britons: Forging the Nation, 1707–1837* (New Haven, CT, and London: Yale Nota Bene, 2nd edn).

Conklin, Alice (1998), 'Colonialism and human rights, a contradiction in terms? The case of France and West Africa, 1895–1914', *American Historical Review,* 103(2): 419–42.

Cooper, Frederick (2001), 'Networks, moral discourse and history', in T. Callaghy, R. Kassimir and R. Latham (eds), *Intervention and Transnationalism in Africa: Global Networks of Power* (Cambridge: Cambridge University Press).

Cooper, Robert (2003), *The Breaking of Nations: Order and Chaos in the Twenty-first Century* (London: Atlantic Monthly Press).

Coupland, Reginald (1964), *The British Anti-Slavery Movement* (London: Frank Cass).

Crick, Bernard R. (1987), *Socialism (Concepts in the Social Sciences)* (Milton Keynes: Open University Press).

Crooks, J. J. (1972), *A History of the Colony of Sierra Leone, Western Africa* (London: Frank Cass).

Cruise O'Brien, Donal (2003), *Symbolic Confrontations: Muslims Imagining the State in Africa* (London: C Hurst).

Cumming, Gordon (2001), *Aid to Africa: French and British Policies from the Cold War to the New Millennium* (Aldershot: Ashgate).

Dahrendorf, Ralph (1968), *Essays in the Theory of Society* (London: Routledge).

Dixon, R., and P. Williams (2001), 'Tough on debt, tough on the causes of debt? New Labour's third way foreign policy', *British Journal of Politics and International Relations,* 3(2): 150–72.

Doty, Roxanne Lynn (1996), *Imperial Encounters: The Politics of Representation in North–South Relations* (Minneapolis: University of Minnesota Press).

Draper, Derek (1997), *Blair's Hundred Days* (London: Faber and Faber).

Duffield, Mark (2002), *Global Governance and the New Wars: The Merging of Development and Security* (London: Zed Books).

Dutfield, Michael (1990), *A Marriage of Inconvenience: The Persecution of Ruth and Seretse Khama* (London: Unwin Hyman Ltd).

Durkheim, Emile (2001), *The Elementary Forms of Religious Life* (Oxford: Oxford University Press).

Ekeh, Peter (1975), 'Colonialism and the two publics: a theoretical statement', *Comparative Studies in Society and History,* 17(1): 92–112.

Etzioni, Amitai (1995), *The Spirit of Community: Rights, Responsibilities and the Communitarian Agenda* (London: Fontana Press).

Foucault, Michel (1988), *Politics, Philosophy, Culture: Interviews and Other Writings, 1977–1984*, edited by Lawrence D. Kritzman (New York: Routledge).

Fourier, Charles (1971), *Design for Utopia: Selected Writings* (New York: Schocken).

Fraser, Peter (1966), *Joseph Chamberlain: Radicalism and Empire, 1868–1914* (London: Cassell).

Freeden, Michael (2003), *Ideology: A Very Short Introduction* (Oxford, Oxford University Press).

Freud, Sigmund (1960), *The Ego and the Id* (translated by Joan Riviere) (London: W. W. Norton and Company).

Frost, Mervyn (1986), *Towards a Normative Theory of International Relations: A Critical Analysis of the Philosophical and Methodological Assumptions in the Discipline with Proposals Towards a Substantive Normative Theory* (Cambridge: Cambridge University Press).

Fukuyama, Francis (1992), *The End of History and the Last Man* (London: Penguin).

Gann, L. H., and Peter Duigan (1978), *The Rulers of British Africa, 1870–1914* (London: Croom Helm).

Giddens, Anthony (1998), *The Third Way: The Renewal of Social Democracy* (Cambridge: Polity Press).

Gordon, Michael (1969), *Conflict and Consensus in Labour's Foreign Policy, 1914–1965* (Stanford: Standford University Press).

Grainger, J. H. (2005), *Tony Blair and the Ideal Type* (Exeter: Imprint Academic).

Gratus, Jack (1973), *The Great White Lie: Slavery, Emancipation and Changing Racial Attitudes* (London: Hutchinson).

Hain, Peter (2001), *The End of Foreign Policy? Britain's Interests, Global Linkages and Natural Limits* (London: Fabian Society).

Hargreaves, Ian, and Ian Christie (eds) (1998), *Tomorrow's Politics: The Third Way and Beyond* (London: Demos).

Healey, Denis (1991), *When Shrimps Learn to Whistle: Signposts for the Nineties* (London: Penguin).

Hegel, Georg Wilhelm Friedrich (1991), *Elements of the Philosophy of Right* (Cambridge: Cambridge University Press).

Hesiod (1978), *Works and Days* (Oxford: Oxford University Press).

Hinden, Rita, and Henry Noel Brailsford (1945), *Fabian Colonial Essays* (London: Allen and Unwin).

Hobson, J. A. (1938), *Imperialism* (London: Allen and Unwin).

Howe, Geoffrey (2008), *Conflict of Loyalty* (London: Politicos Publishing).

Howe, Stephen (1993), *Anti-Colonialism in British Politics: The Left and the End of Empire, 1918–1964* (Oxford: Clarendon Press).

Howse, E. M. (1952), *Saints in Politics: The 'Clapham Set' and the Growth of Freedom* (London: Allen and Unwin).

Hurd, Douglas (2004), *Douglas Hurd: Memoirs* (London: Little, Brown).

Hutchings, Kimberly (1999), *International Political Theory* (London: Sage).

Jacobs, Michael, Adam Lent and Kevin Watkins (eds) (2003), *Progressive Globalisation: Towards an International Social Democracy* (London: Fabian Society).

Jaeger, Hans-Martin (2002), 'Hegel's reluctant realism and the transnationalisation of civil society', *Review of International Studies,* 28: 497–517.

Jones, Tudor (1996), *Remaking the Labour Party: From Gaitskell to Blair* (London: Routledge).

Judd, Denis (1977), *Radical Joe: A life of Joseph Chamberlain* (London: Hamish Hamilton).

Kagan, Robert (2003), *Paradise and Power: America and Europe in the New World*

Order (London: Atlantic).

Kampfner, John (2004), *Blair's Wars* (London: Free Press).

Kaplan, Robert (1994), 'The coming anarchy', *Atlantic Monthly*, 273(2): 44–76.

Kargbo, Michael (2006), *British Foreign Policy and the Conflict in Sierra Leone, 1991–2001* (Oxford: Peter Lang)

Kissinger, Henry (1994), *Diplomacy* (New York: Simon and Schuster).

Klein, Melanie (1998a), 'Love, guilt and reparation', in *Love, Guilt and Reparation, and Other Works, 1921–1945* (London: Vintage), 306–43.

—— (1998b), 'Mourning and its relation to manic-depressive states', in *Love, Guilt and Reparation and Other Works, 1921–1945* (London: Vintage), pp. 344–69.

—— (1998c), 'Weaning', in *Love, Guilt and Reparation and Other Works, 1921–1945* (London: Vintage), pp. 290–305.

Kristeva, Julia (1991), *Strangers to Ourselves* (translated by Leon S. Roudiez) (New York: Columbia University Press).

Kymlicka, Will (2002), *Contemporary Political Philosophy: An Introduction* (Oxford: Oxford University Press).

Lewis, Roy and Yvonne Foy (1971), *The British in Africa: A Social History of the British Overseas* (London: Weidenfeld and Nicolson).

Linklater, Andrew (1998), *The Transformation of Political Community: Ethical Foundations of the Post-Westphalian Era* (Cambridge: Polity Press).

Little, Richard, and Mark Wickham-Jones (2000), *New Labour's Foreign Policy: A New Moral Crusade?* (Manchester: Manchester University Press).

Lugard, Frederick John Dealtry (1926), *The Dual Mandate in British Tropical Africa* (Edinburgh and London: William Blackwood and Sons, 3rd edn).

Machiavelli, Niccolo (1992), *The Prince* (New York: Dover Publications Inc.).

Macmillan, Hugh, and Shula Marks (eds) (1989), *Africa and Empire: W. M. Macmillan, Historian and Social Critic* (Brookfield: Gower).

Major, John (1999), *John Major: The Autobiography* (London: Harper Collins).

Mamdani, M. (1996), *Citizen and Subject: Contemporary Africa and the Legacy of Later Colonialism* (London: James Currey).

Mandelson, Peter, and Roger Liddle (1996), *The Blair Revolution: Can New Labour Deliver?* (London and Boston: Faber and Faber).

Manent, Pierre (2006), *A World Beyond Politics? A Defence of the Nation-State* (Princeton, NJ: Princeton University Press).

Mannheim, Karl (1985), *Ideology and Utopia: An Introduction to the Sociology of Knowledge* (New York: Harvest).

Manuel, Frank Edward (1973), *Utopias and Utopian Thought* (London: Souvenir Press).

Marquand, David (1999), *The Progressive Dilemma: From Lloyd George to Blair* (London: Phoenix Giant, 2nd edn).

Mbembe, J. A. (2001), *On the Postcolony: Studies on the History of Society and Culture* (Berkeley, CA, and London: University of California Press).

Melvern, Linda, and Paul Williams (2004), 'Britannia waived the rules', *African Affairs,* 103(410): 1–22.

Miller, David (1995), *On Nationality* (Oxford: Clarendon Press).

Mistry, Percy S. (2005), 'Reasons for sub-Saharan Africa's development deficit that the Commission for Africa did not consider', *African Affairs,* 104(417): 665–78.

Morgenthau, Hans Joachim (1993), *Politics among Nations: The Struggle for Power and Peace* (New York; London: McGraw-Hill).

Mudimbe, V. Y. (1994), *The Idea of Africa: African Systems of Thought* (London: J. Currey).
Mulgan, Geoff (1994), *Politics in an Antipolitical Age* (Cambridge: Polity Press).
Mumford, Lewis (1922), *The Story of Utopias* (New York: The Viking Press).
Nkrumah, Kwame (1998), *Africa Must Unite* (London: Panaf).
Nyerere, Julius (1967), *The Arusha Declaration and TANU's Policy on Socialism and Self-Reliance* (Dar es Salaam: Tanganyika African National Union).
Owusu, Maxwell (1970), *The Uses and Abuses of Political Power: A Case Study of Continuity and Change in the Politics of Ghana* (Chicago, IL: University of Chicago Press).
Pakenham, Thomas (2001), *The Scramble for Africa, 1876–1912* (London: Phoenix).
Paskins, Barrie (1978), 'Obligation and the understanding of international relations', in Michael Donelan (ed.), *The Reason of States: A Study in International Political Theory* (London: Allen and Unwin).
Perham, Margery Freda (1956), *Lugard* (London: Collins).
Phillips, Anne (1989), *The Enigma of Colonialism: British Policy in West Africa* (London: James Currey).
Phythian, Mark (2007), *The Labour Party, War and International Relations, 1945–2006* (London: Routledge).
Plato (1941), *The Republic* (London: Oxford University Press).
Porteous, Tom (2005), 'British Government policy in sub-Saharan Africa under New Labour', *International Affairs,* 81(2): 281–97.
Porter, Bernard (2007), *The Absent-Minded Imperialists: Empire, Society and Culture in Britain* (Oxford: Oxford University Press).
Ricoeur, Paul (1986), *Lectures on Ideology and Utopia* (New York: Columbia University Press).
Robinson, Ronald Edward, John Gallagher and Alice Denny (1961), *Africa and the Victorians: The Official Mind of Imperialism* (London: Macmillan).
Rodney, Walter (1973), *How Europe Underdeveloped Africa* (London: Bogle-L'Ouverture Publications).
Said, Edward W. (2003), *Orientalism* (London: Penguin).
Segal, Hanna (1986), *Delusion and Artistic Creativity and Other Psychoanalytic Essays* (London: Free Association Books).
—— (1997), *Psychoanalysis, Literature and War: Papers, 1972–95* (London: Routledge).
—— (2006), *Introduction to the Work of Melanie Klein* (London: Karnac Books).
Seldon, Anthony (2004), *Blair* (London: Free Press).
Semmel, Bernard (1960), *Imperialism and Social Reform: English Social-Imperial Thought, 1895–1914* (London: Allen and Unwin).
Short, Clare (2004), *An Honourable Deception? New Labour, Iraq, and the Misuse of Power* (London: Free Press).
Singer, Peter (2002), *One World: The Ethics of Globalization* (New Haven, CT: Yale University Press).
Slater, David, and Morag Bell (2002), 'Aid and the geopolitics of the post-colonial: critical reflections on New Labour's overseas development strategy', *Development and Change,* 33(2): 335–60.
Slim, Hugo (1997), *Doing the Right Thing: Relief Agencies, Moral Dilemmas, and Moral Responsibility in Political Emergencies and War* (Uppsala: Nordiska Afrikainstitutet).

—— (1998) 'Sharing a universal ethic: the principle of humanity in war', *The International Journal of Human Rights,* 2(4): 28–48.

Smith, Steven (1989), *Hegel's Critique of Liberalism* (Chicago, IL: University of Chicago Press).

Sopel, Jon (1995), *Tony Blair: The Moderniser* (London: Bantam).

Swift, Adam (2008), *Political Philosophy: A Beginners' Guide for Students and Politicians* (Cambridge: Polity Press).

Tawney, R. H. (1990), *Religion and the Rise of Capitalism* (London: Penguin Books).

Taylor, Charles (1989), *Sources of the Self: The Making of the Modern Identity* (Cambridge: Cambridge University Press).

Taylor, Ian (2005), '"Advice is judged by results, not by intentions": why Gordon Brown is wrong about Africa', *International Affairs,* 81(2): 299–310.

Taylor, Ian, and Paul Williams (2002), 'The limits of engagement: British foreign policy and the crisis in Zimbabwe', *International Affairs,* 78(3): 547–65.

—— (eds) (2004), *Africa in International Politics: External Involvement on the Continent* (London and New York: Routledge).

Thatcher, Margaret (1993), *The Downing Street Years* (London: Harper Collins).

Utam, Adam (1967), 'Socialism and utopia', in Frank Manuel (ed.) *Utopias and Utopian Thought* (Boston, MA: Beacon Press).

Vickers, Rhiannon (2003), *The Labour Party and the World: The Evolution of Labour's Foreign Policy, 1900–51.* Vol. 1 (Manchester: Manchester University Press).

Villalon, Leonardo, and Philip Huxtable (eds) (1998), *The African State at a Critical Junction: Between Disintegration and Reconfiguration* (London: Lynne Rienner).

Waltz, Kenneth Neal (1959), *Man, the State, and War: A Theoretical Analysis* (New York: Columbia University Press).

Walzer, Michael (1994), *Thick and Thin: Moral Argument at Home and Abroad* (London: University of Notre Dame Press).

Ware, Zoe (2006), 'Reassessing Labour's relationship with sub-Saharan Africa', *The Round Table,* 95(383): 141–52.

Weber, Max (1963), *The Sociology of Religion* (Boston, MA: Beacon Press).

Weil, Simone (2005), *Simone Weil: An Anthology* (London: Penguin Books).

Wickham-Jones, Mark (2000), 'Labour Party politics and foreign policy', in Richard Little and Mark Wickham-Jones (eds), *New Labour's Foreign Policy: A New Moral Crusade?* (Manchester: Manchester University Press): 93–111.

Wilberforce, William (1958), *A Practical View of the Prevailing Religious System of Professed Christians in the Higher and Middle Classes in This Country Contrasted with Real Christianity* (London: SCM Press Ltd).

Williams, Andrew (2006), *Liberalism and War: The Victors and the Vanquished* (London: Routledge).

Williams, David (2000), 'Aid and sovereignty: quasi-states and the international financial institutions', *Review of International Studies,* 26(4): 557–73.

Williams, P. D. (2001), 'Fighting for Freetown: British military intervention in Sierra Leone', *Contemporary Security Policy,* 22(3): 140–68.

—— (2005), 'Blair's Commission for Africa: problems and prospects for UK policy', *The Political Quarterly,* 76(4): 529–39.

Wilson, Peter (2003), *The International Theory of Leonard Woolf: A Study in Twentieth-Century Idealism* (New York and Basingstoke: Palgrave Macmillan).

Woolf, Leonard (1971), *Imperialism and Civilisation* (London and New York: Garland Publishing).

—— (1998), *Empire and Commerce in Africa: A Study in Economic Imperialism* (London: Routledge).

Young, Tom (1995), '"A project to be realised": global liberalism and contemporary Africa', *Millennium: Journal of International Studies*, 24(3): 527–46.

Zolberg, Aristide (1968), 'The structure of political conflict in the new states of tropical Africa', *American Political Science Review*, 62(1): 70–87.

Index

EU authorised representative for GPSR:
Easy Access System Europe, Mustamäe tee 50,
10621 Tallinn, Estonia
gpsr.requests@easproject.com

www.ingramcontent.com/pod-product-compliance
Lightning Source LLC
Chambersburg PA
CBHW061741270326
41928CB00011B/2325

* 9 7 8 0 7 1 9 0 9 1 1 7 9 *